AFRICA, AUSTRALIA, AND THE ISLANDS OF THE PACIFIC

For thousands of years the Sphinx has stood, serene and silent, gazing out over the desert sands. If it could speak, what marvelous tales it could tell of this ancient land!

AFRICA, AUSTRALIA, AND THE ISLANDS OF THE PACIFIC

Nellie B. Allen

YESTERDAY'S CLASSICS

ITHACA, NEW YORK

Cover and arrangement © 2022 Yesterday's Classics, LLC.

This edition, first published in 2022 by Yesterday's Classics, an imprint of Yesterday's Classics, LLC, is an unabridged republication of the text originally published by Ginn and Company in 1924, with editing of the text to conform to modern sensibilities. For the complete listing of the books that are published by Yesterday's Classics, please visit www.yesterdaysclassics.com. Yesterday's Classics is the publishing arm of Gateway to the Classics which presents the complete text of hundreds of classic books for children at www.gatewaytotheclassics.com.

ISBN: 978-1-63334-160-9

Yesterday's Classics, LLC
PO Box 339
Ithaca, NY 14851

PREFACE

Africa is a great commissary for future generations. The highly developed countries of temperate zones are calling each year for additional markets for their manufactures and for increasing amounts of raw materials. Many of these materials—rubber, coffee, sugar, cotton, and cocoa—must come from tropical and semitropical regions. The forests of the torrid zone are the main source of the world's hard-wood supply and of the oil nuts and seeds, gums, resins, and bark, which are used in ever-increasing quantities.

Africa is the greatest land mass which can yield these tropical and semitropical products. It has also vast pastures for flocks and herds which will furnish meat, wool, hides and skins, and dairy products for crowded manufacturing nations.

Because of these reasons the study of Africa is important for our future merchants, manufacturers, and bankers who are at present in our schools. Their attention should be directed to the future of this rapidly developing continent and the place which it will occupy in the economic world. Because this place depends largely on its natural regions and its climate, these points have been emphasized throughout the book. Because the strength and economic wealth of European nations depends to a large extent on their colonies the book is based on colonial interests.

Our young people should have first-hand information regarding our relations with Africa, the products which we receive, the goods which we send, and the demand for men and materials to develop its rich resources. Much valuable material concerning these points can be obtained from government sources. By its use the pupils will gain not only the information they need but also a better idea of the many lines of work carried on by our government. The Department of Agriculture and the Department of Commerce furnish material which may be used in arithmetic classes as well as in geography lessons. The pupils may write letters asking for such material, file this as a part of their library, and prepare and use a card catalogue, work which makes for independence of thought and action.

The ever-changing statistics regarding industries are not given in this book. More permanent figures, of areas, populations, etc., are supplied, with thought-provoking questions regarding them. Teacher and pupils should suggest many more. A review of continents already studied can be carried on through the use of these figures. They are also of much help in problem work. Constant comparisons develop the judgment and tend to make clearer and more permanent the mental pictures of the pupils.

This book is not a mere description of places and people such as might be written by a traveler. The text, maps, and studies are planned and written by a student of geography and an instructor of long standing who knows children and schoolroom problems and the pedagogic principles which underlie the work of the teacher.

That the book may be of great help to both teacher and pupils and may serve to stimulate in both a broader knowledge and a more sympathetic understanding of their world neighbors is the earnest desire of the author.

NELLIE B. ALLEN

ACKNOWLEDGMENTS

Thanks for many valuable suggestions, criticisms, and photographs are due to the following people: Mr. Augustin William Ferrin, formerly Trade Commissioner for the Bureau of Foreign and Domestic Commerce in Australia; Mr. Samuel W. Honaker, formerly Consul in South Africa; Mr. J. H. Muurling, Netherland Indian Government, New York City; Professor C. C. Nutting, University of Iowa; Dr. James A. Robertson, Chief of Near Eastern Division, Bureau of Foreign and Domestic Commerce, Department of Commerce, Washington, D.C.; Dr. H. L. Shantz, United States Department of Agriculture; Mr. Addison E. Southard, formerly Consul at Aden, Arabia, and Jerusalem, Palestine; Mrs. Helen G. Thomas, Clark University School of Geography.

CONTENTS

I. INTRODUCTION 1

II. LIFE IN ANCIENT EGYPT 20

III. LIFE IN MODERN EGYPT 34

IV. BRITISH POSSESSIONS IN AFRICA ... 52

V. ANGLO-EGYPTIAN SUDAN 56

VI. BRITISH EAST AFRICA 65

VII. ZANZIBAR AND ITS CLOVE
PLANTATIONS 84

VIII. THE BRITISH IN SOUTH AFRICA 89

IX. THE UNION OF SOUTH AFRICA 95

X. SOUTHWEST AFRICA,
BECHUANALAND, AND RHODESIA .. 129

XI. BRITISH COLONIES IN WEST
AFRICA 149

XII. OTHER WEST COAST COLONIES
AND ST. HELENA 169

REVIEW OF THE BRITISH
POSSESSIONS 186

CONTENTS

XIII. FRENCH POSSESSIONS IN AFRICA .. 187

XIV. FRENCH EQUATORIAL AFRICA 192

XV. THE FRENCH IN WEST AFRICA 203

XVI. ACROSS THE DESERT FROM
TIMBUKTU TO FEZ 217

XVII. IN THE LAND OF THE MOORS 234

XVIII. IN ALGERIA, THE MOST
IMPORTANT COLONY OF FRANCE .. 253

XIX. TUNIS, THE MOST NORTHERLY
COUNTRY OF AFRICA 273

XX. THE ISLAND OF MADAGASCAR 285

REVIEW OF THE FRENCH
POSSESSIONS 289

XXI. A HOT JOURNEY THROUGH
BELGIAN CONGO 291

XXII. ITALIAN AFRICA AND A TRIP
THROUGH LIBYA 313

XXIII. ERITREA AND THE SOMALI COAST . 327

REVIEW OF THE ITALIAN
POSSESSIONS 337

XXIV. ANGOLA, THE LARGEST COLONY
OF PORTUGAL 339

CONTENTS

XXV. ON THE PLANTATIONS OF MOZAMBIQUE.................. 350

XXVI. ISLAND POSSESSIONS OF PORTUGAL..................... 358

REVIEW OF THE PORTUGUESE POSSESSIONS 365

XXVII. SPANISH POSSESSIONS IN AFRICA .. 366

XXVIII. THE ABYSSINIAN PLATEAU 378

XXIX. THE REPUBLIC OF LIBERIA........ 387

GENERAL REVIEW OF AFRICA... 393

PROBLEMS ON AFRICA 395

XXX. THE GREAT LAND OF AUSTRALIA .. 399

XXXI. A TRIP THROUGH THE ISLAND CONTINENT 410

XXXII. IN GEYSER LAND 429

XXXIII. AMONG THE PACIFIC ISLANDS 438

XXXIV. UNITED STATES POSSESSIONS IN THE PACIFIC................. 448

XXXV. BRITISH POSSESSIONS IN THE PACIFIC 472

CONTENTS

XXXVI. FRENCH POSSESSIONS IN THE
        PACIFIC 478

XXXVII. THE DUTCH EAST INDIES........ 483

        REVIEW OF AUSTRALIA AND
            THE PACIFIC ISLANDS 496

        PROBLEMS ON AUSTRALIA AND
            THE PACIFIC ISLANDS 497

APPENDIX 499
GLOSSARY 507

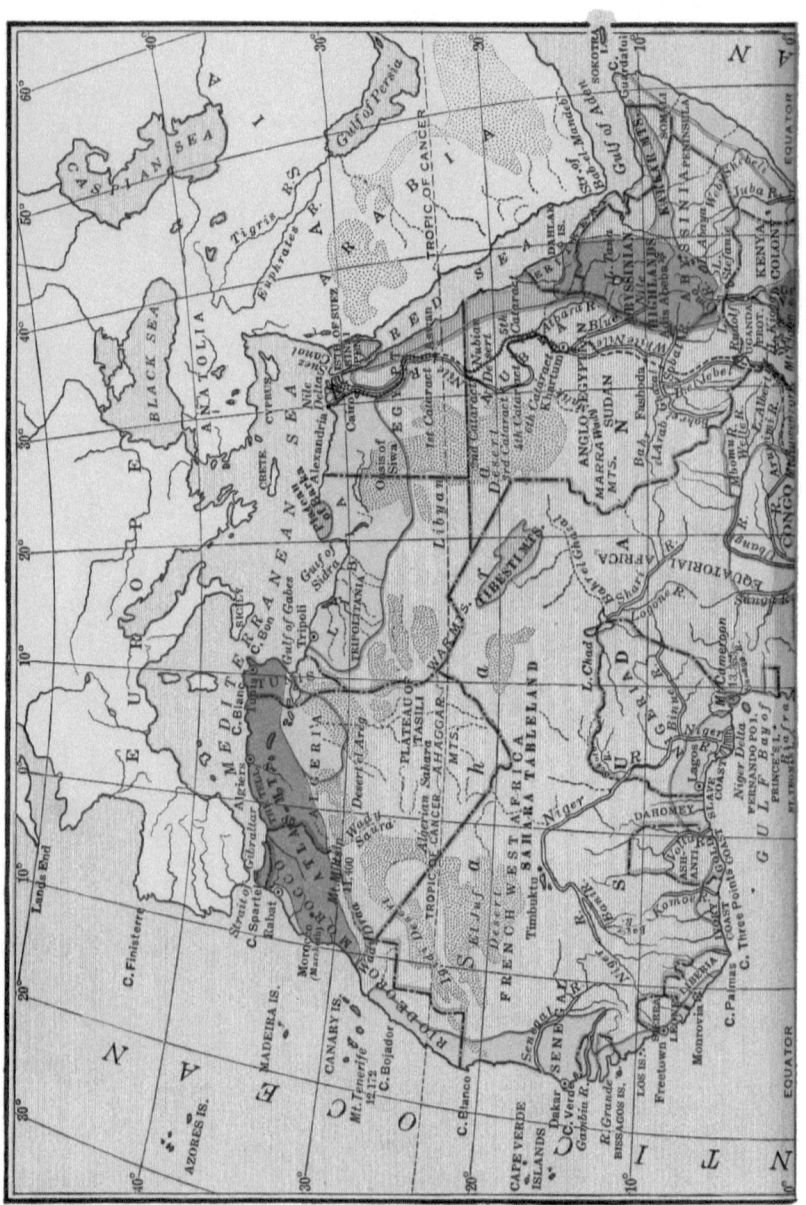

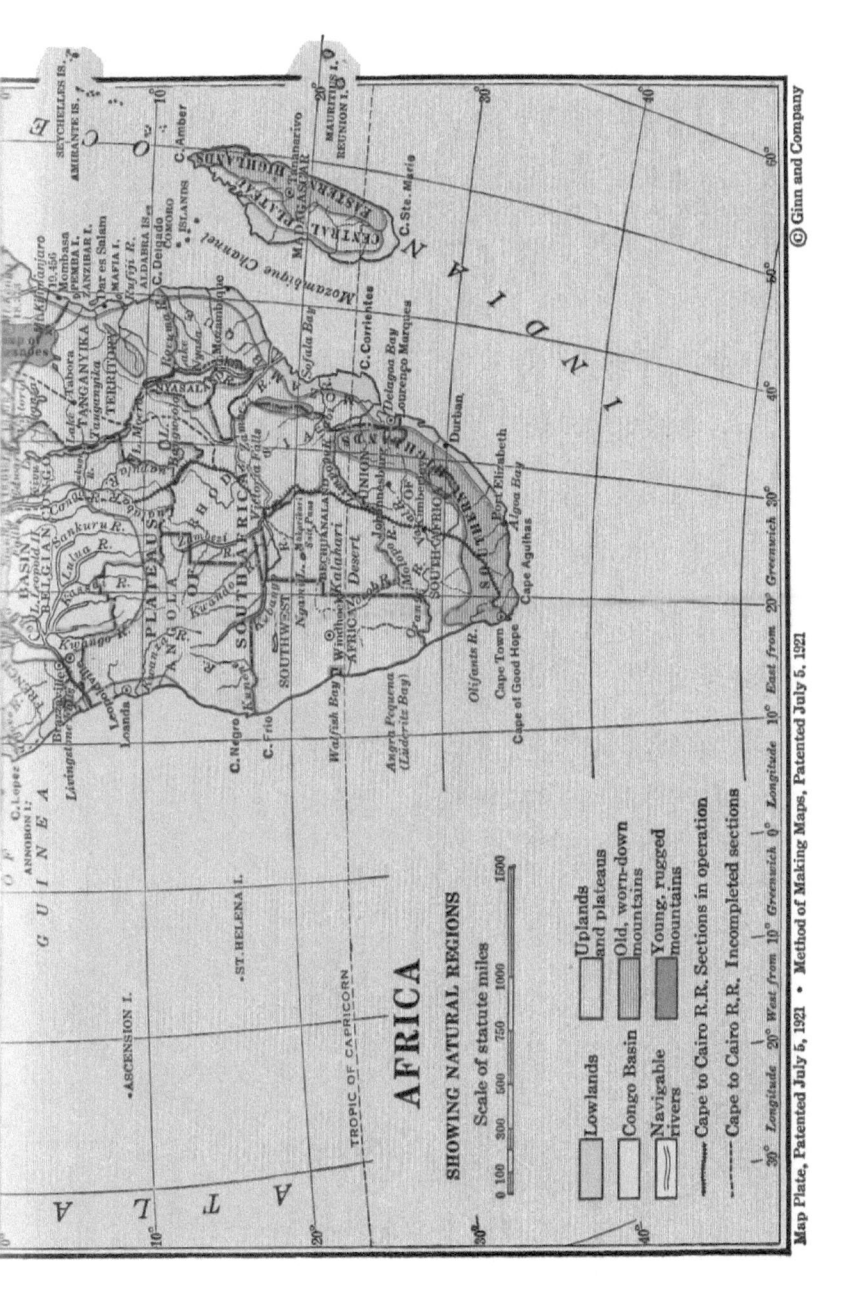

CHAPTER I

INTRODUCTION

We are going to travel in Africa, a continent of great things. It contains some of the largest rivers, lakes, and waterfalls in the world. We shall find there the greatest deserts, the densest tropical forests and jungles, the widest plateaus and grasslands, the richest deposits of minerals, and the largest and fiercest animals. It contains more blacks than any other continent and the smallest people that live anywhere on earth. It is a "colony continent." Almost all its vast area is divided among European nations, who find here room for people from their crowded cities, markets for their manufactured goods, and a rich source of many raw materials for their mills and factories.

For long, long centuries only the northern part of Africa was known, and the rest of the continent was a land of mystery. The great Sahara Desert formed a boundary beyond which few people penetrated. The land to the south was known only along the coast lands and was visited chiefly by slave traders.

What shall we call Africa? It has long been known as the Dark Continent; but today the darkness of ignorance is disappearing before the light of knowledge, which is slowly creeping through the forests and grasslands, into the jungles, and over the deserts.

Vast regions of Africa have been called the Great Thirst Lands; but, though dreary deserts still cover enormous areas, we shall find many places where water is brought in pipes for hundreds of miles for the crops and animals, where thousands of wells have been dug, and where mighty dams and huge reservoirs have been built to store up the surplus water of the rainy season.

Africa is sometimes called the Land of Blinding Sunshine, yet we shall travel for weeks in regions where it rains nearly every day of the year and where the forests are so thick that the sun's rays never penetrate to the shaded, tunnel-like paths which connect the scattered villages.

Another name which has been given to Africa is the Land of the White Helmet. These light head coverings which most of the white men wear in Africa are seen there today in larger numbers than ever before. Protected from the sunshine by their white helmets, men are sailing up the rivers, crossing the deserts, penetrating the forests and jungles, hunting in the grasslands, starting plantations, developing mines, building roads and railroads and bridges, establishing wireless stations and airplane routes, and carrying with them everywhere a knowledge of modern industry and better ways of life.

When we are studying ancient countries, like Egypt, Greece, and Rome, it is well to look back and see what

INTRODUCTION

they have contributed in industry and science, in art and literature, in laws and government, and in other fields to the civilization of the world. But when we are studying new or undeveloped lands, such as make up the most of Africa, it is well to look ahead and learn if we can of what value the region may be in the future and what it may contribute to the welfare of the world.

Many of the leading countries, especially in Europe, are very crowded, farms are small, and most of the people live in the big cities. Larger and larger amounts of fruits and vegetables, cotton, sugar, grain, and animal products, such as meat, wool, hides and skins, and dairy products, must be supplied each year to feed and clothe the increasing population. More minerals must be produced; we need coal, copper, tin, and many others. As the world grows richer more gold and diamonds are used.

Figure 1. This is one of our friends in Egypt. If you visit Cairo, he would like to have you ride on his donkey to see some of the interesting sights in the narrow streets.

Then, too, the countries of the greatest development in Europe and America are located in the temperate zone. On account of the climate it is not possible to produce here many articles needed in the mills and factories, such as rubber, cotton, coffee, cocoa, hard woods, and many gums, oils, and resins. For these the world is dependent on tropical and semitropical lands such as compose large parts of Africa and many Pacific islands.

Figure 2. Boys and girls in northern Africa, where these children live, cannot turn faucets in their houses and get water as you do. They have to go to the fountain.

Much of Africa is an undeveloped region. It has very rich resources, but its exports at present are small compared with what they will be in years to come. The needs and desires of her people and their ability to buy from other countries are small also. In the next half-century you will see wonderful changes in the parts of the world with which this book deals. There will be more roads, railroads, bridges, and motor trucks by

INTRODUCTION

which the people will be able to transport their products cheaply and easily to a market or seaport. Then they will start more plantations and ranches, open mines, and get out lumber and other products from the forests. These industries will vastly increase the amount and value of the exports. The needs of the settlers, their tools, machinery, food products, and building materials, and the materials needed for road-building, bridge-building, and railroad equipment will cause a similar increase in the imports.

The future value of Africa to the rest of the world depends on the work of Mother Nature and the gifts which she has bestowed here. Therefore, before we begin our trip through the continent let us look at these natural features on which the occupations of its people and the value of its products largely depend.

The map which will be of the most help in such a study is the one preceding page 1, showing the natural regions of Africa. As you look at it, notice first of all what an even coast line the continent has. How different is the coast line of Europe, where large gulfs and bays and seas penetrate so far inland that no part of any country except Russia is far from the ocean and from ocean-going vessels. Africa has no indentations which run far inland, and the early explorers who wished to get into the interior received no help from Nature in this direction.

If you will look again at the map, you will see that the most mountainous part is in the east. West of these high lands is a vast crack in the earth's crust beyond which lie other mountains. Nature's mountain-building is not always firm and strong, and here, as in some other parts of the earth, some of the rock strata began to crack and then to slip. Probably it was only a little at a time, but through the long, long ages the crust sank thousands of feet, forming what are called rift valleys. The long chain of lakes which you will find on the map in eastern Africa lies in one of these. Are most valleys formed in this way?

Figure 3. If you should travel in British East Africa, this man might help to carry your baggage. He lives in Uganda. Can you find this on the map on page 68?

Doubtless this breaking of the rock, or faulting, as a scientist would call it, and the slipping and sinking of the crust have been accompanied by earthquakes, for this is one of the chief causes of such catastrophes. The earthquakes in Japan and in Chile, South America, were caused in the same way. This is why earthquakes usually occur in mountainous areas.

The shape of the lakes lying in the rift valley causes them to appear smaller than they are. They really are very large bodies of water. Lake Nyasa is three hundred and fifty miles long, and Lake Tanganyika is

INTRODUCTION

four hundred miles in length and from twenty to forty miles wide. To what place would this lake reach from your home town? If your schoolhouse stood on one side of it, what place would lie on the opposite bank? The Red Sea is the largest body of water that lies in the rift valley. From the scale of miles on the map find out how long it is. Look on page 506 in the Appendix and see how these bodies of water rank in size among the large lakes of the world.

Let us look again at the regional map; this time we will study the surface. You will notice that Africa contains comparatively little lowland, most of which lies around the coast. How does the map tell you this? The Congo Basin, though lower than the surrounding land, lies on the average about a thousand feet above the sea. With the exception of the land in the extreme north and south of the continent, the coastal low lands are hot, damp, and unhealthful. This was another hindrance to explorers in getting into the interior of the continent.

Figure 4. This happy girl lives in French Equatorial Africa, in the part called Cameroons. What does the map of the French possessions on page 188 tell you about this region?

The shading of the regional map tells you that most of Africa is a plateau from one thousand to three or four thousand feet high and that mountains rise from the edge of the plateau near the margin of the continent. Was this arrangement of the surface a help or a hindrance to the explorers? The surface is high in the east and north in the regions of the Abyssinian and Atlas mountains, lower in the south, where the Southern Highlands are, and still lower in the west, where you find Mt. Cameroon.

The rivers of Africa, cutting their way through the high lands and the hard rocks of the plateau down to the lower coast lands, have falls and rapids, making them unnavigable. This hindered for many years the exploration of interior Africa.

The even coast line, the unhealthful coastal lowlands, the marginal highlands, the unnavigable rivers, and the great deserts and jungles were the chief reasons why the exploration of Africa was so long delayed.

One of the chief factors in determining what help Africa can be in supplying other parts of the world with needed materials is the climate. More than anything else the temperature and rainfall influence the products of a region. More of Africa than of any other continent lies in the hot part of the world. You will notice that the equator crosses it near the center, that only comparatively small areas lie in the temperate zones, and that these portions are in the warmer rather than in the cooler parts of those belts.

The low coastal regions in and near the torrid zone

INTRODUCTION

are hot all the year round. You remember, however, that much of Africa is a plateau, higher and therefore cooler than the low coastal plains. Before we can decide what the people do who live in the coastal regions and on the higher plateaus, how they live, and what products they raise we shall have to notice the winds of Africa, for these are among the most important of Mother Nature's workers.

Figure 5. These children of Morocco are having just as much fun as if they were riding on flying horses. Where is Morocco?

You know that in the torrid zone easterly winds prevail. North of the equator they blow from the northeast, and south of the equator they come from the southeast. Before reaching the part of Africa which lies in the Northern Hemisphere these winds have been blowing for thousands of miles over the dry lands of inland Asia, and consequently they contain little moisture. Moreover, as they are coming from cooler

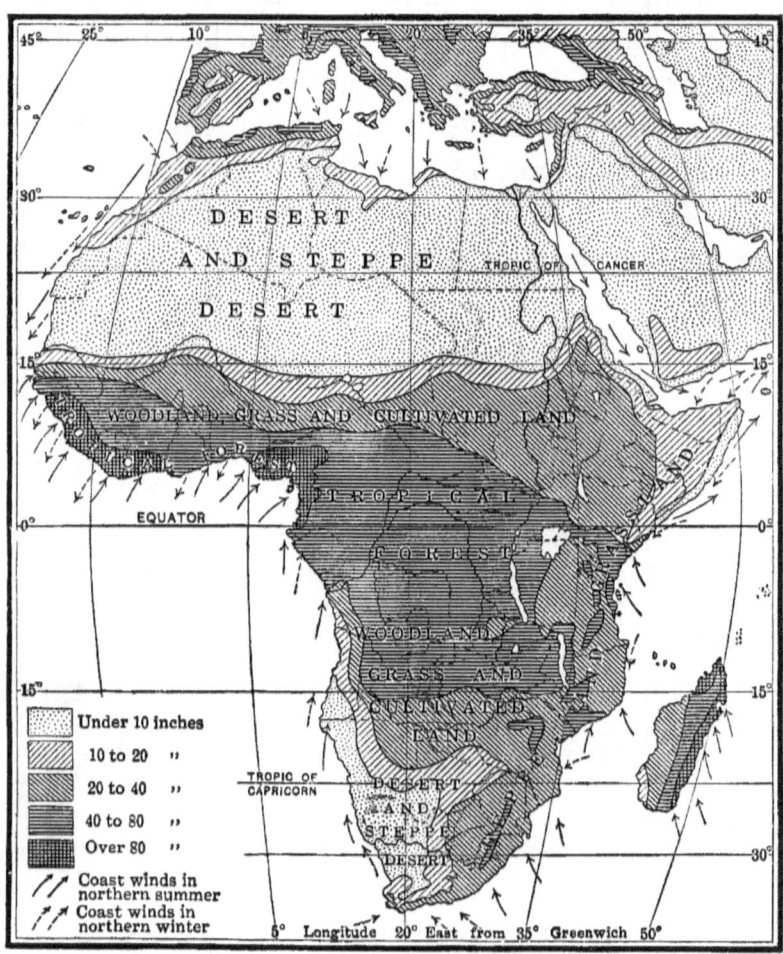

Figure 6. Rainfall map of Africa. Where is the heaviest rainfall in Africa? What grows here? Why are there few forests in other parts of Africa? Which coast of southern Africa receives the greater amount of rain? Why? (See page 12.) Along which coast of this part of the continent do the greater number of people live? (See map on page 11.) Why? What kind of a region is much of the northern part of Africa? Why? (See pages 9 and 12.)

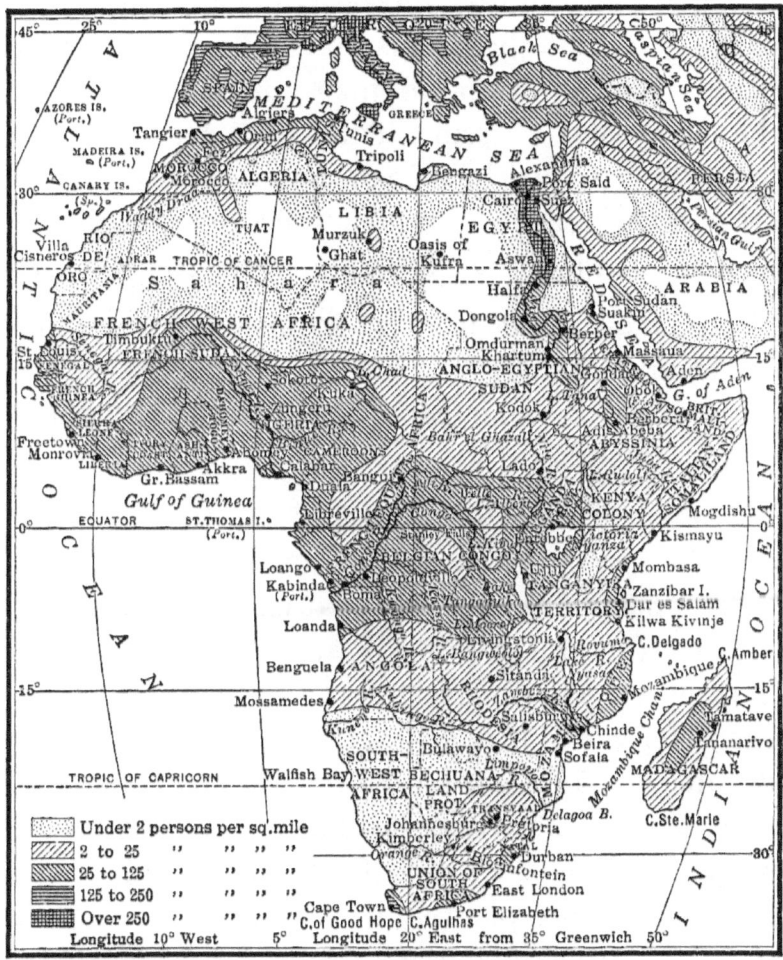

Figure 7. Population map of Africa. In what part of Africa is the densest population? Of what region is this area a part? (See map on page 10.) Why do more people live here than anywhere else? In what part of the continent are there the fewest people? Why? How dense is the population in Central Africa? What kind of a region is this?

to warmer regions they are constantly increasing their capacity to hold their moisture, and unless they are chilled by passing over mountains they give no rain to the thirsty land. Therefore in northern Africa we have the great desert of Sahara. In the interior of Sahara there are some mountain ranges high enough to chill the winds as they blow over them, and here some rain falls.

The moist winds from the Mediterranean are shut out from the Sahara by the Atlas Mountains, and the local winds which come from the Atlantic do not blow very far inland.

In parts of the desert sharp, heavy showers occur once in a while. These last but a short time, and the water quickly sinks into the ground. When the snows melt or the rains fall on the Atlas Mountains or on the ranges in the Sahara, rivers flow down their slopes. The water which they contain soon evaporates in the dry air, or sinks into the loose soil where it flows along as underground streams. It is this underground water which furnishes the supply for the wells and springs which make life possible on the oases and enable caravans to travel over the desert.

Similar wind conditions prevail to form the desert in the south. The trade winds from the Indian Ocean are chilled by the highlands along the eastern coast of the continent and drop their moisture on their seaward slopes. Therefore this part of Africa receives more rain than the western portions. You will see this by looking at the rainfall map on page 10.

Central Africa is located in the equatorial rain belt.

INTRODUCTION

Here the warm, light air, full of moisture, becomes chilled as it rises, and drops its vapor in heavy rains. As the sun moves north in summer the rainy belt follows it nearly to the border of the Sahara. In winter the rains follow the sun southward. Thus, as the map shows you, Central Africa receives a heavy rainfall throughout the year. This grows lighter toward the Tropics, where little or no rainfall occurs.

Because of the heat and the heavy rainfall in Central Africa we shall find there deep forests and jungles. On both sides of the forest region, where the rainfall is lighter, there are vast areas of grasslands, and still farther north and south, where there is little or no rain, are the two great deserts. Beyond these we come to mountain ranges,—the Atlas in the north and the Southern Highlands in the south. Climbing these we find on their coastal slopes well-watered, fertile lands, which are among the most productive areas of Africa.

Figure 8. Abyssinia is one of the few independent countries of Africa. The people there do not fight with other countries, but some of the tribes often have war with others. Could you use such a long spear?

AFRICA, AUSTRALIA, ISLANDS OF PACIFIC

What we have learned about the position, surface, and climate of this great continent teaches us many very interesting things about its products. In its hot, tropical regions millions of natives are raising peanuts, gathering coconuts and drying the meat, and collecting seeds and nuts. These products and the oil which they yield are exported from tropical Africa in enormous quantities and are manufactured into many useful articles, such as butter substitutes, soap, candles, glycerin, and cosmetics.

In the hot part of Africa there are many large cocoa plantations, the product from which is fast outstripping that of South American countries. We shall find hundreds of natives tapping rubber trees and carrying the hardened sheets and biscuits on their backs to the nearest trader's station. In places we shall wonder if we have not been suddenly transported to Louisiana or Texas, for the sights on the cotton and sugar plantations are very similar to those in our Southern states.

As we go from village to village we shall notice the people gathering beeswax and honey, for the sweet tropical blossoms attract immense numbers of bees. We shall see the natives also collecting gums and resins, which are useful in making druggists' supplies, varnishes, and other articles. In the forests we shall find them felling African mahogany trees and loading them on ships bound for European ports.

The grasslands of Africa will some day be ranked among the most important grazing lands of the world. The natives here are raising millions of cattle, sheep, goats, and camels, and in the future their numbers will

INTRODUCTION

be greatly increased. The climate of these grasslands, particularly on the southern plateau, is pleasant and suitable for light-skinned people, who do not thrive in the lower, hotter regions.

In the northern part of Africa, between the Atlas Mountains and the Mediterranean Sea, are fine farms, vineyards, and orchards which remind us of those in southern European countries. On the well-watered slopes of the Southern Highlands we shall see splendid farms where grain and fruit are raised.

Figure 9. These Arab children live in the desert part of Tunis. What things in your city do you think would seem strange to them?

Mother Nature has hidden in the ground in many parts of Africa rich mineral treasures. Africa produces 95 percent of the world's supply of diamonds and more than half of its gold. It has coal beds covering an area almost twice as large as that of our states which border Mexico and the Gulf of Mexico. Its copper deposits equal those of Europe and North America combined, while its beds of iron are several times greater than those in the United States. Besides these there are beds of tin, graphite, lead and zinc, phosphates, manganese, and chrome ore.

The waters of Africa form another tremendously valuable resource. On its navigable rivers and lakes one could sail twice the distance around the earth at the equator. Its falls and rapids will yield an almost unbelievable amount of water power, from which can be generated enough electricity to light its cities, run its cars, and propel the machinery in its mills and factories.

In spite of its large cities, its flourishing industries, and the great undertakings going on there, Africa contains many miles of grasslands as yet unoccupied, large forests and jungles where no foreigner has ever set foot, and great stretches of desert as yet unirrigated where water can be supplied.

To help in its development Africa will have everything that Europe and America did not have in their early days, such as locomotives, steamboats, motor trucks, tractors, airplanes, machinery of all kinds, and telegraphs and telephones and wireless telegraphy.

All these things will cause the growth of industries, cities, and communications in Africa to be much more rapid than has ever been possible in the development of any other continent. Changes are taking place very

INTRODUCTION

rapidly in this great land mass, and you will have to read papers and magazines if you wish to keep your knowledge accurate and up-to-date.

In this chapter you have seen the pictures of some of our African neighbors. In our journeys we shall see many others at work and at play in the forests and deserts and grasslands. As we travel through the continent we shall understand better the necessity for a greater knowledge of these people who are already supplying us with large quantities of raw materials and who in the future will send us enormously greater amounts. As the years go by and their knowledge of other countries and peoples increases, their desire for foreign products will increase also, and we shall send to them larger and larger quantities of manufactured articles from our mills and factories and foundries.

SUGGESTIONS FOR STUDY

I

1. The wonders of Africa.

2. Appropriate names for Africa.

3. Future importance of tropical and semitropical lands.

4. The coast line and its influence.

5. Natural regions.

6. Effects of the surface on the rivers.

7. Winds and rainfall.

8. Resources and products.

9. Aids in the development of Africa.

II

1. How does Africa rank in size among the continents (see Appendix, page 504)?

2. Where is the region of greatest rainfall in Africa (see map on page 10)?

3. Why does the eastern coast of southern Africa receive more rain than the eastern coast in the northern part of the continent?

4. Name the three largest rivers of Africa (see Appendix, page 506). Into what waters do the lakes in the great rift valley flow?

5. Among the early explorers of Africa were Mungo Park, David Livingstone, and Henry M. Stanley. What do cyclopedias tell you about these men? What other African explorers do they mention? Have you ever read any of the books which these men have written?

6. Can you find out the use of chrome ore? phosphates? graphite? manganese? These are all important minerals.

INTRODUCTION

III

QUESTIONS ON THE REGIONAL MAP

1. Of what does most of the surface of Africa consist? What two divisions of this plateau region do you find given on the map? What nations control these? To whom does most of the Congo Basin belong?

2. What highland region is in the north of Africa? What countries are included in it? To whom do they belong? What divisions of Africa are included in the Southern Highlands? They are a part of what commonwealth? What great highlands lie in East Africa? In what divisions are they located?

3. What divisions are included in the widest part of the coastal plain? In what divisions is this plain so narrow that it does not appear on the map?

4. What hindrances to navigation do you notice on the Nile? on the Congo? on the Zambezi? Explain why these falls are located as they are.

5. How can you tell on the map that only a small part of Africa lies outside the torrid zone?

CHAPTER II

LIFE IN ANCIENT EGYPT

Long ages ago, even thousands of years before Christ was born in Bethlehem, a great nation lived in the valley of the Nile River. The name of this part of Africa is Egypt. The history of the Egyptians extends back for seven thousand years, and even before this they had an art, a religion, and a literature of their own. While Europe was still peopled with barbarians, the Egyptian priests had a knowledge of science, of mathematics and astronomy, and of sculpture and architecture. The workers of the nation possessed a mechanical skill which enabled them to build temples and monuments, palaces and tombs, at which the world still wonders. At Memphis and Thebes, the two chief cities of ancient Egypt, are ruins of buildings so wonderful that stories of their size and beauty seem almost like fairy tales. The ruined city of Karnak across the river from the plain of Thebes was a city of temples. The oldest building there was begun more than two thousand years before the birth of Christ. It grew for centuries, as each successive ruler in adding to its beauties did his best to outdo anything that any king before him had done. Gateways, courts, chapels, halls, sacred lakes, rows of giant columns, lines of massive statues, and avenues of sphinxes were added year by year and century by century to the original temple. The gateway to the main building is a hundred and fifty feet high and three hundred and fifty feet wide. Compare this with the size of your school building and you will have some idea of the size of this pylon, as the gateway is called. The pylon is only the entrance to courts so vast that large temples stood in them and to halls so great that it seems impossible to find adequate words to describe them.

Figure 10. This is a little Egyptian village which now stands on the sands where once rose the temples and palaces of the ancient city of Memphis.

The early Egyptians were governed by rulers who lived in luxury in beautiful palaces. Indeed, the royal palace was more like a small town than a house. In one building dwelt the king and his many servants; in another were the rooms of state, where councils of high officials were held, and the banqueting halls, where feasts were given; a third, surrounded with beautiful trees and lovely lakes, was the home of the queen and

Figure 11. These men are tending sheep on the plains near Cairo. See the great pyramids in the distance. Why were they built? How old are they (see page 28)?

the young princes and princesses. There were also the stables, where were kept hundreds of splendid horses, and the buildings which housed the royal chariots. The storehouses for the grain and provisions stood in long rows. All these buildings and many more were needed, for if we may judge by the titles of the officials and servants, there were hundreds of people attached to the royal house. Among these were guards, councilors, gatekeepers, chamberlains, lords in waiting who received visitors, and waiting women for the queen

Figure 12. This is the gateway to the temple of Karnak. Can you see the carvings which cover it? What was said about this gateway, or pylon, on page 21?

and the royal children. There were spinners and weavers, bleachers, washers, wigmakers, metal workers, keepers of the diadem, lords of the bedchamber, fan bearers, cupbearers, scribes, physicians, wine-makers, cooks, and scores of other "butchers and bakers and candlestick makers."

When the ruler left his palace it was in a beautifully ornamented sedan chair borne on poles resting on the shoulders of courtiers clad in beautiful garments, or in a golden chariot drawn by prancing horses. Fan bearers on either side waved enormous fans, and runners with long staves in their hands ran ahead to clear the way through the crowd which had gathered to see the display. Perhaps behind the king's chariot came those of the queen and the royal children. These in turn were followed by gorgeous carriages filled with court ladies.

Now let us go inside the royal palace, a thing that the common people of these ancient days never dreamed of doing. The great rooms were beautifully furnished and decorated. The walls were covered with tiles or draped with rich hangings of wonderful tapestries. Costly rugs woven by women in far-away Turkish tents lay on the floors. Couches were covered with material embroidered by slaves. Chairs and tables were of ebony wood inlaid with ivory and had feet and legs carved in imitation of those of a lion. On tall stands of carved ebony were golden vessels of incense, which was burned to perfume the air.

The poorer people of Egypt were the slaves of the nobility. They had to labor at whatever work their masters assigned. They built temples, palaces, and tombs; they worked in the quarries, cutting the stones which were used in these buildings; they mixed the mud of the Nile River with straw and made bricks, which they dried in the sun.

The Egyptian peasants lived in little mud huts with earth floors in much the same way as many of them do today. They raised barley, wheat, and corn, and ground the grain by hand into coarse flour. Out of this the women made little flat cakes just as we may see them doing today in many parts of Egypt. The vine was very carefully tended, for otherwise there would be no wine to fill the great stone jars in the royal palaces or to offer to the gods in return for their protection. The flax fields were irrigated and cultivated, and the women spun and wove the fiber into fine linen for the garments of the priests and the nobility and for the wrappings of the dead. The people molded their dishes from the clay near the river, and coppersmiths in their little booths hammered copper into pans, jars, and vases just as we shall see them doing in the bazaars of Cairo. In parts of the country the men hunted the elephant and the giraffe, and killed the awkward hippopotamus on the banks of the river. Most of the traffic was carried on the Nile River or along its banks, as the desert which lay on either side of the narrow valley was desolate and dangerous.

The papyrus plant, which grew by the river, was very useful to the ancient Egyptians. The tender new shoots were eaten, and the stalks were used for building the little huts and for making canoes. The fiber was used for paper. The possession of this writing material was a great advantage to the Egyptians. Other nations had to carve their records and accounts on heavy stone tablets, which were difficult to move. The Egyptians made wide use of the papyrus scrolls which, when rolled, were easily carried from place to place.

Figure 13. At flood time the river overflows the land so that the trees rise out of the water. What causes the floods of the Nile (see pages 26 and 40-41)?

The whole life of the ancient Egyptians centered around the Nile River. Then, as now, the tropical rains poured down on the mountains of Abyssinia, and the swollen branches, thick with the mud scoured from the hills, rushed down the steep slopes into the valley. The Nile rose higher and higher. Soon the banks were covered; and the water spread farther and farther over the land, dropping there the rich soil which it carried.

The people anxiously awaited the rising of the river and rejoiced as the flood covered the valley. Their very life depended on it, for without this life-giving water the fertile valley of Egypt would be like the bare, brown desert which stretched away on either side.

Egypt was so densely populated that land not reached by the flood waters of the Nile had to be irrigated in order that food crops might be raised. All day and day after day, in the heat of the Egyptian sun, the peasants lifted the heavy skin buckets of water from the canals and emptied them into ditches to flow to the thirsty land.

When they could be spared from the crops the Egyptians had to perform other hard labors for their rulers. If the king wished to make a record for himself as a conqueror of nations, the common people made up his army. If he wished to outdo any previous ruler in the magnificence of his palace or in the size and beauty of his royal city, the peasants quarried stone and built the houses, the palaces, the temples, and the city walls. If the king wished a safe tomb in which his body might lie, the peasants labored by thousands to haul the stones and pile them in place.

The Egyptians believed that the soul or spirit of a person existed after death and would at some time wish to return to the body which it had occupied. Therefore the bodies, especially those of the rulers and nobles, who were then thought to be much more important than the common people, were carefully preserved. They were treated with spices and ointments and wrapped

AFRICA, AUSTRALIA, ISLANDS OF PACIFIC

in bandages and cloths dipped in certain preparations. In the museums of several countries we can see these mummies, as they are called. Is it not wonderful to think of actually seeing the body of a person who lived four or five thousand years ago and knowing how he looked?

In order to keep his mummified body safely, each monarch built the strongest tomb possible. In very early times these were pits in the sand. Later, tombs were made in the rocks and cliffs. But the most wonderful tombs—in fact, the most wonderful buildings in the whole world—are the great pyramids which stand in the desert near Cairo.

Of the hundred pyramid tombs in Egypt the three on the opposite side of the Nile from the great city of Cairo are much better known than the others. The largest of these was built by old King Cheops, who ruled over Egypt nearly three thousand years before Christ was born. It covers more than thirteen acres, is about four hundred and eighty feet high, and each one of its four sides is more than seven hundred feet long. Compare this area and these distances with something near your school and try to imagine what the Great Pyramid would look like and how much ground it would cover if it stood there.

The four corners of the Great Pyramid point exactly north, south, east, and west. By means of the shadows the priests could determine the exact noon, the longest and shortest days, the date of the beginning of each season, and other things which helped in the daily lives of the people. Can you tell when it is noon by the

LIFE IN ANCIENT EGYPT

Figure 14. Large jars fastened to the rope dip up the water in the ditch below and pour it into the ditch which you can see on the surface. The oxen, driven by a woman, lift and lower the buckets. Thousands of years ago one might have seen Egyptians watering their fields in just the same way.

direction of your shadow, or the date of the shortest day by the length of your shadow?

Not far from the Great Pyramid is the Sphinx, another monument of ancient Egypt. It is a statue with the head of a man and the body of a lion. It is so enormous that if you should stand on one of the huge ears you could not see over the top of the head. The body is more than a hundred and seventy feet long. How does this compare with the length of your schoolhouse? The sphinx has stood for centuries, calm and majestic, looking out over the lonely desert. Do you not wish that its stone lips could move and tell us the story of its life?

None of the rulers or great men of ancient Egypt wished to be forgotten or to have their great deeds, their wars, and their conquests pass out of the minds of the people. Every where on the walls of temples and tombs, on pillars and gateways, are pictures carved of the gods whom the Egyptians worshiped and of the kings and their courts, their slaves, their wives, their journeys, and their victories. Men have spent their lives in studying these pictures, and from them they have learned much about the life and the most important deeds of each monarch.

Besides the pictures which appear on many Egyptian ruins, there was found on walls and tablets a curious kind of writing which for a long time no one was able to read. At last a tablet of black stone inscribed with hieroglyphics, as the characters in this writing are called, was found in some ruins near the Rosetta mouth of the Nile River. This Rosetta stone also bears an inscription in demotic, the writing used by the Egyptian people, and beneath the Egyptian writing the same text is repeated in Greek, which, as you know, many people can read. This furnished a key to the Egyptian writing, and by studying both languages the text of the hieroglyphics was translated. Then some scholars found that they could read other inscriptions where the same characters appeared. With this as a beginning great progress has been made in translating Egyptian inscriptions and through them learning more and more of the life and customs of this ancient and interesting people.

Much information has also been gained from tombs

LIFE IN ANCIENT EGYPT

Figure 15. These workmen are drilling out stone vessels. The hieroglyphics between them record their conversation. One says, "This is a very lovely vase"; the other replies, "It is, indeed."

in which the kings were buried. In these tombs not only the bodies were placed but also many articles which the royal family used. Can you find in magazines printed during 1923 and 1924 what were some of the things found in the tomb of King Tutankhamen which was opened at that time? Many rolls of papyrus have also been preserved. One roll, the largest document ever found, is a hundred and thirty feet long. It contains an account of the doings of the great King Rameses and gives a description of the wealth and income of the temples in his time.

Not so many years ago most of the ruins, carvings, and tablets which tell us so much about ancient Egypt were unknown. Many of them were buried deep in the sands of the desert or hidden under the villages of the present inhabitants. Under the dust and dirt and the mud houses of the people there are doubtless other ruins which some day may tell us even more about these ancient people of the Nile valley. It seems wonderful to read the very writing, handle the tools, and see the people who lived thousands of years ago.

When we examine the beautiful things which were made by these people, see the buildings which they built, and read descriptions of what they did, it makes us wonder what we are doing which will last six or seven thousand years. What do you suppose that people living thousands of years from today will find still standing in our country? What will our records tell them about us? Are we doing greater things than did these ancient Egyptians? Will our records show us to be of a finer character than were these people who lived so long ago in the Nile valley?

SUGGESTIONS FOR STUDY

I

1. History of Egypt.

2. Ancient cities and buildings.

3. Life in ancient Egypt.

4. Historical records.

5. The Nile River.

6. The pyramid tombs and the Sphinx.

7. Picture writing and hieroglyphics.

II

1. The flooding of most rivers is a cause of sorrow because of the damage which results. Why have the Egyptians always regarded the flooding of the Nile as a blessing?

2. How old is our nation? The recorded history of England may be said to begin with the invasion of the famous Roman general Julius Cæsar, in 55 B.C. How many years is it since then? The Chinese claim that their history dates back to 2800 B.C. According to this how old is the Chinese nation?

3. How does the age of each nation mentioned above compare with that of Egypt?

III

Make a list of the places mentioned in this chapter. From it select the ones which you think are so important that you should always remember them.

CHAPTER III

LIFE IN MODERN EGYPT

During the long centuries that the Egyptians have lived and worked in the Nile valley they have been ruled by many nations. Today, for the first time in two thousand years, they are once more independent. The British, the last nation which ruled Egypt, made many improvements in the country. They levied just taxes, built dams and canals and enlarged the irrigated area, increased crops, extended railroads, improved sanitary conditions, and did many other things to make the life of the people more comfortable. We must wait and see whether the country under native Egyptian officials will continue to prosper.

We shall begin our journey through Egypt at Alexandria, a great seaport of nearly half a million people and, next to Cairo, the largest city of Africa. In many ways Alexandria is a modern city, and the scenes at the busy docks are much like those which we might see in large commercial cities in other continents.

Compared with some of the ruined cities of Egypt this is a very young city, but compared with the cities of the United States it is very old, for it was founded when Alexander the Great conquered Egypt, more than three hundred years before the birth of Christ. It once was a magnificent place with palaces, gardens, public baths, and temples. It was a center of learning, and scholars from all over the known world came here to study. When the Arabs conquered Egypt, Alexandria contained the world's largest library, in which were thousands of papyrus rolls filled with Egyptian records. All these were destroyed by order of the Arab general, and thus was lost a means for learning much about the ancient Egyptians.

The trade of Alexandria is very important. On the wharves are the ivory tusks of elephants, killed far to the south, and ostrich feathers from the Sudan. There are quantities of grain and sugar also and great numbers of bales of cotton. Cotton is the chief export of Egypt, and we shall see it growing in many places as we ride through the country.

The great city of Cairo is about a hundred miles from Alexandria, across the low delta lands of the Nile River. From the car windows we see here and there villages of little mud huts, cotton fields white with bolls of fiber, tall, waving sugar cane, and the soft green of the growing rice. All the fields are connected with one another and with the river by canals and ditches which carry the water necessary for the crops.

Cairo is situated at the head of the Nile delta, where the river separates into several branches through which it makes its way to the sea (see map on page 219). Let us take a donkey ride through old Cairo. The donkey boys soon recognize us as Americans, and we hire donkeys with good American names, such as George Washington, Teddy, Uncle Sam, and Yankee Doodle. If we were English or German or French, the same donkeys might be called Wellington or Bismarck or Napoleon.

Each donkey boy runs beside his animal and with whip and voice urges it continually to a better pace. The trip is interesting, but we are almost glad when it is over. The streets are so narrow that we are frequently crowded against the wall by porters with great bundles on their backs and by heavily loaded donkeys and camels. At every turn beggars cry for gifts, and venders of fruit and water carriers with their goatskin bags advertise their wares with loud voices. How should you like to wear turbans instead of hats, like those tall Arabs? Do you think that you could carry a great water jar on your head without spilling a drop, as those straight graceful girls do?

The bazaars are more crowded even than the streets through which we have come. What odd little stores line the narrow alleys! They are much like those which we have seen in western and central Asia (see Allen's "Asia"). Each store is so small that the proprietor, sitting cross-legged in the center, can reach everything around him. Many of the little places are workshops also, in which the men make the things which they sell. In one street all the men are making brass dishes, and the noise of the hammers is deafening. In another street the jewelers are at work. In a third the leather workers are making slippers, saddles, bridles, and bags.

Figure 16. This is an old street in Cairo. See how narrow it is! Notice the tall minarets of the mosque on the corner. On the high balcony of the nearest one a priest calls the people to prayer.

The merchants are very polite. They see that we are foreigners, however, and put high prices on all their goods. We bargain with them for some time before they come down to a reasonable figure so that we can buy. While the bargaining is going on, some of them offer us coffee which is very sweet and thick.

Cairo is a Mohammedan city and contains many Mohammedan churches, or mosques. Each has its tower, or minaret, from which the priest calls the people to prayer several times a day, and its court containing water, where the Mohammedans wash their hands and feet before they enter to worship. If we go into a mosque, we must either take off our shoes or put over them slippers which the guide provides so that we may not defile their sacred place. We may not believe as the Mohammedans do, but it is well for us to respect their customs, as we should wish them to do if they were visiting our country.

In the newer part of Cairo the wide boulevards, beautiful parks, and modern shops are very attractive. Our hotel is as fine and has as many conveniences as hotels in our country. The scenes from our windows, however, are very different from anything which we could see in a European or American city. Dark-robed Bedouins from the desert ride by on their silent-footed camels, covering with a cloud of dust a splendid automobile standing near. Here is a group of American tourists, and just behind them is a turbaned sheik on his donkey. Nearly run over by the carriage of that Egyptian official is a juggler crouched in the dust doing some wonderful tricks for the group watching him. There goes a snake charmer with his bag of snakes, and behind him comes a traveling salesman introducing some articles manufactured in Birmingham, England

(See Allen's "New Europe"). Truly Cairo is a place of contrasts, and not only Cairo but Egypt as well, and not only Egypt but other African countries. Always with the old we shall find the new. So rapidly are changes taking place in these lands that side by side with ancient customs we find those which are modern.

Figure 17. This is a modern street in Cairo. Contrast it with the previous one. Note the sidewalk, curbing, and up-to-date buildings.

All around Cairo stretches the brown desert. The life, the noise, the activities of the great city, are a sharp contrast to the emptiness and the silence of the vast sea of sand which surrounds it. The great Sahara stretches from the Atlantic Ocean on the west to the Red Sea on the east. Egypt is a part of it. In all this immense desert area there are no permanent towns and cities and farms except on the scattered oases and in the narrow valley watered by the floods of the Nile River.

Egypt is nearly as large as the states of Wyoming, Colorado, Utah, and Idaho. Its settled, cultivated part is only about as large as four Yellowstone Parks. Look at the map of the states mentioned above and see what a small fraction of their area would be covered by four parks the size of Yellowstone. All the rest of Egypt belongs to the desert and is peopled only by wandering tribes. The wonderful history of the ancient country of which you read in the last chapter belongs to the Egypt of the Nile valley.

Egypt is often called the Gift of the Nile. Were it not for the great river and its annual floods, the country would be like the rest of the Sahara, bare and brown. We do not wonder that the ancient Egyptians looked on the yearly flooding of the Nile as a miracle and worshiped the gods who controlled it. They knew nothing of the source of the great stream and of the heavy tropical rains which poured down the slopes of Abyssinia and changed into torrents the small streams which make up the branches of the Nile.

During the spring and summer months the sun shines vertically over the part of the torrid zone north of the equator. The heat becomes very great, and as heat hastens evaporation, enormous quantities of vapor are taken up into the air from the warm surface of the Indian Ocean.

The easterly trade winds which prevail in the torrid zone blow in from the ocean over the land, bringing this moisture with them. Much of Abyssinia is covered with high mountains, whose cool tops chill the winds and cause them to drop their moisture. Thus heavy rains pour down the steep slopes of the Abyssinian highlands into streams which later join the Blue Nile. This river, rushing along with its floods of water and its tons of soil scoured from the hills, joins the White Nile at Khartum (see map on page 68). Below this point no tributary enters the Nile in its long journey to the sea except the Atbara, which runs nearly dry during part of the year, but which in the rainy season helps to flood the main stream.

Other rivers are as useful as the Nile for navigation; others have an equal or a greater amount of water power; others water the land in their valleys; but no other river in the world has for thousands of years turned a desert into a prosperous farming country supporting one of the densest populations on earth.

In early June the Nile begins to rise and continues to increase in height during July and August. In September the water reaches its maximum height at Aswan (see map on page 68) and about a month later at Cairo. In an unfavorable year the Nile rises about twenty-one feet at Cairo and in an average year about twenty-five feet. If it rises twenty-eight or thirty feet, the embankments are in danger and have to be watched day and night.

During the flood season the tall palms grow out of the water; boats sail over fields which a few weeks later will be green with waving corn or dotted with vegetable gardens; mammoth gateways of ancient ruins and colossal statues stand in still waters which reflect below other gateways and statues as large and beautiful.

If for some reason the tropical rains in Abyssinia are less plentiful than usual and the river fails to rise to its usual height, some fields will be left dry, and no crops can be raised there until another season. Eagerly the people watch their river. Plenty or starvation depends upon its height. Even in very ancient times means of measuring it were devised and records were kept of its height. These were very necessary, for the tax rate depended on the height of the waters. Can you see why this was the only fair way in which the taxes could be adjusted? In several places we can still see the old Nilometers used centuries ago by the Egyptians. On an island near Cairo there is a circular building containing a well in which the water rises to the height of the river outside. Thus the amount of the flood could be determined with accuracy.

For thousands of years in the Nile valley irrigation from the natural flooding of the river has been practiced. On either side the land is divided by earth banks into low fields or basins. During the floods, water covers them from three to five feet deep. The silt in the water gradually settles, and a thin layer of rich soil is spread over the soaked ground. This coating of soil is nearly as valuable as the water itself, for it enables the farmer to raise his crops year after year without other fertilizer.

It is November before the land is dry enough for planting. Then the seed is sown, and so well has the ground been soaked that it sprouts and grows until harvest time.

The people who depend on Nature's flooding of

the land can raise crops only in the winter, for in the summer the fields are baked and hardened and cracked by the drying heat of the sun. These winter crops are chiefly grains, cereals, and vegetables, and clover for the cattle. None of Egypt's most famous crops, such as cotton, corn, rice, and millet, are produced to any great extent by this method of irrigation. These more important products are raised in the summer or autumn, and in order to produce them the ground is irrigated in other ways.

To irrigate fields not reached by the floods, the ancient Egyptians lifted water from the river by means of water wheels turned by oxen, and many peasants today follow the same method. At every turn of the wheel a series of earthen pitchers are raised and, one after another, empty themselves into a trough through which the water flows to the thirsty land. Sometimes other contrivances are used. A common one which you see in Figure 18 consists of a long pole weighted at one end and supporting a bucket at the other. When the weighted end is raised, the bucket sinks into the water; when the heavy

Figure 18. For thousands of years Egyptians have watered their crops in just such ways as this. Describe other methods.

AFRICA, AUSTRALIA, ISLANDS OF PACIFIC

end is pulled down, the bucket rises and its contents are emptied into a small trough or ditch.

Sometimes the farmers irrigate their fields by even simpler methods. A man standing in the water fills a bucket by hand and empties it into a higher canal. All over Egypt thousands of men and boys are working all day long and day after day lifting water from the river and canals by these and other methods.

Only small areas can be irrigated by such handwork as this. To enlarge the amount of cultivated land and to increase the crops which can be produced, great dams have been built in several places on the Nile. The

Figure 19. Behind this Aswan dam a great lake of water is stored. There are 180 sluices in the dam such as you see in the picture. Each one is 20 feet high. They can be opened or closed by means of huge sliding doors operated by electricity. What is the use of the sluices?

water collects behind these dams, or barrages, in large reservoirs, and from these it flows in canals and ditches to the farmers' fields. In the flood season the canals and ditches are filled naturally from the overflow of the river. When the Nile is low the water in the reservoirs is let out and used.

Figure 20. Why is the land which you see in this picture green with growing crops, while that on the other side of the great pyramids is a part of the desert?

One of the oldest barrages on the Nile is located near Cairo, where the river separates into its delta branches. The canals leading from this barrage irrigate large portions of the low, rich delta lands.

The dam at Aswan, farther up the river, is the finest of its kind in the world. It is as wonderful as some of the ancient temples and tombs and far more useful to the Egyptians. It is built of stone and cement and is more than a mile long and sixty feet high. At its base it is eighty feet thick, narrowing slightly toward the top, which, however, is broad enough for a road. Imagine the dam in the street before your school building. To what place would it reach? How high would it be compared with your schoolhouse? How wide would it be compared with the width of the street?

Figure 21. Three thousand years ago one might have seen Egyptians dressed like these in the picture and using the same kind of plow and yoke, driving their slow, patient oxen over the fields watered and fertilized by the Nile River.

At the time of low water the Nile flows peacefully through the sluices (Figure 19). When the floods come the sluice gates are arranged so that only a certain amount of water is allowed to flow through, and the rest is stored in the great reservoir. When the river has become low again this water is let out and distributed over the land, irrigating many thousand acres which formerly were soaked only at flood time or were a part of the great desert. The water held up by the dam drops its muddy load to the bottom of the reservoir. The sluices were built in the bottom of the dam so that mud and water might flow out together and thus fertilize as well as irrigate the land.

Figure 22. This picture shows you some of the shipping at Port Said. Where is this place? Why should there be so many vessels here?

In the thousands of villages in the Nile valley everyone is busy, and all the work is in some way connected with the great river. As we ride over the land and see the fields where camels, donkeys, water buffaloes, sheep, and goats are feeding, we must remember that without the Nile these fields would be a sandy waste and the people could raise no flocks and herds. As we meet droves of donkeys laden with grass, and camels piled high with loads of grain, we must not forget that were it not for the Nile there would be no such loads for them to carry. As we wander through the villages made up of little houses of sundried bricks, we notice the groves of date palms. We know that these trees, from which many of the people derive their only income, are also the gift of the Nile. As we watch the women at work in the villages, grinding the grain and making the flat, round cakes which serve as bread, we realize that there would be no bread, no women grinding grain, no children playing in the dirt, and no villages of little huts were it not for this wonderful African river.

In our trip through the Nile valley we have been astonished at the number and size of the fields where cotton is growing. The dry air, the continual sunshine, the Nile water, and the rich soil all combine to produce a long silky fiber which is very valuable in manufacturing. Next to the United States and India, Egypt produces more cotton than any other country in the world. As you have read, the Egyptians cultivate also large grain and vegetable crops and much sugar, but the cotton crop exceeds all of them in value.

Before we leave Egypt for other parts of Africa we must take a look at the Suez Canal, that most important artificial waterway which forms a part of the main route between western Europe and eastern Asia and Australia.

The Isthmus of Suez, across which the canal was cut, is a neck of land about seventy-five miles wide, low and sandy, without vegetation or fresh water. Several dry lake beds, some of which were thirty feet below the level of the sea, lay in the route of the canal. The water of the Red Sea was let into these lakes, and they now form a part of the waterway.

It is a hundred and one miles from the lighthouse at Port Said to the Red Sea at Suez, and the lakes occupy about a third of this distance. The canal proper is much narrower than the part through the lakes. Every few miles wider sections were built so that vessels can safely pass one another. In order that the wash of the water from the ships may not injure the embankments along the sides of the canal, vessels go slowly; and though we start in the early morning the lights will be twinkling along the route long before we reach Suez, at the southern end.

It was difficult to carry on such an undertaking as the building of this canal in the desert, where everything necessary for the thousands of laborers—food, water, tools, and machinery—had to be brought long distances. What a wonderful thing it is that men could cut a trench through this isthmus, separate two continents, join two seas, and shorten the trip from western Europe to southern and eastern Asia by thousands of miles!

The Suez Canal is so important to their trade that the British feel that they must always be in a position to protect it. In the Anglo-Egyptian treaty made in 1922, regarding the independence of Egypt, regulations concerning the protection of the canal were included.

Our visit to Egypt has been most interesting, but we must leave it for other lands, for Africa is a large continent, and it will take us a long time to visit all its divisions and see what the people in them are doing. An old Egyptian proverb says, "Who drinks the Nile waters will return." We may not care to drink the water of the famous river, but we hope that we may at some future time return to this ancient land and learn more of its former greatness and its present-day importance.

SUGGESTIONS FOR STUDY

I

1. The port of Alexandria.

2. The old city of Cairo.

3. Egypt, a part of the Sahara Desert.

4. The Nile floods.

5. Irrigation and the Aswan dam.

6. Products of Egypt.

7. The Suez Canal.

II

1. Alexandria was named for Alexander the Great. Who was he? What did he do to earn his title? When did he live?

2. With what city in the United States does Alexandria compare in size? Cairo? (See Appendix, pages 501 and 504.)

3. How does the Nile River rank in length among great world rivers (see Appendix, page 506)?

4. Why is the Suez Canal of great importance to England? Find out who built it. What other canal did he attempt to build?

5. On what waters should you sail in going from London to Bombay, India?

6. Why was the Panama Canal more difficult to build than the Suez Canal (see Allen's "North America" and "South America")?

III

Make a list of the places mentioned in this chapter. Arrange them by countries, cities, rivers, mountains, etc. From these places select those which you think are so important that you should always be able to locate them and know something about them.

CHAPTER IV

BRITISH POSSESSIONS IN AFRICA

It will take us a long time to visit all the lands which are under the control of the British, for they cover an immense area (see map on page 55). The British possessions in southern Africa are half the size of the United States, while the Anglo-Egyptian Sudan alone would cover an entire third of its area. British East Africa would cover the rest of the country and make a second layer over Texas, while other British lands in the east and the west would continue the second layer over several other states.

Study Table I in the Appendix. How many people live in British Africa? How does the number compare with the population of the United States (see Table IV, page 503)? Which division of British Africa contains the most people?

We shall find nothing monotonous in our journey in British territory, for the colonies are very different one from another. Some are high and some low, some are wet and some dry. In them we shall see tropical forests, cool, grassy plateaus, and hot, swampy coast lands. We shall find miners getting gold, copper, and diamonds from some of the richest mines in the world. We can watch wild animals feeding on the high plains and domestic flocks and herds in the pastures. We shall travel through lands uninhabited save for wild creatures, visit villages of native tribes who live as they did before Europeans landed on the African shores, and rest in cities as modern and as cultured as any in our own country.

AFRICA, AUSTRALIA, ISLANDS OF PACIFIC

STUDIES ON THE BRITISH POSSESSIONS

1. Sketch an outline map of Africa and show on it the British possessions (see map opposite). Write the name of each of the divisions.

2. Which British possessions lie in the north of Africa? in the east? in the south? in the west? Name some British islands.

3. Which possessions lie in the torrid zone? Which lie in two zones?

4. Which divisions are largely included in the low coast lands (see regional map preceding page 1)? Which consist largely of plateaus? Which have extensive grasslands? Which extend into the tropical forests?

5. Referring to Table I in the Appendix, write the names of the British possessions in the order of their size. Which is the largest? Which is the next in size? Which is the smallest?

6. Using Table I in the Appendix, find the total area of the British possessions in Africa. How does this compare with the area of the British Isles?

7. Using the table mentioned in question 6, find the total population of British Africa. How does this compare with the population of the British Isles?

BRITISH POSSESSIONS IN AFRICA

8. Which division of British Africa is the largest? How do you account for the fact that fewer people live in this division than in the larger colonies of British East Africa or Nigeria?

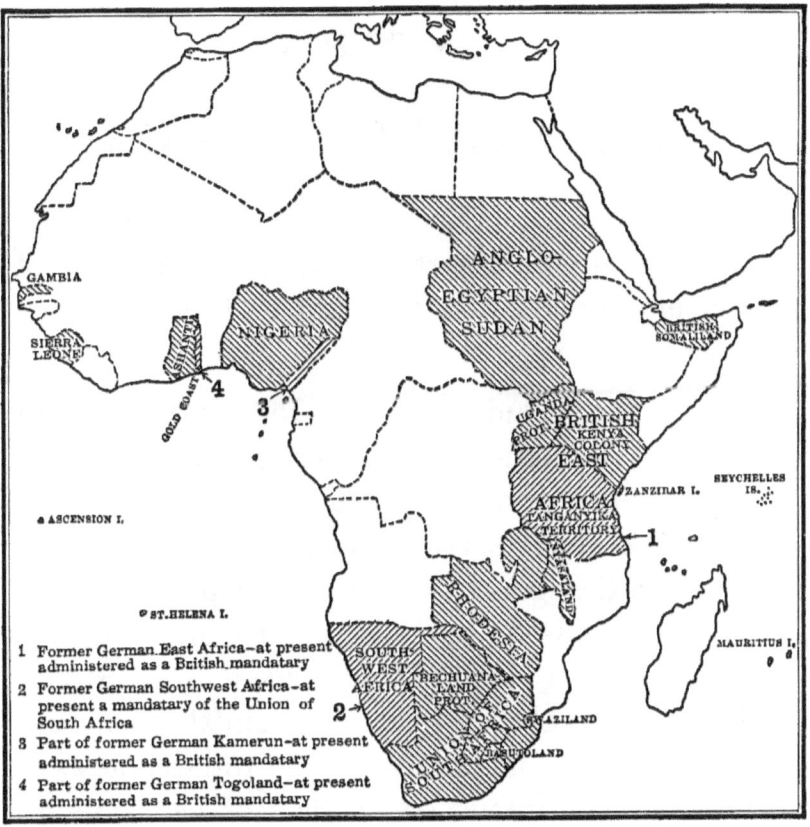

Figure 23. British Africa. Compare this map with the regional and rainfall maps. Which of the British possessions are in the temperate zone? Which have considerable rainfall? Which are partly deserts?

CHAPTER V

ANGLO-EGYPTIAN SUDAN

The Anglo-Egyptian Sudan is a part of the great Sudan region which stretches across Africa south of the Sahara from the Atlantic Ocean to the Red Sea (see map preceding page 1).

The African Sudan includes the great grassland area which lies between the desert of Sahara and the tropical forest region. South of the equator, between the southern boundary of the tropical forest and the desert, there is another grassland area (see map on page 10). These grass lands are semiarid regions, drier near the deserts and more plentifully watered on the forest side. Over large parts of these regions the rainfall is sufficient for native grasses but not enough to produce forests or to make agriculture successful. Many of the people are wandering tribes who move with their flocks and herds from one oasis to another. Other tribes have settled homes on the oases and raise vegetables, fruit, cotton, and grain.

We can go a part of the way through Egypt and the Anglo-Egyptian Sudan by train. This road is a part of the great Cape-to-Cairo Railroad, which in the not-far-distant future will connect Cairo in the north with Cape Town in the extreme south of the continent. This railroad has been built hundreds of miles southward from Cairo and for an even longer distance northward from Cape Town (see map preceding page 1, and Appendix, page 501). When the two ends are joined in Central Africa, the great ribbon of steel will extend the entire length of the continent. Many side branches will sometime be built to the seaports on the eastern and western coasts, and the great artery of commerce will be a wonderful help in opening up and developing the rich resources of the interior of the continent.

As we enter the Anglo-Egyptian Sudan the sights from the car windows are much like those which we

Figure 24. In parts of the Anglo-Egyptian Sudan the people are adopting modern methods of work, but much is still done in crude ways. The picture shows you what passes for a sawmill there. Did you ever see a saw like the one in the picture?

saw in Egypt. Tall palm trees, each crowned with its bushy tuft of leaves hiding bunches of yellow dates, cast their reflection in the water. Mud villages dot the valley, women grind the grain between two flat stones, and donkeys plod along nearly hidden by their heavy loads. Men and boys work beside the river, raising the water and pouring it into ditches which carry it to their fields. Where the Nile water can be used there are people and villages and growing crops. Beyond this stretches the desert.

Figure 25. This is a little desert village near Khartum. The houses are built of mud, for there is no other material here. Where is Khartum?

By referring again to the map you will see that at Halfa, on the boundary of Egypt, the river makes a bend to the west, while the railroad takes a more direct course to Berber. The railroad is especially useful in this region, for the Nile is broken here by several cataracts, making navigation impossible except at the time of high floods, and dangerous even at that period. How many of these cataracts do you find on the map? "Rapids," perhaps, would be a more appropriate name, for there are no high falls here, but the water rushes madly along in its rocky bed down the steep grades.

How long do you suppose it will be before this water will be harnessed and its power used to move machinery in mills and factories, to light cities, and to run electric cars? All this will surely come in time to the Anglo-Egyptian Sudan as it has to other lands.

In the peninsula to the west bounded by the great loop of the Nile we see goats, camels, and sheep feeding in the pastures, for this is a fine grassland peopled by several tribes. The natives in this and other parts of the

Figure 26. These children do not look very different from boys and girls in our schools. This is a little mission school at Khartum. It is directed by people from the United States.

Sudan are raising more and more cattle each year. The government is helping in this industry by improving the breeds, eliminating diseases, and making it easier for the people to market their stock and sell the hides and skins. Some of the natives raise ostriches and others hunt the wild birds for their feathers, which are an important export.

Khartum is the capital and the most important city in the Anglo-Egyptian Sudan. Its location tells the reason for much of its importance. In this continent of few roads and railroads, rivers and caravan routes are of great importance; and Khartum is situated at the junction of the Blue Nile and the White Nile, where several routes meet. Look at the map on page 220 and you will see that one of the caravan routes leads westward across the Sudan from Khartum to the trading center of Timbuktu.

One of the products which we see in large quantities at Khartum waiting to be shipped away is gum arabic. Perhaps you can obtain some from a druggist so that you may have some idea what it looks like. We use yearly thousands of pounds of this hard, yellowish-white substance in medicines, confectionery, and in the manufacture of textiles to give a luster and finish to the cloth. Gum arabic comes from trees which grow in the Sudan, in parts of eastern Africa, in Arabia, and in some other regions. The natives tap the trees and collect the sticky sap, which hardens on exposure to the air. They sift out the dirt and sand and let the hardened gum lie for weeks in the sunshine until it turns from amber yellow to nearly white. Many tons of gum arabic are thus collected from the Sudan each year.

When you studied South America you probably read about the vegetable-ivory nuts of Ecuador from which buttons are manufactured (see Allen's "South America"). There are palm trees in the Sudan that produce nuts which are used for the same purpose. These are collected by the natives, and large quantities are exported.

Figure 27. The picture shows you a pottery at Omdurman. Can you find this place on the map? The people here make many of their dishes from the clay near the Nile.

You read on page 48 that Egypt is a very important cotton-producing country. The natives of the Anglo-Egyptian Sudan have learned how to cultivate the crop, and with the extension of irrigation the amount of cotton produced here is increasing every year.

As we go farther south both the heat and the rainfall increase. How near to the equator is the southern boundary of the Anglo-Egyptian Sudan? The forests along the Nile are deeper also. All through this African forest many varieties of rubber plants and trees grow, and rubber, as you will read later, is a very important product of Central Africa. Many natives in this part of the Sudan spend much of their time in gathering the milky juice, smoking it over their little fires, and carrying the rubber to the trader in the nearest village.

As you know, the elephant is one of the common animals in Central Africa and we are now far enough south to be near its haunts. Many roam through the southern part of the Anglo-Egyptian Sudan, and the natives hunt them for the valuable ivory of the tusks.

Our next trip will take us into British East Africa. Instead of continuing farther south in the Sudan we will return to Alexandria and there take passage on some vessel bound for the eastern coast of the continent. As we sail southward we pass the Somali coast. The British control a part of Somaliland, and you will read about this region in Chapter XXIII. Farther south in British East Africa we shall find railroads which will take us into the interior.

SUGGESTIONS FOR STUDY

I

1. The Sudan.

2. The Cape-to-Cairo Railroad.

3. Cataracts of the Nile.

4. Occupations and products of the Anglo-Egyptian Sudan.

5. Khartum and its importance.

II

1. Why are the British so interested in increasing the cotton production in their colonies? In what British possessions is the climate suitable for cotton-raising?

2. By what route does the cotton from the Anglo-Egyptian Sudan reach London?

3. Using the scale of the map on page 68, find how long from north to south the Anglo-Egyptian Sudan is. To what place would this distance reach from your home?

4. How many countries the size of the Anglo-Egyptian Sudan would it take to cover the United States (see Appendix, pages 499 and 503)?

III

Make a list of the places mentioned in this chapter. Arrange them by countries, cities, rivers, mountains, etc. From the list select the places which you think are so important that you should always be able to locate them and know something about them.

CHAPTER VI

BRITISH EAST AFRICA

SEVERAL divisions make up what is now known as British East Africa. The best known is Kenya Colony, which, before the World War, was called British East Africa. Uganda Protectorate lies farther inland, north of Lake Victoria. To the south is Tanganyika Territory. This was formerly under German control and was called German East Africa, but it was taken by the Allies during the World War.

British East Africa is a big-game country, a region where lions, antelopes, giraffes, zebras, hippopotamuses, rhinoceroses, and other wild animals abound. It was to this part of Africa that Theodore Roosevelt came for a hunting trip after the close of his term as president of the United States. He sent back to museums in the United States many fine specimens, among which were some of rare, little-known animals. So popular has the hunting of big game in this part of Africa become that companies in Mombasa and Nairobi (see map on page 68), towns which you will visit later, make a business of fitting out expeditions with porters, tents, food, and other supplies.

Figure 28. This picture shows Theodore Roosevelt on a hunting trip with some of his native helpers. He is in the "big-game country." Describe it.

We will enter British East Africa through the port of Mombasa. As we sail into the harbor we see the buildings standing out bold and white against the luxuriant greenery. Festoons of tropical vines hang over the gray rocks, tall palms fringe the shore, and groups of native huts nestle beneath the coconut trees.

All parts of the town are interesting to a stranger. There is the old Portuguese section near the water, with its narrow streets, whitewashed walls, balconies, and carved doors. In the Arab quarter narrow, crooked alleys wind between tall white buildings, and in the high minaret of the mosque near by we hear the cry of the priest, or muezzin, calling the faithful to prayer. Behind the Arab quarter are thousands of the little grass and mud huts of the natives; while above, on the bluff where the breeze from the sea tempers the heat, are the bungalows of the few Europeans who live in this part of tropical Africa.

The scenes in the streets furnish a continual entertainment. In the market places the natives sit cross-legged behind their piles of vegetables and fruit. Dark, turbaned Hindus from southern Asia bargain with customers in their little shops; unclothed children

Figure 29. A traveler slipped quietly up in a rowboat and took the picture of this big "hippo." His expression indicates that the photographer forgot to tell him to smile.

play in the dirt of the narrow alleys; tall, straight Arabs in loose, flowing gowns and white turbans walk slowly by; water carriers swing their pails at either end of long, slender poles balanced across their shoulders; and black women, each wearing a single garment of bright-colored cotton cloth, carry a heavy weight of ornaments on their arms, necks, and in their ears. Should you like jewelry like that shown in the picture?

Figure 30. This woman is a native of East Africa. How do you like her jewelry of copper wire? Notice how she carries her baby.

Mombasa is a very important port. Those ships at the wharves are unloading cotton cloth, farming tools, grain and flour, machinery, building materials, and other articles which the people in this new country need. On the wharves and in the warehouses are products from all parts of the colony. We see many bales of cotton, bundles of hides and skins, fibers of various kinds, ivory, copra, coffee, and nuts and seeds from which oil may be extracted. There are also large quantities of sisal fiber such as you have seen in Mexico. All these products will increase as the country is developed. At the present time cotton is the most important export. Many of the natives raise cotton on their little farms, and large modern plantations have been started.

Some of the tribes in the interior of the colony raise many cattle and goats and bring the hides and skins to the ports on the shores of Lake Victoria. The vessels plying on the lake call at these ports, take on the goods collected there, and carry them across the lake to Kisumu. From here they are taken by train down to Mombasa (see map on page 68).

In the cleared areas near Mombasa we visit large plantations where coffee, rice, corn, coconuts, tobacco, spices, rubber, and various fruits are raised. We notice that most of the native farms are small. The large plantations, like those around Mombasa, are usually owned by Europeans, who use modern tools and methods and hire the natives as laborers.

While we are here on the coast lands let us visit a coconut plantation. The tall, straight trunks of the trees are often from seventy-five to a hundred feet high, and the leaves are from ten to fifteen feet long. How does the width of your schoolroom compare with the length of one of the longest leaves? The natives eat the coconuts and drink the milk which they contain. They use the husks of the nuts for fuel and also make them into brushes. They make ropes and mats from the fiber and dishes from the shells. They build their houses from the wood of the tree and thatch their roofs with its long leaves. They use the leaves also for baskets and mats. Is there any tree or plant which grows near your home that you can use in so many ways?

All these products are of very great importance to the people who live in the lands where the coconut tree grows. The people of Europe and America value much more highly the oil which can be extracted from the meat of the nut, and it is to obtain this oil that so many large coconut plantations have been started in Africa, southern Asia, and the Pacific islands.

When the nuts are ripe the natives climb the trees and gather them. They cut them open and let the moist, white meat dry in the hot sunshine. This dried coconut meat, called copra, is put into bags and shipped to the United States and European countries, where the oil is extracted. In some places, where the industry has grown to be of great importance, oil mills have been built, and

Figure 31. Yes, this is Africa. This is the motor bus which runs between Entebbe and Kampala. Find these places on the map.

the oil, instead of the copra, is shipped away. Here in the United States we use enormous quantities of coconut oil for soaps, medicines, cosmetics, shampoo preparations, and other manufactures. From the Philippine Islands we get millions of pounds of both copra and oil, and we import about as much more from other lands.

In all the hot parts of Africa you will notice many banana trees. It would be as hard for the native of tropical lands to get along without bananas as it would for the Chinese to do without his rice, the nomad of the desert to do without his dates, or for you to do without your bread and butter. Every village has its banana grove. The people cook the fruit when green, roast it when ripe, and crush the dried bananas into meal. The leaves serve for tablecloths, as a thatch for roofs, and as coverings for baskets. The fiber is made into ropes, hats, shields, and baskets. The sap yields a substance which answers the purposes of soap; the stems furnish material for fences, and the pith, for sponges.

We shall find the people of East Africa even more interesting than their products. Many Arabs live in the coast lands, for intercourse with Arabia has been carried on here for centuries. To this part of the country have come also Hindus from India. They are traders, merchants, and bankers. Many ships leave the ports of India for Mombasa, bringing people from that country to British East Africa and goods for the Hindu merchants to sell in their little shops.

The greater part of the population of British East Africa, however, is made up of native African tribes.

Most of them now wear some cotton garment, though some are scantily clad and a few still dress in a cloth made from the bark of a tree. They strip this off in large pieces, soak it in water until it is soft, and then pound it on a log. Soon the outer, rougher part comes off, leaving the inner bark, which is as fine and soft as cloth.

Figure 32. These women are dressmaking, and when they get their bark-cloth dresses made, they will be in the latest style. How do they make cloth from bark?

Some of the natives live on the fruits and fish of the region, some have gardens where they raise grain and vegetables and cotton, while others own cattle, sheep, and goats. There are many wild animals lurking around the pasture lands where the flocks and herds feed, and the herders must always be on the watch for such enemies.

The Masai are, perhaps, the best known of all the pastoral tribes. The younger men and boys tend the large herds of cattle. At night they drive them into the village, which is surrounded by a hedge of thorn bush. The little mud huts are arranged in a circle inside the hedge and another thorn hedge stretches from hut to hut. Within this inner inclosure the animals are kept for the night. Yet in spite of all these precautions lions or leopards sometimes leap over or break down the protecting hedges, stampede the herd, and capture a good dinner.

There is little furniture in the native huts. The floor is of earth, and the bed is a raised earth platform covered with coarse fiber mats. The stove is a platform of clay on which is a circle of stones with a little fire burning in the middle. Over this a woman is baking some small cakes. It has taken her a long time to grind the corn between two stones and to gather the fuel for her fire. In all her work, whether in the hut or in the field, whether standing or stooping, she carries her baby tied onto her back. It tips this way and that, it jogs up and down with her every motion, it may cry or laugh, but there it stays from morning till night and has to make the best of it.

Now we will start on our trip from Mombasa up to Lake Victoria. The railroad runs through hot, damp jungles, over grassy plains, between wooded mountains, and along deep gorges filled with flooded streams and bordered by creeper-covered trees. Every few miles we pass trim little stations with their tall water tanks and gay flower beds shut in on all sides save one by the impenetrable bush. Once in a while we see a grove of rubber trees or a cotton plantation or pass a field of sisal where natives are cutting the long leaves and hanging the fiber to dry in the hot sunshine. We pass villages made up of scores of little round huts on which long-leaved banana trees cast flickering shadows. Women with yards of copper wire wound around arms and legs are busy grinding grain, and scantily clad children playing in the dirt stare at the moving train.

We climb slowly up the steep grades through the high scrub desert covered with thorn bushes to the higher grassy plains beyond. Many cattle and flocks of sheep and goats are feeding in the pastures. The farms and plantations and ranches are long distances apart, but these distances will gradually become shorter as more settlers occupy the land. The railroad is a thread of civilization which connects seaports with the scattered inland settlements and carries comforts and necessities to the people there.

As we climb we realize that at last we are in the great African game country. From the car windows we catch sight of an ostrich racing with the train. Members of the antelope family—the hartebeest and the curious wildebeest, with a mane and tail like a horse and a body like a cow—feed in the distance. Zebras lift their heads to watch the train, and tall giraffes nibble at the tender leaves on the trees.

Figure 33. It took much time and patience to get near enough to this zebra to take his picture without his knowing it.

The animals have sometimes caused trouble along the railroad line. Giraffes have found the telegraph wires convenient for neck scratching, and elephants have been known to pull up the poles. Because of the ants these are of iron instead of wood. For miles through the rolling grass country, even until we come to the wire fence which surrounds Nairobi, we catch glimpses of African game.

Figure 34. Elephants like to bathe. The water is refreshing in the hot land where they live. These animals are not far from Mt. Kenya. In what latitude is it?

One of the most beautiful sights on the trip up to Nairobi is Mt. Kilimanjaro, the highest mountain of Africa. Its white, snow-capped head towers far up toward the blue sky. A railroad from Tanga, a seaport on the coast, runs past the mountain, and a hotel has been built at its base for tourists who wish to climb or hunt. Signposts point out the trail up the mountain, and little huts have been built in various places, where the tired climber may find shelter and rest. The forests around the base and on the lower slopes of Mt. Kilimanjaro will some day be of great value, for they are made up of fine hard woods out of which beautiful furniture and ornaments can be made.

Nairobi, a mile and a half higher and three hundred miles farther west than Mombasa, is situated where the railroad enters the higher hills beyond. The wild game feed up to its very doors, and the roar of lions is not an uncommon sound. Instead of hunting foxes, as they do in their old homes, Englishmen here go leopard-hunting. Natives in all shades of black and brown make up the largest part of the population. Some of the light-skinned people are traders or farmers who have come here to live, scientists who are studying the vegetation and animal life and collecting specimens for museums in Europe and America, and sportsmen who are getting their outfits ready to start on hunting trips into the wilderness. How should you like to go on a trip to hunt lions in the grasslands, elephants in the forest, hippopotamuses in the reed-grown swamps, buffaloes in the thickets, and rhinoceroses in the bush?

In the streets we pass humpbacked oxen drawing heavy two-wheeled carts, and muscular boys drawing "rickshaws" such as we might see in Japan. We like to watch the native women carrying their loads of firewood. The ornaments of wire on their arms and legs and necks look to us like a heavier burden than the loads of wood on their heads.

Equally interesting with the sights in Nairobi are those in the native villages outside the town. From these villages come the porters, gun bearers, and men wanted for other work on long, hard trips. What the ox wagon has been to the settlers of South Africa and the camel caravan to the travelers on the trackless desert, the strong, patient native has been to the explorer, the settler, and the hunter of East Africa.

In the midst of the vast plain to the north of Nairobi rises Mt. Kenya, a rocky, volcanic mass with a snowy crown rising sharp and clear against the sky. Its slopes are clothed with forests and with thickets of bamboo sixty feet high. These may prove useful in the future in the manufacture of paper.

Our railroad ends at Kisumu on the shores of Lake Victoria. All the vessels which sail on this great lake were brought here in pieces and put together on its shores. Lake Victoria is the birthplace of the famous Nile. After it leaves the lake over Ripon Falls the river is broad and deep, and flows with a strong current over a series of rapids.

The town of Jinja in Uganda is located near where the Nile leaves Lake Victoria. At present Jinja is only a small place, but some day, perhaps far in the future, it will be an important center with mills and factories and warehouses. There is power enough in the Nile River as it rushes down its rocky stairway at Ripon Falls to gin all the cotton, weave all the fiber, and saw all the wood in Uganda.

In a trip through Uganda we notice banana trees

everywhere. We see many natives at work on their little farms. Some are pulling peanut vines and picking off the nuts. Some of the women are harvesting rice. Men, women, and children are picking the fluffy white fiber in the cotton fields, and boys and girls are tending the flocks and herds in the pastures. Later the men will carry the peanuts, the cotton fiber, and the hides and skins down to Lake Victoria to be taken by boat and rail down to Mombasa. Here they will be loaded on big ocean vessels bound for England and other countries.

We will take a coasting vessel at Mombasa for Dar es Salam, a port farther south. It is hard for us to realize that Dar es Salam is the gateway of a country which is as yet largely undeveloped. The harbor is one of the best on the coast. Concrete wharves border the water, and large warehouses stand waiting to be filled. The town is pleasant and well laid out with parks, gardens, and wide streets bordered with flowering trees. The houses of the Europeans are neat white buildings with screened piazzas and tiled roofs.

From Dar es Salam a fine caravan route leads up through the hills, across the high plains, and down to Lake Tanganyika in the long rift valley. More important than this road is the railroad which connects the seaport and Kigoma, the most important port on the inland lake (see map on page 68). Leaving Dar es Salam we ride by great coconut plantations, and others where cocoa, sugar, and sisal fiber are grown. Traveling up the slopes toward the interior we pass plantations of coffee trees covered thick with their red, cherry-like fruit; and still farther up, on the grassy plains where the tsetse fly, carrier of the dreaded sleeping-sickness, does not come, we see cattle, sheep, and goats.

Figure 35. On the low, hot coast lands of East Africa there are many coffee plantations. See how the young coffee plants are protected from the hot sun by the taller banana trees.

As we read of these important products we must not forget that much of the country is as yet uncultivated, wild beasts abound, the deep forests are scarcely touched, and comparatively little has been done to develop the land. Only a few thousand Europeans live among the millions of natives. Many of these native tribes produce little except small amounts of beans, corn, peanuts, sugar, and sweet potatoes for their own food supply. Some of the men are porters and make long trips, carrying the products of the country to the railroad, or taking tools, cotton cloth, machinery, and camping outfits into the interior.

Ujiji, on Lake Tanganyika, was formerly a great

Arab trading center where quantities of ivory and large numbers of slaves were bought and sold. It is now a big native village of twenty-five thousand people. Years ago Henry M. Stanley, searching through the interior of Central Africa for David Livingstone, the famous explorer, found him here at Ujiji dangerously sick and completely exhausted from the hardships he had suffered. These men traveled across Africa in continual danger from native tribes, wild animals, poisonous insects, deadly sickness, and the fierce heat. Should you have had the courage to face such dangers and hardships as they did?

NYASALAND

Touching British East Africa on the south is Nyasaland, a small British protectorate. We could travel for many miles through this land by river or on good roads which the English have built and visit large, flourishing plantations where hundreds of thousands of pounds of coffee and tobacco are raised. Cotton plantations are growing larger and more numerous each year, and tea cultivation is no longer an experiment, but a valuable industry. As in other British possessions many of these large plantations are run by foreigners. The natives are slowly learning their ways and are beginning to start small farms of their own and to raise products which the foreigners will buy. On the higher lands of the interior there are good pastures where the natives raise many cattle and sheep and where in future years many more will feed.

SUGGESTIONS FOR STUDY

I

1. Divisions of British East Africa.

2. Big game.

3. Surface and vegetation.

4. The port of Mombasa.

5. Farms and plantations.

6. People of East Africa.

7. From Mombasa to Nairobi.

8. Kisumu and Lake Victoria.

9. Uganda Protectorate.

10. Dar es Salam and the trip inland.

11. Lake Tanganyika and its ports.

12. British Nyasaland.

II

1. Find on the map the divisions which make up British East Africa. Which is the largest? the smallest?

2. What is the area of British East Africa (see Table I, page 499)?

How does it compare in size with the state in which you live?

3. In what zone is British East Africa? How do you account for the permanent snow caps on Mt. Kenya and Mt. Kilimanjaro? How high are these mountains (see page 505)? What is the nearest mountain to your home with which you can compare them in height? How does Kilimanjaro rank among the mountains of the world?

4. What oils or fats do you use in your home which are made from vegetable material? Do you use any made from animal sources?

5. How does Lake Victoria rank among other large lakes (see page 506)?

6. What waters does Nyasaland touch?

III

Make a list of the places mentioned in this chapter. Arrange them by countries, cities, rivers, mountains, etc. From the list select the places which you think are so important that you should always be able to locate them and know something about them.

CHAPTER VII

ZANZIBAR AND ITS CLOVE PLANTATIONS

BETWEEN twenty and thirty miles off the coast of British East Africa there is a chain of beautiful coral islands. Zanzibar is the most important of these and perhaps the only one whose name you have ever heard. It is a lovely place about as large as the little state of Rhode Island. What a good time you would have there among the fruit trees and gardens! Oranges, lemons, limes, pineapples, and coconuts grow here. These fruits you already know and like to eat, but how about shaddocks, custard apples, guavas, jack fruit, and mangoes?

Besides fruits, the people of Zanzibar raise peanuts, sugar cane, sweet potatoes, tomatoes, nutmegs, ginger, and, more important than any other product, great quantities of cloves. Millions of pounds of cloves come from Zanzibar and Pemba, a smaller island some thirty miles farther north. The Molukkas, or Spice Islands, in the Pacific and the island of Madagascar, which you will visit later, furnish the rest of the world's supply. It seems hardly possible that people can use twelve million pounds of cloves from these places every year.

Cloves are the dried flower buds of a little tree. People have tried to raise the clove tree in many parts of the world, but the soil and climate in the islands of Zanzibar and Pemba suit it better than those of any other lands. There are millions of trees here, and their care and cultivation is the chief occupation of most of the natives.

Figure 36. This is a clove orchard in Zanzibar. What is a clove?

The owners of the clove plantations watch the little buds carefully. When they first appear they are green; soon they turn yellow, and then red. Now they are ready to be picked, and everybody flocks into the orchards. The people chatter and laugh and have good times while their fingers fly among the scarlet buds. Perhaps you could pick strawberries or blueberries faster than could boys or girls from Zanzibar, but they could probably pick more clove buds in a day than you could. After the picking, the buds are dried until they are hard and brown. Then they are packed and shipped away.

If you like color, you will enjoy the city of Zanzibar. The blue ocean stretches in front, the beach is white, and the square Arab houses are built of white stone. Bright colored awnings project into the narrow streets, which are thronged with dark-skinned natives dressed in blue, yellow, and purple draperies. All this is set in the deep, rich green of tropical trees and vines and plants aglow with their brilliant flowers.

The port of Zanzibar is located on the western side of the island. For many years it has been an important center for the commerce between eastern Africa and India and Arabia. Since railroads have been built into the interior of Africa from other ports, Zanzibar has lost some of its importance in foreign trade. On account of its position, however, it will continue to be of importance as a center of local trade along the eastern coast of the continent.

Years ago the Sultan of Zanzibar grew rich from the profits of the ivory and slave trade. Blacks were captured in the interior, loaded with ivory tusks, and forced to march down to the coast. Here both they and their loads were put on vessels in the harbor of the city of Zanzibar and carried to other lands, where the blacks were sold as slaves. This slave trade no longer exists, but ivory still forms an important export from the mainland.

ZANZIBAR AND ITS CLOVE PLANTATIONS

Figure 37. Down from the higher land where the elephants roam, these men have brought the great ivory tusks to the coast to be shipped away. For what is ivory used?

SUGGESTIONS FOR STUDY

I

1. Fruits of Zanzibar.

2. The clove industry.

3. The port of Zanzibar.

II

1. On what waters will a vessel sail in going from the Molukka Islands to China? to Rotterdam in Holland?

2. On what waters will a vessel sail in going from Zanzibar to London? What will form the cargoes going and returning?

III

Make a list of the places mentioned in this chapter. From it select those which you think are so important that you should always be able to locate them and know something about them.

CHAPTER VIII

THE BRITISH IN SOUTH AFRICA

Our next trip in the British colonies will take us into South Africa. Cape Town, the most important seaport in this part of the continent, is as far south of the equator as Los Angeles in California is north of it. Because of this southerly position many things will seem odd to us who live in the Northern Hemisphere.

The Great Dipper and other constellations near it which are familiar objects to people who live in the United States cannot be seen in South Africa. They have disappeared below the northern horizon; while a strange group of stars, the Southern Cross, never seen in the United States, glitters in the southern sky.

In all lands people have their hot season and their longest days when the sun is highest in their sky. In the United States and other countries north of the equator this occurs in June and July. At this time the people who live south of the equator must look low in their northern sky to see the sun, and its rays must fall slantingly on them. Therefore this is their winter season. On the other hand, in December the sun shines vertically over the heads of people who live south of the equator, and they are having their summer season. At this time of the year, as you know, the people of the United States see the sun at noon-time low in their southern sky. Its journey across our skies is short, and its slanting rays give us but little heat; therefore our days are short and our weather is cold.

It would seem strange to us who live in the northern United States to have our coolest weather at Fourth of July time and to celebrate Christmas in the hot sunshine with picnics and boating and all sorts of out-of-door sports. But we must not forget that our winter Christmas, with its short days and cold weather, would seem just as odd to the boys and girls of South Africa.

Cape Town is the front door to the British possessions in South Africa. Most important of all the divisions here is the Union of South Africa, made up of the provinces of the Cape of Good Hope, the Orange Free State, Natal, and the Transvaal. Rhodesia is divided into two parts. Northern Rhodesia is a colony of the British Commonwealth, while Southern Rhodesia is a dominion like Canada, Newfoundland, Australia, New Zealand, the Irish Free State, and the Union of South Africa. A dominion is self-supporting, makes its own laws, and provides for its own defense. Bechuanaland and some smaller divisions are parts of the British Commonwealth, as well as Southwest Africa, before the World War a German possession but now a protectorate of the Union of South Africa.

Though the area of British South Africa is so great, the population is scanty and averages only about eight to a square mile.

You read in Chapter I about the great plateau of South Africa, and of the mountains, the Southern Highlands, which stretch around the southern end of the continent and up along the eastern coast beyond the tropic of Capricorn. All this area is in the belt where the trade winds blow in from the southeast, bringing with them much moisture from the Indian Ocean. As you can see from the map the mountains stand directly in the path of these winds. Consequently much of the moisture which the winds carry is dropped on the southern and eastern slopes, and little remains in the air to be scattered over the high plateaus which stretch away to the Atlantic coast (see the rainfall map on page 10 and the regional map preceding page 1).

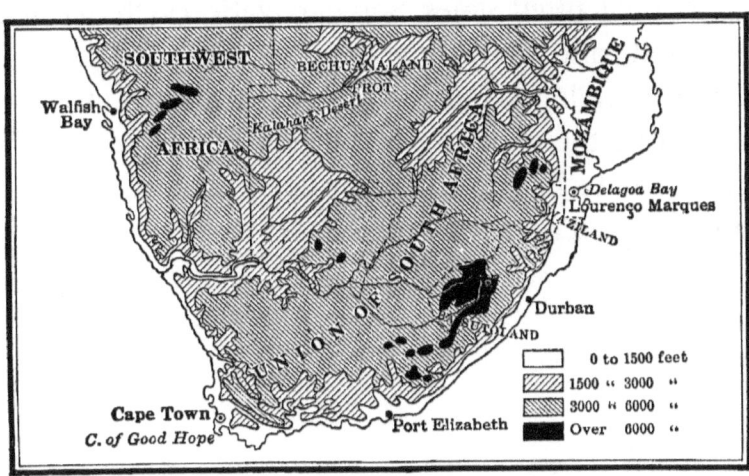

Figure 38. This map shows you the plateau of South Africa. How high is the greater part of it? How does it compare in height with the place where you live?

Most of Southwest Africa and Bechuanaland, and parts of the Union of South Africa, are true desert areas which receive little or no rainfall and produce no vegetation except low thorny shrubs. Other areas receive sufficient rainfall for the growth of grass, but this soon turns brown and withers. A large part of what is known as the Kalahari Desert is land of this type. In the north, nearer the equator, the veldt (as the plateau in South Africa is called) receives more rain. With the increase of moisture the grassland gradually merges into the tropical forest, just as it does in the Northern Hemisphere (see page 56).

Water is the greatest need of southern Africa. When the snow melts on the mountains the rivers rise and rush away to the sea, carrying the precious water with them. By building reservoirs men can store it and use it for growing crops as they have done in the western part of the United States. Some irrigation systems have been built, and many more are planned, so the amount of cultivated land is steadily increasing. As in our own great West, there will always be large areas too far from any water to be reclaimed or so situated that water cannot be led to them.

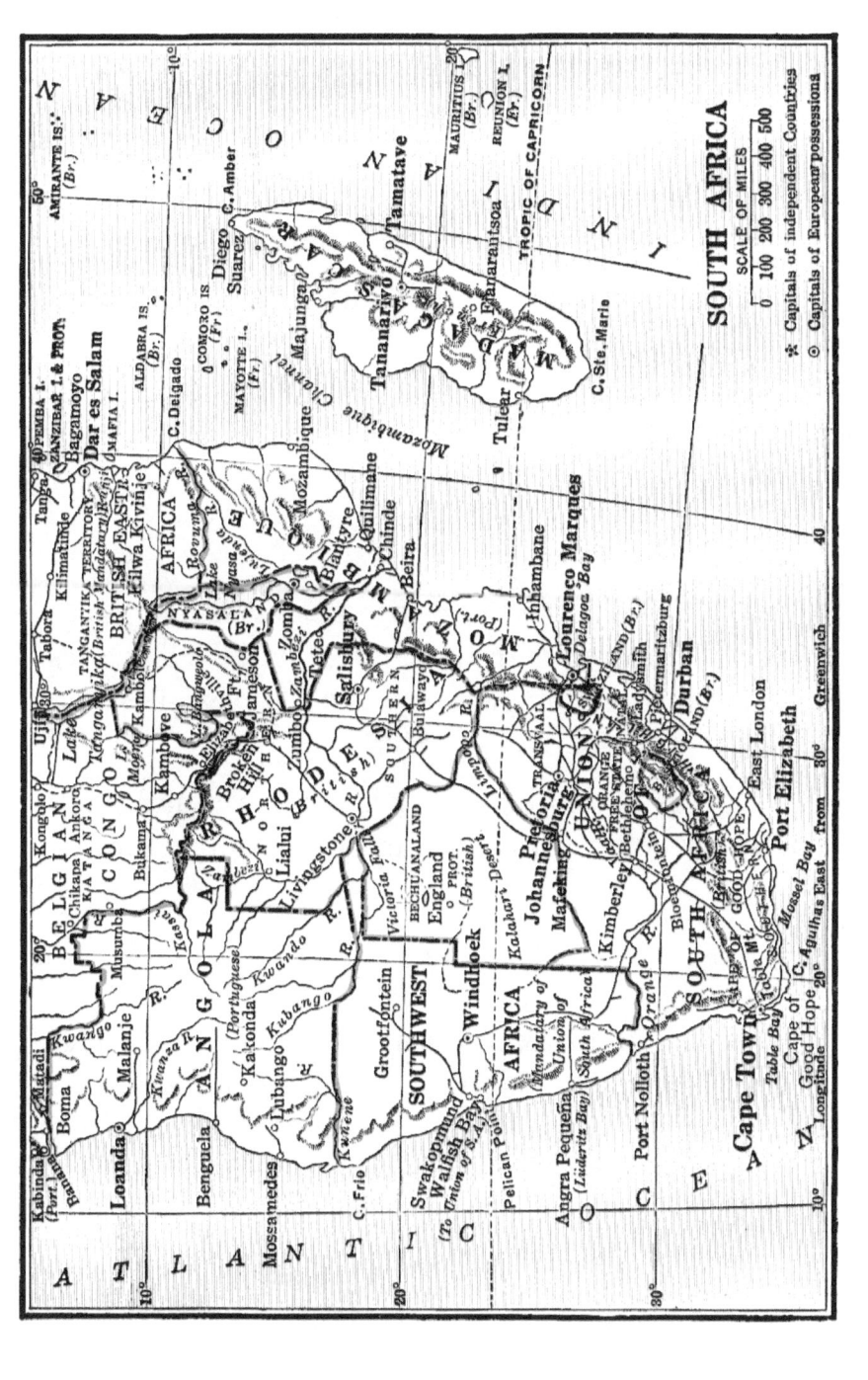

SUGGESTIONS FOR STUDY

I

1. Seasons in the Southern Hemisphere.

2. British possessions in South Africa.

3. Surface and climate.

4. Irrigation.

II

1. How large are the British possessions in South Africa compared with the United States? How does the population compare (see Table I, page 499, and Table IV, page 503)?

2. Why do more people live in the east and south of British South Africa than in the interior and west?

III

Make a list of the places mentioned in this chapter. Arrange them by countries, cities, rivers, mountains, etc. From the list select those which you think are so important that you should always be able to locate them and know something about them.

CHAPTER IX

THE UNION OF SOUTH AFRICA

The Province of the Cape of Good Hope

For many years before the discovery of South Africa the nations of Europe had been carrying on a great trade with the Far East. Their route lay through the Mediterranean Sea and thence overland by caravans through the deserts of Central Asia. When the Mohammedan tribes who founded the Turkish empire swept westward from Asia, occupied the peninsula between the Black and Mediterranean seas, and captured the city of Constantinople, they blocked these sea and overland routes, made war on the Christian merchants, and captured their vessels and caravans.

The rich overland trade with the East being thus destroyed, the seafaring nations of Europe began searching for ocean routes which would lead them to eastern Asia. With this purpose in mind a Portuguese, Bartholomew Dias, set out for the East in 1486, six years before Christopher Columbus, with the same object in view, sailed to the west. Making his way southward along the western coast of Africa, Dias discovered the bold, rocky promontory which we know as the Cape of Good Hope. He met with heavy storms and winds as he tried to round the cape, and so called it the Cape of Storms. King Henry of Portugal was so pleased that the southern end of the long, continental mass of land which blocked the way to the East had been reached that he gave the projection what he thought was a more fitting name, the Cape of Good Hope.

A few years after the voyage of Dias another Portuguese, Vasco da Gama, rounded the Cape of Good Hope and made some discoveries along the eastern coast of Africa.

In 1652 some people from Holland landed at Cape Town and made a small settlement. The Dutch were then, as they are now, a very important commercial nation and made long voyages to their possessions in the East, carrying back to European peoples spices, silks, tea, and other luxuries. In those days of small sailing vessels the voyage from Holland to eastern Asia and the East Indies was so long that it was impossible to carry food and water enough for the trip. Therefore the settlement at the southern end of Africa was an important one to captains who needed to obtain fresh provisions for the remainder of the voyage.

The settlement at Cape Town prospered. More Dutch settlers came from time to time and, attracted by the climate of the plateau and the grasses which grew there, went gradually farther and farther into the interior. For many years the region was a Dutch colony. Many of the light-skinned people in South Africa today are Boers, descendants of these early Dutch settlers. When South Africa came into the possession of the British in 1806, some of the Boers traveled, or trekked, as they called it, farther north, where they might be free from English control. Beyond the Orange River they established the Orange Free State and beyond the Vaal River the Transvaal. One after another these divisions and others in South Africa have come to be a part of the British Commonwealth.

Cape Town today is a large, important city and one of the beauty places of the earth. All around the city are deep woods, lovely orchards and farms, and vineyards. In front of it lie the blue, rippling waters of the bay and directly behind it rise the western ranges of the Southern Highlands.

Table Mountain is very appropriately named, for its top is remarkably flat and often covered with a tablecloth of white clouds formed by the condensation of the moisture in the air blowing in from the sea.

Cape Town is as modern as any city in Europe or America. It has fine stores like those in our great cities at home. The houses of Parliament are large and imposing. The broad streets, the beautiful residences, the parks and gardens and beaches, and the views from Table Mountain and Lion's Head are all very attractive. On the great pier which stretches out into the bay we listen to splendid concerts. In the museum we visit an

Figure 39. These buildings are the Houses of Parliament in Cape Town. See Table Mountain rising behind them. With the sea in front and the mountains behind, what a beautiful place Cape Town must be!

interesting collection of African animals. We explore the castle, the oldest building in the colony, the first stone of which was laid in 1666.

We are interested in the people of all colors whom we meet on the streets of Cape Town. Among them are light-skinned Englishmen and Boers, and darker-skinned Hindus from India. Also included are brown-skinned laborers who are the descendants of people brought here in early days from the Dutch colonies in the East Indies. More numerous than any of these are the dark-skinned people of the native tribes.

The many vessels in the harbor of Cape Town will carry the goods stored in the warehouses and on the wharves to all parts of the world. There are larger amounts of animal products than of anything else—cattle hides, sheepskins and goatskins, meat, hair, and wool. There are also quantities of sugar, fruit, tobacco, corn and wheat, and ostrich feathers. Every year millions of dollars' worth of gold and diamonds are also sent out of Cape Town.

Figure 40. These workers are picking grapes in a vineyard near Cape Town. What is said on page 119 about the fruit industry here?

The train which we take from Cape Town climbs from the low coast land to the higher veldt. As we climb we notice how the vegetation changes with the height. In the lower plains are great vineyards and orchards like those in southern California; on the higher terraces there are large grain farms; and still higher, where it is cooler and drier, we see many sheep and cattle feeding in the pastures. On many of the farms we notice the irrigation ditches which bring the water for the crops.

Now we are on the high, dusty veldt. For hours and even for days we can ride northward over this vast plateau. Away in the distance are dim blue mountains. Sometimes the track runs near curious flat-topped hills, called kopjes, and again no hills or mountains are in sight in all the wide sweep of plain.

Figure 41. This picture shows you the inside of a jam factory in the Cape Province. What is done with the thousands of jars of jam and preserved fruits prepared in South Africa?

Scientists tell us that ages and ages ago this entire plateau of South Africa was as high as the tops of the flat kopjes. Through all the long centuries, Nature's workers—the rain, the frost, the sunshine, and the streams—have been wearing down the land to its present level. The kopjes, made of harder rock less easily worn away, remain, like the mesas and buttes in the western United States, to tell us of this great work of Nature and of the enormous amounts of soil which have

THE UNION OF SOUTH AFRICA

been washed into the sea (see Allen's "North America").

Except where settlers have planted trees on their farms and around their houses, the great veldt is bare. Low bushes and grass grow on the unshaded plain, and in the long droughts become brown and withered. Many of these desert plants, however, have a way of storing up their moisture and sap and are sweet and juicy, furnishing excellent food for the flocks and herds of the ranchmen.

Farther north large areas of the plateau are too barren even for ranching. The wind lifts clouds of dust, twists them into spiral columns, and carries them along over the parched earth. From time to time the train crosses bridges spanning dry river beds. At another time of the year these gullied channels might be full of rushing water. Except the Zambezi, the Orange, and the Limpopo (see map on page 93), few rivers of South Africa flow for the entire year. For months they are only a series of water holes or dry, rocky channels.

There are many large ranches on the veldt. When you put on your warm woolen coat or sweater do you ever wonder where the wool of which they are made comes from? We raise large numbers of sheep in the United States, but our factories require so much wool that we import millions of pounds from Argentina, Australia and New Zealand, China, and South Africa. Do you suppose that some of the wool of which your coat is made came from the sheep on a South African farm?

Not only our warm woolen garments but our shoes

as well may serve to remind us of our neighbors in South Africa. Though we have many cattle and sheep and some goats on our own great plains, they do not furnish leather enough for our busy shoe factories, and we import hides and skins from many countries. Some of these come from animals raised on South African farms.

Figure 42. Many sheep feed on the plateau of South Africa. Here you see thousands of bags of wool in a wool market in Port Elizabeth. Where will it be sent?

Besides the cattle and sheep many farmers in South Africa raise Angora goats, whose long, fine hair, called mohair, is very valuable in manufacturing. Much of it is used in making plush for covering seats in railroad and electric cars and automobiles. South Africa raises more Angora goats than any other country, but the industry is spreading as people in other lands learn more of the value of this hair.

THE UNION OF SOUTH AFRICA

Somewhere on every farm and ranch on the veldt there must be a well, a water hole, or a dam built to store up surplus water. In times of very long droughts the water may be nearly or entirely exhausted. In such cases the water for the use of the family may have to be brought for long distances, and many of the animals which cannot be supplied may die.

The owners of most of the ranches are light-skinned Boers or Englishmen. Much of Africa is so hot that light-skinned people find the climate problematic. Not so in South Africa. Though much of it is in the torrid zone the interior plateau is so high that the climate is delightful. The clear, dry air is bracing, and though the days are hot the nights are always cool. Americans and Europeans can live and work here as well as they can in their own countries.

Figure 43. Could you carry as heavy bundles on your heads as the people in this picture are carrying?

Many of the laborers on the ranches are native blacks of South Africa. They tend the flocks and herds, plant and harvest the crops, milk the cows and drive them to the pastures. We may happen to see some of these men driving heavy wagons, filled with corn or wool and drawn by several pairs of long-horned oxen, to the nearest railroad station, which is often many miles away from the ranch.

Once in a while our train stops at a village, and we find the sight of the tree-lined streets very pleasant after our long ride over the unshaded plain. Though small, these villages are often important centers of trade. Here the cattleman from his ranch, the farmer from his fruitful acres, and the native from his kraal come to buy and sell. On the wide, dusty road leading out into the open, sunny country around we see a heavy ox wagon loaded with wool come slowly creeping into the village. Perhaps it came from a nearby ranch, for some of these natives now have farms and ranches of their own.

The government of South Africa has set apart areas in the different provinces where the natives may live, much as we in the United States have set apart our Indian reservations. Others live in villages on the veldt. Many of the blacks live and work on the ranches and farms of the English and Boers. Others own large flocks and herds and are prosperous farmers. Some live in the cities and towns, work for the foreigners, and dress as they do. Some of the natives are going to school and are learning there more of modern ways. There are so many more natives in South Africa than there are foreigners that the problem of their education and uplift is an important one which will take many years to solve.

By taking the train from Cape Town northward through the province of the Cape of Good Hope we missed seeing Port Elizabeth, an important seaport of South Africa (see map on page 93). Let us now take a side trip on the branch railroad which runs down to this city.

For some time before we get to the coast we realize that Port Elizabeth is an important commercial city. At every station there are quantities of freight waiting to be put onto the southbound trains. We see piles of hides and skins, bales of wool, and many ostrich feathers. We have seen so many Angora goats feeding on the plateau, and at the stations so many bales filled with their long, silky hair, that we are not surprised to learn that Port Elizabeth exports more mohair than any city in the world.

See those great birds with their long legs and out stretched wings running along beside the train. They are ostriches, and there are hundreds of them off there on the plain. South Africa is famous for ostrich farms and for the lovely plumes taken from the birds.

Let us visit an ostrich farm. There are high fences around the fields to prevent the birds from getting out. See the nest in the sand filled with eggs. Many eggs also are in the incubators, where little ostriches are hatched as we hatch chickens. Should you like an ostrich egg for your breakfast? It is as good as a hen's egg; but if you ate a whole one, you would have a very hearty meal, for it is larger than a dozen hens' eggs.

When it is time to pluck the feathers the workmen drive the birds one by one into a small pen. A cloth is drawn over the ostrich's head to blindfold it while the

Figure 44. This is a scene on an ostrich farm. Notice what long straight legs the birds have. These enable them to run fast and kick hard.

men cut off the long, beautiful wing feathers and the shorter ones in the tail. More than a hundred feathers and many short tips are taken from one bird.

Sorting and grading the plumes is dusty work, but it must be done before they are tied up in bundles and sent to Port Elizabeth to be shipped away. This city is the center of the South African ostrich trade. Never before in our lives have we seen so many ostrich feathers. Great storerooms are filled with them, and it seems to us that there are feathers enough here to trim a hat and make a fan for every woman and girl in the world.

Port Elizabeth has been called the Liverpool of South Africa. It is a great center of trade for the eastern portion of the Cape Province and a large part of the interior. It is connected by rail with Kimberley and the rich mining country around. Its position with relation to the diamond fields and other parts of the interior and to the other sea ports gives it great advantages for commerce.

Almost on the boundary between the Cape Province and the Orange Free State is the city of Kimberley, famous for its diamond mines, which are the richest in the world. Since 1867, when they were first discovered, tons of diamonds worth many million dollars have been obtained.

There are many interesting stories told of the discovery of diamonds in South Africa. One of these is about a hunter who, while stopping overnight in a farmhouse, saw on the table some shining stones which the children had picked up on the bank of a stream

Figure 45. The picture shows you an ostrich-feather sale in Port Elizabeth. What was said about feathers and Port Elizabeth on page 106?

Figure 46. This is an old mine in Kimberley used when diamonds were dug out of the soil near the surface of the ground. As the miners dug deeper and deeper, great pits like this were made. Why was this method abandoned for underground mining?

which flowed close by. As the hunter admired the stones the farmer gave them to him, and this gift of a few pebbles, which turned out to be diamonds, made him a very wealthy man.

A second story tells of another hunter who stopped at the house of a farmer. Seeing something glistening in the mud walls, he dug it out and found that it was a large diamond. The farmer tore down his house and dug out the diamonds in its walls and thus became rich.

Like the first gold prospectors of California and Alaska, the early diamond miners of South Africa searched for the gems in the loose gravel and sands near the river beds. As they dug deeper and deeper the

THE UNION OF SOUTH AFRICA

miners came to a hard, bluish clay under the surface soil. When this was reached most of them thought that their good luck was over and sold their claims for what they could get. It is this same blue earth, however, which has since furnished the diamonds of South Africa. It has to be blasted out, and as the digging became deeper the cost of mining grew greater, so that large amounts of money were required to meet the expense. Therefore most of the mining is carried on by a few big companies.

See that inclosed space or compound over near the mine. There are hundreds of men inside chatting, smoking, playing, eating, and otherwise amusing themselves. In the early days many diamonds were stolen by the workmen. Valuable stones are small and are easily secreted in the hair or mouth. Sometimes they were swallowed. To prevent theft today the workmen

Figure 47. Here you see some of the wire entanglements surrounding a diamond mine. What is their use?

live in these fenced compounds, which lead directly into the mines, and they cannot leave the compounds until their contract expires. When this time comes they are kept in confinement for some days and then are carefully examined before they are allowed to depart. The men know all this before they sign their contracts, but the high wages and the comfortable life in the compounds attract them.

Figure 48. This is the inside of a compound in which the diamond miners live. The men are cooking their suppers. What is said of these compounds on pages 109 and 110?

Let us go down into one of the mines. The mines have the most modern machinery for lifting and lowering the men and the rock and for lighting and ventilation. The elevator drops us swiftly hundreds of feet to the level where the miners are working. As we walk through the long passages we see some miners drilling the holes for explosives. Farther on other men with pickaxes are breaking up the rock which has been blasted out, and still others are loading it onto cars. These cars run to the shaft and are taken up to the surface. Arriving there the rock is dumped in a field inclosed by a high wire fence. This field is closely guarded, and no one is allowed to go in or out, for there are hundreds of diamonds hidden there.

The blue rock is left here for some weeks. Sometimes it is sprinkled with water and rolled or harrowed. All these things, with the action of the sun and air, help to soften it and cause it to crumble.

When soft enough to be worked, the earth is mixed with water and put into the mixing machines, which washes away much of the finer, lighter soil. When as much as possible has been removed, the coarser material, which contains the diamonds, is passed over sloping, shaking tables which are covered with grease. The diamonds stick to the grease, while the worthless material slides away. Then the grease is melted and thus the diamonds are recovered. The sorters find diamonds of all sizes and colors—white, yellow, green, blue, pink, and black. The white and the yellow are the most valuable for gems, but all the stones find many uses. A diamond is the hardest substance known and will cut any other material, so the stones are very valuable in manufacturing and are used for cutting, drilling, and engraving. Perhaps your dentist may have some tool with a diamond point which he uses for drilling your teeth when filling them. The most important industrial use of the stones is in gem cutting and rock drilling.

In puzzling out Nature's secrets about diamonds, scientists have discovered that the gems occur in the earth and rock which fill the craters of ancient volcanoes. These round volcanic pipes stretch far down into the interior of the earth. The largest of them is near Pretoria, and it was here that the great Cullinan diamond, the largest ever mined, was obtained. It was four inches long and two inches wide and was worth two and a half million dollars. How should you like to dig out of the earth a gem like that?

From the appearance of a sparkling diamond you would hardly think that it is formed of the same material as a lump of coal or the lead in your pencil. Yet these three substances are all composed of carbon. A diamond is pure crystallized carbon. What processes the agents of Mother Nature in their underground workshops employed to fashion diamonds out of the same material from which they formed coal is one of her secrets. It is certain, however, that intense heat and tremendous pressure were necessary and that these were connected with the outbursts of underground volcanoes.

The diamonds and gold of South Africa have drawn many people to this part of the world. They needed homes and supplies, and thus cities grew. Many of the people who came here to search for gold and diamonds have become farmers and ranchers, and thus these industries have developed.

The mineral deposits in our Western states had a similar influence in attracting many people to that part of our country (see Allen's "North America"). Yet the gold which is mined today in California and Colorado is of little value compared with the products of the farms in those states. In the future this will be true in South Africa. Diamonds, gold, and silver are not the most valuable things on earth, though many people seem to think so, but they often serve to draw men to regions where other and more useful industries may be developed.

Like many of our Western cities, Kimberley was originally a camp which grew up around the mines. Its location is not very pleasant, for it lies in the midst of a vast sandy plateau. Instead of rainstorms, dust storms often occur, and Kimberley housekeepers close every door and window to keep out the fine dust.

Kimberley owes its birth and its growth to the diamonds around it, and there was no choice concerning its location. It has accomplished marvels under the circumstances and has grown into a thriving modern city.

Orange Free State

The diamonds extend for some distance into the Orange Free State, another of the four provinces which make up the Union of South Africa. Like the other British possessions here, it consists chiefly of high, rolling plains from three to five thousand feet above sea level. At this height the climate is cool and pleasant. The best farms are located in the east and south, where the trade winds bring considerable rain, while in the drier west there are many ranches with wide areas of pasture land.

Figure 49. You may think that this is a picture of a great wheat farm in the United States. The reaper which the man is using was made in our country, but the farm is in the Orange Free State.

The Orange Free State is often called the Granary of South Africa. Many of the farmers are Scotch and are thrifty and prosperous. Some of the farms and ranches cover thousands of acres. Near the ranch houses are great fields of waving corn and yellow wheat. Corn is one of the important crops of South Africa, and wheat, which has always been imported in large amounts, is being raised in greater and greater quantities. Much wheat is ground into flour in mills run by power from the mountain streams.

Beyond the fields of grain are rolling pasture lands where cattle and sheep feed. Many of the ranchmen raise their cattle for beef; others, located nearer villages and towns, raise dairy cattle and make butter and cheese. In some of the villages through which we have come we have seen large creameries, to which the farmers bring their milk instead of making the dairy products at home.

Going north toward Bloemfontein, the capital of the province, the veldt is a reddish-brown plain of grass with no tree or high hill in sight. Once in a while we cross a stream which we can trace far into the distance by the line of green which borders it on either side. Now and then we stop at a village station. The large numbers of bales of wool and mohair and the bundles of hides and skins waiting shipment on the coast-bound trains tell us that there must be many cattle and large flocks of sheep and Angora goats feeding off on the wide plains. These products will be taken down to East London, a prosperous seaport in the Cape Province, and shipped to European countries. Some of the wool will come to Boston, which, next to London, is the greatest wool port in the world.

Bloemfontein is the most important city in the Orange Free State. The height, forty-five hundred feet above the sea, the dry air, and the many sunny days make the climate very healthful and attract so many visitors to the city that it has become popular as a health resort.

Bloemfontein is laid out in squares with a large market place in the center. You would enjoy visiting the market some morning and seeing the fruit, vegetables, and grain and the cattle and sheep and wool which the farmers for miles around have brought in.

Many of the natives whom we see in Bloemfontein have come from Basutoland, which joins the Orange Free State on the southeast. If I tell you that Basutoland is often called the Switzerland of South Africa, you will know what kind of region it is. The route from Bloemfontein into this colony takes us through a splendid ranching country and past villages around which the Basutos cultivate large fields of corn and wheat.

As we continue our journey farther into Basutoland the country grows more hilly, and the mountains rise higher and higher until at last we can see the snow-covered peaks of the highest mountains of South Africa gleaming white and rose-pink in the light of the setting sun.

In the future Basutoland will be a popular land for tourists, who will enjoy its invigorating air, its beautiful mountains, its lovely rivers, its splashing falls, and its green valleys.

Natal

We have already visited two of the provinces of the Union of South Africa. Between the ocean on the east and the Orange Free State and Basutoland on the west is another province, Natal, a land of rolling hills and broad valleys, green meadows, swift rivers and brooks, and high waterfalls. Vasco da Gama, the Portuguese explorer, touched the coast here in 1497 on Christmas

Day, the birthday, or natal day, of Christ, and for this reason he named the land Natal.

This province is often called the Garden of South Africa. It has many fine farms, comfortable homes, and prosperous farmers. It is well adapted for farming because the trade winds blow over it, dropping their moisture as they cross the Southern Highlands.

By whatever route we descend from the high interior to the coast lands we shall notice that immediately on leaving the higher level the air is warmer and softer. The crops also differ on the different levels, as do the views and the scenery. Behind us on the higher, drier plateau are the great cattle and sheep ranches. Farther down, on the sheltered hillsides, we see long rows of tea plants, and natives picking the tender green leaves. We think of China, Japan, and India as the great tea countries of the world, and many people do not know that today South Africa is producing several million pounds each year. Like other tea-producing countries, Natal has sunny hillsides, fertile soil, balmy sunshine, plenty of moisture, and native workmen who labor for low wages. Therefore in the future we may expect to see a great increase in the tea produced here.

There are coffee plantations also on the sunny slopes, and large fields of tobacco where the ground is completely hidden by the long leaves. As everywhere else in South Africa, there are large fields of corn, the chief farm product in this part of the continent. On the broad terraces between the plateau and the coast are many ostrich farms where valuable birds are raised.

Figure 50. These are bales of tobacco leaf brought here to be shipped away. Tobacco is becoming an important crop in South Africa.

As we journey farther down the slopes, where the air is warmer, we ride past large well-kept plantations where many acres are covered with tall, waving sugar cane. Some cane is grown in the warm parts of other provinces, but the greater part of the many thousand tons of sugar which are produced in South Africa comes from Natal.

Those rows of trees with the long, drooping leaves off there in the distance are banana trees. These are grown all over South Africa as ornaments in gardens and parks, but here on the coast lands of Natal are modern plantations where large amounts of fruits are produced. We see, too, large fields of pineapples and visit the canneries which have been built for preserving the fruit. This industry is as yet not so important here as it is in the Cape Province, where the fruit is raised and canned in great quantities and shipped from East London and Port Elizabeth.

The number of orange, peach, plum, pear, and apple trees in South Africa runs well into the millions. With the large crops from these orchards, and with the development of the pineapple and banana industries, South Africa is becoming one of the important fruit-producing areas of the world. The importance of her fruit crop is greatly increased by the fact that her growing and harvesting seasons come when King Winter reigns in northern countries. Therefore the shipments from South Africa reach the markets of England when fruit there is scarce and prices high.

You remember that our dried fruits, our prunes,

Figure 51. Doesn't this look like California, with the mountains in the distance and the fruit drying in the sun? Do you think the boxes contain prunes, apricots, or raisins?

apricots, and raisins, come chiefly from California (see Allen's "North America"). No rain falls there during the growing and harvesting seasons, and the fruit is picked and dried in the sunshine with little danger of decay from being wet. There are similar large areas in South Africa where, because of the climate, the dried-fruit industry has become important. Already large quantities of raisins, currants, prunes, and apricots are shipped away, and in the future these amounts will be greatly increased.

Durban is the port of Natal and holds a very important place in the trade of South Africa. In your sight-seeing trips through the city you may choose an automobile, a horse-drawn cab, an electric car, or a jinrikisha. The drivers and drawers differ as much as do the vehicles. Not all of them are dark-skinned natives. Some are Hindus from India, and still others are natives from the East Indies and the Malay Peninsula.

On the wharves at Durban we notice great bundles of dried bark. This has come from a species of the acacia tree which grows in the province. The bark will be taken to England, where it will be put through processes to extract from it a tanning preparation useful in the manufacture of leather. The wood of the tree is used for props and supports in mines and for building purposes.

On the wharves we see also large quantities of corn, bags of sugar, boxes of tea, bales of wool, and bundles of hides. There are vessels here taking on coal, for this is one of the important products of Natal. In this land so far away from the great coal-producing countries of the world these coal deposits are very valuable. Natal has also rich beds of other minerals which will in the future yield large returns.

Figure 52. Do you not wish that you could join the crowds here on the beach at Durban? What other interesting sights might you see in the city?

Durban is not only an important commercial city but a famous pleasure resort as well, and it has many big hotels and places of amusement. On its splendid beaches men, women, and children dive through the rolling breakers, shoot the chutes into large swimming pools, bury one another in the fine, white sand, and get splendid coats of tan as they while away the hours in the sunshine.

Joining Natal on the north is Swaziland, a little colony governed by the Union of South Africa. Swaziland is a well-watered, healthful region well adapted to farming and grazing. On the veldt the grass is green all the year, and the natives here raise many cattle and sheep. Hundreds of farmers from the higher, colder parts of Swaziland and from the Transvaal bring sheep here for winter grazing. The blacks who live on the lower veldt raise grain, sugar, coffee, and other semitropical products. We should see here large fields of corn and farms where peanuts are grown. On the lower coast lands, which are hot and damp, the people raise considerable cotton.

Swaziland is a good illustration of the fact that the height of a place affects its climate and thus helps to determine its crops. Do you live in a high or a low region? How has the height of your section of your home state influenced the occupations of the people who live there?

The Transvaal

Our next visit will be to the Transvaal, the fourth province of the Union of South Africa, and its great city of Johannesburg. Next to Cairo and Alexandria in Egypt, Johannesburg is the largest city on the continent. It is a city built on gold. There is gold, to be sure, in other parts of the Transvaal and in other parts of Africa, but the reef or ridge around Johannesburg contains what are thought to be the richest deposits in the world. Hundreds of thousands of men are engaged in work which in some way is connected with these gold mines, which have given Africa the highest rank among the continents in gold production.

THE UNION OF SOUTH AFRICA

In the early days of the colony the only industry in the region where Johannesburg stands was farming and stock raising. The rainfall was scanty, and in times of long droughts many animals died. There were no railroads, markets were very far away, and the farmers were not very prosperous. Then, in 1886, the gold rush began. Land became more valuable, houses were built, and roads, railroads, bridges, telegraphs, schools, churches, stores, and banks followed. As the settlement grew larger and transportation to the coast easier, men began to take up land and raise cattle, grain, fruit, and vegetables. Realizing that the people needed many articles which had to be brought from places long distances away, men began manufacturing, and the industry has steadily increased. Because of these conditions Johannesburg has grown rapidly into a large,

Figure 53. This is the great open market in Johannesburg. See the ox teams! What goods do you think they have brought in from the country around for the people to buy?

rich, modern, pleasure-loving, money-making city. It is more than a mile above the level of the ocean; the air, though hot in the middle of the day, is so clear and bracing that it makes one feel like doing hard work and accomplishing great things. Do you think that such a climate would have any influence on the growth of the city?

One cannot approach Johannesburg without realizing that mining is the most important industry in the region. We see the tall chimneys, the piles of waste rock from the mines, the buildings containing the machinery for crushing the ore and for separating and treating the gold. These evidences of the gold industry extend for many miles along the rocky ridge, or Rand, as it is often called.

The gold deposits in different parts of Africa have been known and worked for ages. Probably the gold which was used to decorate King Solomon's wonderful temple in Jerusalem came from Africa. The English coins known as guineas received their name because they were made from gold found in the lands bordering on the Gulf of Guinea.

The ancient people who first carried on mining in South Africa had few tools or conveniences for separating the gold from the rock. They built charcoal fires over the hard rock which contained the gold. When the rock was thoroughly heated they poured water on it, which cooled it and caused it to crack, and thus made it easier for the workmen to break it up. How different these early methods are from the modern mines with their deep shafts, their long tunnels lighted by electricity, the expensive machinery, and the chemical processes for recovering the gold!

Figure 54. This is one of the great tanks into which the crushed ore goes for its cyanide bath. The cyanide in the water separates the gold from the worthless material. Beside the tank is a waste dump.

Not only are there rich gold deposits in the Transvaal but silver also is abundant. Coal beds divide and encircle the gold fields so that there is plenty of fuel at hand to run the machinery connected with the mines. Iron and copper are worked also. The Transvaal is one of the regions which we must always remember for its rich mineral deposits.

Pretoria, the capital of the Transvaal and the headquarters of the government of the Union of South Africa, is about forty miles north of Johannesburg. On the trip between the two cities we pass splendid farms surrounded by fields of grain. Many acres are covered with grapevines carefully pruned and supported and loaded with delicious fruit. In the sheltered valleys are groves of oranges, lemons, and other tree fruits. We see fields where men are pulling the dried vines and harvesting fine crops of peanuts, which are crushed for their oil. Tobacco is produced in increasing quantities each year in the Transvaal and other parts of South Africa. Cotton is another crop which farmers in the warmer areas can raise successfully and which has increased tremendously in a few years.

On the drier areas of the veldt cattle raising is the most profitable industry, and large creameries are being established where farmers may bring the milk from their ranches to be made into butter and cheese.

Pretoria is a typical Dutch South African city. Like many other towns of that region it is built in a valley to protect it from the fierce winds which sweep across the open veldt. It is thus considerably warmer than Johannesburg, which stands on the plateau. The city is laid out in squares, with straight streets well shaded with many varieties of trees. The public buildings are a fine group overlooking the city.

SUGGESTIONS FOR STUDY

I

1. The search for ocean routes to the East.

2. Cape Town.

3. The surface of South Africa.

4. Ranching on the veldt.

5. Port Elizabeth.

6. Ostrich farming.

7. Kimberley and diamonds.

8. A trip through the Orange Free State.

9. Bloemfontein and East London.

10. Basutoland and Swaziland.

11. Occupations in Natal.

12. The fruit industry of South Africa.

13. The port of Durban.

14. Johannesburg and gold mining.

15. From Johannesburg to Pretoria.

II

1. Name the divisions of the Union of South Africa. Which is the largest? the smallest? the most northerly? the most southerly?

2. Name the chief city of each province; the chief products.

3. Where are the best farms? Where are the ranches situated? Where are the crops grown which need the warmest climate? What are some of these crops?

AFRICA, AUSTRALIA, ISLANDS OF PACIFIC

4. How many years before the settlement of Cape Town was Alexandria founded (see pages 35 and 96)? Why should you expect to find older places in North Africa than in the southern part of the continent?

5. People in the cities of South Africa are building up the manufacturing industries there. Why is it better for a country to manufacture its own products than to ship away the raw materials and import manufactured goods?

6. Of what leather are your shoes made? Can you find out from what country the skins came?

7. With what might you load a vessel at Durban for London? Should you send the vessel over the same route that a ship from Cape Town would take?

8. Why are the best farms of the Orange Free State in the east and south and the ranches in the west?

9. Why has Boston become such an important wool port (see Allen's "North America" and "United States")?

10. Compare the size of Natal with some states in the United States. What contrasts between Natal and these states can you name?

III

Make a list of the places mentioned in this chapter. Arrange them by countries, cities, rivers, mountains, etc. From the list select those which you think are so important that you should always be able to locate them.

CHAPTER X

SOUTHWEST AFRICA, BECHUANALAND, AND RHODESIA

Southwest Africa

On the map on page 93 you will find a branch line of the Cape-to-Cairo Railroad which leads west along the valley of the Orange River into Southwest Africa. Before the World War this was a German colony. It is now a part of the British Commonwealth and is governed by the Union of South Africa.

Southwest Africa is thinly peopled, and we shall see few cities and towns along our route and find the people on the farms and ranches living far away from any neighbors. Only about a tenth of the people are light-skinned. The blacks belong to many different tribes. Some are Bushmen and Hottentots, odd-looking people with woolly hair which grows in tufts. Most of them have no settled homes, but move from place to place in search of water and the game which they kill for food.

In the northerly parts of the country there are other tribes who live in settled villages, raise grain and vegetables, and have large flocks and herds.

The route through Southwest Africa leads us into regions where rain seldom falls and where clouds of dust race across the plateau, sifting into every crack and crevice. All this country is dry, the southern part particularly so. Rains are few and far between, but when they do come they change the dry river beds into roaring torrents of water which runs to waste

Figure 55. In trouble, isn't he? Do you think he will pull out? He is a mining engineer on a prospecting tour in Southwest Africa. There are no roads in this part of the country, and the car had to follow a dry river bed. The automobile was made in the United States.

into the sea. Much water from the flooded rivers sinks into the ground, and the people dig wells to supply themselves and the animals which they raise. In some parts of the country we should see many windmills for pumping water.

Some day the water which now runs to waste will be stored in reservoirs and led in canals and ditches over the thirsty land. Then there will be more farms here on which the people will raise crops similar to those grown in other parts of South Africa. What are some of these?

At present stock raising is the chief industry, and many cattle, sheep, and goats find food in the dry grasses and low shrubs which cover the plateau. Some of the farmers raise pigs and are breeding horses and camels. Others have started ostrich farms. The government is helping to increase the numbers and improve the quality of the livestock by importing animals of fine breeds from other lands and by teaching the natives how to care for their flocks and herds.

The railroad route runs through Windhoek, the capital, situated on the plateau surrounded by a circle of mountains. The town is a center for a large farming district, and many cattle and sheep are often seen in its streets. The farmers bring in their wool and other produce in large covered wagons drawn by twenty or more oxen. Both animals and wagons are gray with dust, and the faces of the men are tanned by exposure and wrinkled by the wind and sand and the glare of the sunshine.

It is a day's ride on the train from Windhoek down to Swakopmund on the Atlantic coast. Much of the way lies through a gray, barren land. Now and then we pass a native village where the huts, made of bentwood sticks, remind us of wicker bird cages. Beside each hut is an iron kettle in which the women cook the meals over an open fire shared by several families. There are other villages out on the plain, and we see heavy ox wagons coming toward the station bringing grain, tobacco, and wool.

Swakopmund, named from the little Swakop River, is the sandiest town we have ever seen. In whatever direction we look we are sure to see sand, and if we step off the wooden pavement our shoes are filled with it. On the beach the great waves rolling in from the ocean beat and pound the sand hard and smooth. Swakopmund

Figure 56. We are still in Southwest Africa. You can see what a barren land much of it is. This is a construction train building some railroad track near a copper mine in the northern part.

has no good harbor, and the surf and breakers make the coast a dangerous one. Walfish Bay, a short distance away, has a fine harbor protected by an encircling arm of land.

Those dark-colored buildings on the shore are the headquarters of the whaling industry. Many whales are caught in the South Atlantic, large quantities of oil are extracted from the blubber, and the refuse and bones are made into fertilizer. Seals also are caught, and several thousand skins are exported each year.

At Swakopmund we notice another railroad besides the one on which we have come from the Cape Province. This will take us into the northern part of Southwest Africa, where there are rich copper mines. The colony is known to contain deposits of lead, tin, gold, sulphur, and iron, but thus far more has been done toward mining the copper than any of the other minerals.

In the southern part of the colony we could visit mines where diamonds are obtained, and at present these are more valuable than any other exports. These gems are scattered in the gravels near the surface of the ground and are obtained as the diamonds were in the early days of mining around Kimberley. It may be that richer deposits will be found buried deep in the earth and that in the future the gems will be obtained from mines fitted with shafts and tunnels as the Kimberley mines are.

AFRICA, AUSTRALIA, ISLANDS OF PACIFIC

BECHUANALAND

The main line of the Cape-to-Cairo Railroad takes us into Bechuanaland, another British possession. Bechuanaland is not as important as some smaller colonies, for much of it is too dry for farming, and in the south and west there are true desert areas. Here there are miles of hot, dry sand where the only vegetation is a kind of shrub and where the only water supply is in muddy water holes a hundred miles or more apart.

As we travel toward the equator the desert changes gradually into grasslands, and still farther north the equatorial forests begin (see page 10). Many parts of northern Bechuanaland are well wooded and beautiful and capable of sustaining a dense population. The grasslands make good pastures, and many of the natives in this part of the colony raise cattle, sheep, and goats, driving them from place to place in search of food and water.

Some natives live in parts of the desert where you and I should die of starvation. The poor Bakalahari know every plant and root and bulb which grows here. Some they eat, and from others they quench their thirst. One of the most useful plants is called the water root, and many lives have been saved by the water it contains. Its large bulb is six inches or more in diameter. The native digs it up with a sharp stick and drinks the water it contains. Some of the roots and bulbs are eaten by wild animals, whose keen sense of smell guides them to the juicy plants.

Nearly all the people in Bechuanaland are black. They belong to different tribes, each of which is governed by its chief. A commissioner from England lives in Mafeking on the southern border and represents the king and the authority of the British.

As in the other dry regions of South Africa, stock raising is the most important industry, and many of the natives have large flocks and herds. Wherever there are streams or water holes there are native villages. The little huts are often built of a circle of small tree trunks interwoven with bark and perhaps plastered with mud. The men tend the flocks and herds and hunt wild animals, while the women gather fuel, prepare the food, and cultivate the garden patches. Always around the settled villages we see fields of corn.

For many years the corn crop in the drier regions of our Middle Western states was not very successful. In some seasons large quantities were raised, while in years of lesser rainfall the crop was a failure. Finally some native corn, such as is raised on the South African plateau, was brought to the United States and planted in parts of the Central Plain and the Great Plains where the rainfall is light and uncertain. This variety, brought from a semiarid climate, has proved a great success and is now grown over large areas.

On maps of the United States which were made a good many years ago a very large area between the Rocky Mountains and the Sierra Nevada system was marked as a great desert. As water has been stored up in large reservoirs and led over the land, farms have sprung up, cities and towns have been built, and, though large areas of barren land still remain, the desert has grown gradually smaller.

In reading about Bechuanaland we must try to keep constantly in mind that similar changes must come in the future to large parts of this region. As lands become more and more thickly settled, and as the cities of the world grow larger, people will need greater and ever greater supplies of food and clothing materials, such as grains, meat, hides and skins, wool, cotton, and fruit. When the need becomes great enough, men will go into the dry areas and try in some way to make up for the lack of Nature's supplies. They will lead water in canals and ditches from hundreds of miles away to the thirsty lands and use the rich soils to produce needed crops. They will build roads, railroads, bridges, schools, and churches, and in these and other ways try to make life as pleasant and comfortable there as it is in the reclaimed areas in the western part of the United States. It may be many years before such changes will take place in regions like Bechuanaland, but no doubt they will come there in time.

Rhodesia

If we continue northward on the Cape-to-Cairo Railroad we shall come to Rhodesia. The colony of Northern Rhodesia and the Dominion of Southern Rhodesia make this the largest division in this part of the continent. A map of Rhodesia made on the same scale as one of the United States would cover the four states of Washington, Oregon, California, and Nevada.

All of Rhodesia lies in the torrid zone. It is not so hot, however, as one might expect from its position, for most of it is from half a mile to a mile above sea level. It is a healthful country, a place where white men can live and work as well as in Europe or America.

During the summer season, from December to April, the days are very hot, and heavy rains fall which fill lakes and reservoirs. During the rest of the year it is much cooler, especially in June and July, and generally dry. If, as sometimes happens, less rain falls in the summer than usual, the water supply becomes exhausted before the next year's rains come, and many of the animals die of thirst. As the country develops, more and larger irrigation systems will be built so that this danger may be avoided.

Here and there as the train glides along over the plateau we see cattle and sheep browsing on the dry grass. Nearer the ranch houses are big fields of corn and smaller ones of wheat. At the stations there are large quantities of grain which the southbound trains will carry to cities and towns along the route and to the seaports to be shipped away. The great wagons which have brought the grain in from the farms miles away on the veldt are standing beside the station, while the tired oxen rest in the shade. When railroads run nearer to the farms, and roads are built so that motor trucks can be used, much time will be saved which may be put into other useful work.

The first important place which we reach in

Southern Rhodesia is Bulawayo, once a famous native city where the chief tribe of the region had its headquarters. Rhodesia looks forward to a great future, and the town of Bulawayo was planned accordingly. The streets, stretching like red ribbons across the town, are from ninety to a hundred and twenty feet wide. How does this width compare with that of the street on which your schoolhouse is situated? Many trees have been planted to shade the streets, and pleasant houses and gardens lie behind them.

Figure 57. This is the main street in Bulawayo. The statue in the distance is one of Cecil Rhodes. From the street, the buildings, the trees, etc., what do you think about this place?

You would enjoy looking at the exhibit of African animals in the museum here at Bulawayo. You would like also to watch or join in the games on the tennis and croquet grounds. Even more interesting are the polo games and the horse races. English people, you know, are fond of outdoor sports, and in many English colonies care has been taken to provide the people who are living so far from their homeland with the exercise and games to which they are accustomed.

Bulawayo is the chief commercial center of Southern Rhodesia. Here are brought the gold, asbestos, chrome ore, copper, and other minerals from the rich mines of the colony, and the corn, tobacco, cattle, and hides and skins from the farms. We might see here also bags of sugar and coffee, bales of cotton, and rolls of rubber, for these valuable products are increasing every year.

The northbound trains leave here at Bulawayo goods of many kinds: clothing, boots and shoes, arms

Figure 58. These are some modern coke ovens in Southern Rhodesia. The neighboring coal mines yield several million tons each year. What do these facts tell you about industrial possibilities here?

and ammunition, blasting compounds and candles for the mines, machinery for mines and railroads, electrical appliances, agricultural tools and implements, furniture, and food supplies. Most of these come from the British Isles, some from the Union of South Africa, and some from the United States.

At Bulawayo the railroad forks (see map on page 93). The main line swings west and north, and a branch line winds east and thence down to the port of Beira in Mozambique. We will take this branch road for a visit to Salisbury, the capital of Southern Rhodesia. Though well within the torrid zone Salisbury is nearly a mile above sea level and is therefore not extremely hot. The better buildings are of brick, though we see also many of corrugated iron, which is used here to a large extent for building purposes. Ants cannot devour it, heat and dampness do not affect it as much as they do wood, and sheets of it are easily transported.

From the country around, the farmers bring their corn, tobacco, wool, meat, and skins to Salisbury, where they are sold to buyers who send them to Beira or to the more southerly ports for export.

In Bulawayo we saw on the main street a splendid bronze statue of Cecil Rhodes (see Figure 57). This "pioneer of continents" is standing bareheaded, hands clasped behind him, gazing over the town which he created. We admired the statue, but in our trip through Rhodesia we shall see other memorials of this man, not only monuments erected to his memory but great works accomplished—railroads, bridges, and towns, which his imagination saw and his intellect helped to bring into being.

Rhodesia is a living monument to Cecil Rhodes in the name which it bears. The railroad on which we are riding is another memorial to this English statesman. If we go back to Bulawayo and take the main line of the railroad northward across the Zambezi, we shall see another monument to his wisdom and foresight. This is the famous bridge built across the river just below the falls.

Figure 59. Imagine yourself sitting in a train on this bridge looking at the falls and listening to the roar of the water. Locate the bridge in Figure 61.

Victoria Falls, named in honor of that good English queen, is one of the most wonderful sights in the world. When more than ten miles away we can hear the roar of the water as it takes its mighty leap over the cliff nearly four hundred feet high. The bridge which spans the Zambezi River is the highest of its kind in the world, and from it a good view of the falls can be obtained.

As we listen to the roar of the falls and gaze on the wonderful sight, we think what the tremendous

Figure 60. This is what you could see from the bridge in Figure 59. What great men saw visions in these mighty falls?

power of the falling water can do in the future for the development of Rhodesia. The power in this water can generate enough electricity to light mines, move trains and cars, illuminate cities and towns, and run all the mills and factories which will ever be built in this South African country.

The natives named the falls the Smoking Waters, for the shifting clouds of spray which rise from the gorge resemble smoke. The rays of the sun shining on the spray turn the white smoke into rainbows, which spread their beautiful arches over the falls. The witch doctors of the native tribes, gazing into the misty rainbows, pretended to see in them visions which gave them not only great wisdom but a knowledge of the future.

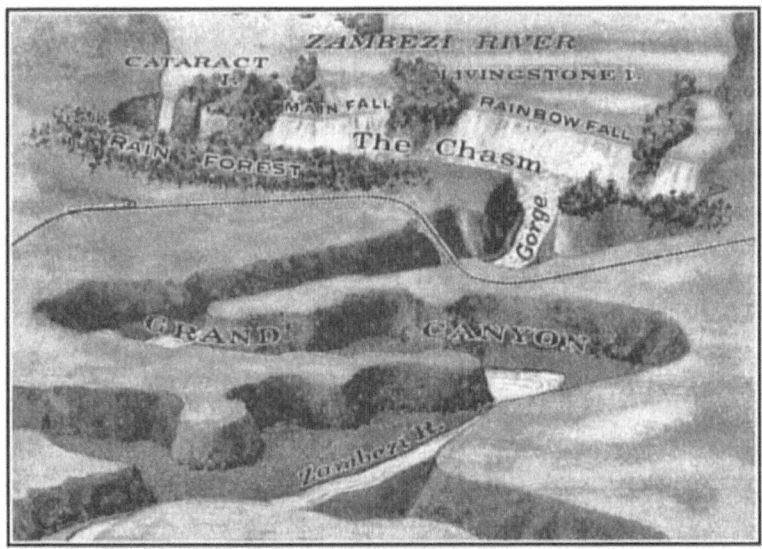

Figure 61. This is a drawing of Victoria Falls, the gorge and canyon of the Zambezi River, and the railroad and bridge. What man dreamed of this railroad and worked to make his dream come true?

David Livingstone, the first white man to penetrate this wild country, discovered the mighty cataract. Like the native witch doctors, he also gazed into the mist and the rainbows and saw visions of the future—long processions of people of civilized nations going deeper and deeper into the Dark Continent, sailing up the long rivers, making their way over high mountains, and penetrating the swamps and jungles. Each of them bore a torch whose light gleamed in the darkness. This was Livingstone's vision—that after him would come those people who would carry to the natives of Africa the torch of knowledge which should scatter the darkness of ignorance. As more and more of the Africans are learning the ways of civilization, Livingstone's dream is coming true.

Looking into the same misty rainbow over Victoria Falls, Cecil Rhodes saw his vision—two shining rails of steel gleaming on the high plains, running through dark forests, tunneling mountains, bridging rushing rivers, and linking together all parts of this vast continent from Cairo in the north to Cape Town on the southern coast.

Wonderful dreams! But had these men not set to work to make their dreams come true, the Dark Continent might still be dark and the visions a long way from being fulfilled. Have you ever dreamed of something fine which you should like to see accomplished? It is fine to dream such things, but it is finer still to work to make the dreams come true.

The colony of Northern Rhodesia and the Dominion of Southern Rhodesia are divided by the Zambezi River.

The town of Livingstone, on the left bank of the river, is the capital of the northern division.

Northern Rhodesia is larger than the southern colony, but it is less developed. Were we to leave the train we should find few roads. All goods are brought to the stations by wagons or native carriers. The plateau is dust covered and parched with heat in the dry months and deep with mud in the rainy season. Yet, like Southern Rhodesia, this great interior plateau is already becoming an important cattle country, and there are many ranches owned by both natives and colonists.

As in other parts of South Africa, corn is raised on many farms. In parts of the warmer, northern portion the rubber tree grows well and cotton of a fine quality can be raised. Northern Rhodesia also reaches into the tropical forests, where there are trees valuable for their splendid hard woods. From others dyes, gums, and fibers can be obtained.

In this part of the colony there are many wild animals such as we saw in our trip through British East Africa. Elephant-hunting is common here, and ivory is an important export.

Stock raising and agriculture will always be important occupations in both divisions of Rhodesia, but Nature has stored away so many minerals in the rocks and soils that mining is sure to grow in importance. Coal, copper, and iron, the most useful of minerals, are found in abundance, while in Southern Rhodesia are rich gold reefs, or ridges, similar to those in the Transvaal.

You will notice on the map that the Cape-to-Cairo Rail road, on which we have been riding, extends directly across Northern Rhodesia to Broken Hill, near the northern border, and thence into the Belgian Congo. This railroad has had a wonderful influence in drawing settlers farther and farther north and making people acquainted with the rich resources of this land. In the future, Rhodesia will become one of the important divisions of the continent. Over its vast stretches great numbers of cattle, sheep, horses, and goats will feed. Large fields of tobacco will cover the ground with their big leaves; cotton plantations will furnish materials for clothing; rubber plantations will be started; and vineyards and orchards will yield delicious fruits. Like the other divisions of South Africa, Rhodesia will become increasingly important in supplying products to help feed the world and in furnishing mills and factories with raw materials for manufacture.

SUGGESTIONS FOR STUDY

I

1. Southwest Africa: people, climate, and occupations.
2. Towns and harbors.
3. Mineral wealth.
4. Bechuanaland.

SOUTHWEST AFRICA

5. Native corn.

6. Southern Rhodesia and its cities.

7. Victoria Falls.

8. Northern Rhodesia.

9. Future development of these lands.

II

1. Using the scale of your map on page 93, find the distance from Cape Town to the northern boundary of Rhodesia. To what place in the United States would this distance reach from New York City?

2. Why should there be snow on the mountain tops of South Africa when little or no rain falls on the plains?

3. Why do more people live in the Union of South Africa than in Bechuanaland or Rhodesia?

4. How can you tell on the map that all of Rhodesia lies in the torrid zone?

5. To what important ports do branches of the Cape-to-Cairo Railroad lead? In what divisions are these ports? What freight does the railroad take to them?

6. Write to the Department of Commerce in Washington asking for information concerning the exports from the British colonies in South Africa to the United States; the imports to South Africa from the United States.

AFRICA, AUSTRALIA, ISLANDS OF PACIFIC

III

Make a list of the places mentioned in this chapter. Arrange them by countries, cities, rivers, mountains, etc. From the list select those which you think are so important that you should always be able to locate them and know something about them.

CHAPTER XI

BRITISH COLONIES IN WEST AFRICA

Our next trip in British territory will take us into a region very different from that which we have just visited. We will sail northward on the Atlantic Ocean, past the northern boundary of Southwest Africa and along the coast of the Gulf of Guinea. For hundreds of miles we see few settlements and, in many places, no trace of a foreign presence; yet, with the exception of Liberia, every foot of land is claimed by some European nation whose territory runs back from the swamps on the coast through dense forests into the higher, drier grasslands of the interior.

We have reason to be greatly interested in the people, products, and conditions of West Africa. Perhaps the rubber for the tires on your automobile or bicycle came from these lands. The oil used in your soap or salad may have been made from seeds and nuts which grew here. The beans which furnished your morning cup of cocoa may have come from a West African plantation.

For long years the heavy surf of great ocean rollers,

the swamps and jungles, the unhealthy climate, the insect pests, and the unwelcoming natives isolated West Africa from the rest of the world. In spite of these handicaps the Europeans have persisted in their efforts to get the palm oil, the rubber, the cocoa, the gold, and the other valuable products of the region. They have built piers and break waters, cleared the jungles and started plantations, built roads and railroads into the interior, and established trading stations where natives can sell the products of farms and forests.

The first British possession which we reach in our northward sail is Nigeria, the largest and the most important British colony in West Africa. A little farther west lies the Gold Coast and Ashanti. Just around the bend in the African coast lies Sierra Leone, and farther north shaped somewhat like your thumb, is the little colony of Gambia.

These British possessions lie in the torrid zone, and in the low coast lands the weather is hot all the year round. Farther inland the land is higher and therefore somewhat cooler. There is no real winter and summer here; but, as in other tropical regions, the year is divided into rainy and dry seasons. During the rainy season the rivers overflow their banks and extend far inland, changing large areas of lowlands into lakes and swamps.

There are no great cities here, and large areas are either entirely uninhabited or peopled by uncivilized tribes; yet these lands are of great value, and the ocean trade which is carried on between their ports and England mounts into hundreds of millions of dollars.

Let us take a trip into the different divisions, find out how the few English people live who are stationed in these hot lands, visit the native villages, and learn why England has thought it worth while to build roads and railroads, warehouses and wharves, and make other improvements in this part of Africa.

Our first visit will be to Nigeria. This colony takes its name from the great Niger River, which flows through it. This river is one of many in West Africa which flow from the highlands of the interior down to the coast, bringing with them large quantities of silt. More than a hundred miles from the sea the Niger, overburdened with its load, begins to drop the silt in its channel, filling it up so that the river forks into a multitude of small streams. Only one of these is navigable for seagoing vessels.

The amount of silt which the Niger brings down is so great that its delta plain is enormous, one of the largest in the world. Much of this low, hot, swampy land is covered with mangrove trees. On either side of the sluggish river are greenish-black walls of these forests, looking, as one writer says, as if standing on stilts, with their branches tucked up out of the wet, leaving their roots exposed in mid-air. When the tide comes in, the brown muddy water rises higher and higher. Soon there are no banks in sight. One can go in canoes far into the country or from one native village to another. The heat is intense, mosquitoes and flies buzz and sting, and crocodiles sleep in the slimy mud.

As the tide ebbs, the lower branches and the trunk

are left with a thick coating of mud. Finally the gray twisted roots appear and then the wet brown earth. Dead branches and roots mixed with the soil brought down by the stream help to build up the land. Seeds fall on the muddy earth and grow, and thus, bit by bit, the coast of Africa is widened.

Farther inland, even before one reaches the place where the main stream divides into its delta mouths, the mangroves begin to give place to other forests beautiful in form and coloring. Here, among many others, the African mahogany trees overtop the graceful raffias and oil palms. So many palm nuts and so much oil have been shipped from this region that the delta streams of the Niger have long been called the Oil Rivers.

Figure 62. *These children in West Africa like to do out-of-door exercises as well as you do. This is a mission school. Missionaries are teaching the natives of Africa many things which will make their lives happier and better.*

In these delta lands settlements are few and widely separated. There are many miles of pathless jungles and forests where no one has trodden. What courage the early explorers and traders and missionaries must have had! They made their way through these gloomy stretches, facing death from disease, from native tribes, from poisonous insects, and from fierce animals in order that they might add more facts to the world's knowledge, more products to its manufacturing materials, more markets for manufactured goods, and more peoples to our world neighbors.

Once in a while we pass a little village in a clearing in the forest. Little children are swimming and diving in the river, and women are shelling the nuts of the oil palm. Some of the men put out to the vessel in their dugout canoes to trade fruit or nuts or cocoa for cloth and tools and other articles which they need in their simple lives.

Farther inland the land is higher, and the green hills rise into dark rugged mountains. Here the Niger, broken with many small islands, hidden rocks, and swift rapids, cuts its way through a gorge in the highlands. Here, in the pleasanter lands of the interior, are larger villages, a greater variety of industries, and natives who are more enterprising than the coastal tribes.

We should find a sail up the great river into the interior a long, slow, tiresome trip. Our best way to get acquainted with Nigeria is to travel on the railroad which runs from Lagos on the coast through the heart of Nigeria to Kano in the north (see map on page 193).

Lagos is the capital and the most important seaport of Nigeria. As we approach it from the ocean we see first the lighthouse which guards the coast. The winds are strong here, and the high surf which breaks on the shore is often dangerous to shipping. On a cliff facing the sea is a government hospital and sanitarium, reminding us that we are in one of the most unhealthful places to be found anywhere on earth. Foreigners have died here by thousands on the dreaded "west coast." The death rate, though still high, is much lower than formerly, for the nations who control these lands have done a great deal to protect the health of the Europeans who live here. They have built hospitals, ice plants, and good houses with screened piazzas to keep out the disease-carrying mosquitoes. They have drained land, built sewers, and installed a water supply.

In the native quarter the houses are of bamboo, with roofs of palm leaves or corrugated iron. As in every native town there are crowds of people trading and gossiping in the bazaars. The inhabitants are of many different tribes, and one hears a jargon of dialects and languages. Some of the women are buying yams, which are as good as potatoes. Others are purchasing manioc root, which they will grind into flour and make into bread. There goes a strong, handsome woman with a baby tied fast on her back and her arms full of coconuts, manioc root, and bananas. Those tall, straight blacks dressed in dark-blue robes belong to the Hausa tribe. They have come here from their homes hundreds of miles farther north, perhaps from Kano in northern Nigeria or from Timbuktu on the edge of the Sahara.

They will exchange the ivory, silks, and woolen stuffs which they have brought for some bright-colored cotton cloth or some cooking utensils.

On the wharves at Lagos we notice great piles of rubber being loaded on vessels bound for England. In the coastal forests there are many rubber trees and vines. Some of the vines have stems as thick as a man's leg, which twist themselves like huge serpents around the trunks of the forest trees and hang in long festoons from the branches, helping to shut out the light and sunshine from the moist, steaming earth.

On our way northward from Lagos we stop at several trading centers. The size of such towns has little to do with their importance. They may be only small places containing a few people, and yet they may carry on a large trade with the villages around.

Trade is the greatest industry of West Africa. With the exception of peanuts, cocoa, and ginger, the natives produce little from cultivated lands. The great trade here is in forest products, such as palm nuts and wild rubber.

At the trading stations where we stop, the "factories," as the warehouses are called, are in compounds surrounded by high fences. One warehouse may be for the goods which the natives bring in and another for the foreign goods which they wish to buy. Under a large open shed are scales for weighing. Some of the natives have come from villages long distances away. They have been several days on the journey, carrying on their heads or backs bags of peanuts or palm nuts or bundles of hides and skins. They will rest here for a while, buy food for the return trip and goods to take to their villages, and then start back to their homes.

Could you peep into the warehouses at the trading stations, you would see, besides the hides and skins, the beeswax, and the groundnuts, or peanuts, as you would call them, many casks of oil and tons of the kernels which come from the fruit of the oil palm tree. Palm nuts and palm oil are the most important exports of Nigeria. You would find them in every trading station along the railroad and in every seaport of Nigeria and other West African colonies. You would find them, too, in the trading posts along the Niger River and other streams and in the traders' villages scattered along the forest paths.

The city of Hull in England imports more seeds and nuts and from them crushes out more oil than any other city in the world. Millions of dollars' worth of such products come each year to this one city. Marseille in southern France, Hamburg in Germany, and many other cities in Europe and the United States import immense quantities. From cotton seeds, coconuts, castor beans, soy beans, peanuts, palm nuts, and other fruits, seeds, and nuts less well known, oil is prepared in enormous quantities, even millions of tons. This is used for making butter substitutes, cooking fats, and salad oils, and for manufacturing soaps, candles, and lubricating oils. Sometime when you are washing your hands with some fragrant soap in which palm oil is used let your imagination take you across the Atlantic into the African wilds where the oil palm grows.

Around nearly every village we shall find oil palm trees growing. A bunch of oil palm nuts weighs anywhere from twenty to fifty pounds and may contain a thousand nuts, which look somewhat like huge cherries.

The native climbs the tall oil palm trees and cuts off the bunches of fruit, which grow near the base of the leaves. He lowers them to the ground, carries them to the edge of the path, and covers them with palm leaves. Here they will lie until he is ready to take them to the village.

Figure 63. Could you climb that palm tree as easily as this man is climbing it? He fastens his fiber rope around the tree and around himself and, jerking the rope higher and higher, walks up to the big bunches of fruit.

Through many forest paths the men bring the bunches to the village. The women cut off the fruit and put it into large earthen pots, which they fill with water and set over the fires which they have prepared. When the fruit is thoroughly cooked they turn it, with some water, into a large trough, where the pulp is either trodden or pounded into a soft, greasy mass. As the pulp is mashed the oil which it contains gradually rises in fatty masses to the surface of the water. The women scoop it off with their hands into a jar, which they put over a fire to boil. Soon all the water is evaporated, leaving only the clear fat, which is strained into other jars.

The villagers save some of the fat to use for cooking. They also need some to rub on their bodies. This protects the skin from the heat of the sun, the drenching rains, and the bites of insects. The unstrained fat mixed with dirt and fiber they burn in their lamps.

The men carry most of the oil to the nearest trading post. If the village is near a stream they put the oil into casks, which they roll down to the water's edge. Later the casks are loaded on the little steamer which calls here every few weeks.

You remember that the whole fruit was put into the trough, and the treading or pounding not only mashed the pulpy part but also separated it from the nuts which the pulp contained. These nuts are taken from the trough and spread out to dry in the sunshine. When thoroughly dried the women break open the hard shell with a stone or a piece of iron and take out the kernels. Though the work is tiresome, I imagine that they have a good time chatting and laughing while the piles of kernels and shells grow gradually larger.

Thousands and even hundreds of thousands of tons of kernels are sent to European cities, and the oil is extracted in the oil mills there. The cake or meal left after the oil is pressed out is a nourishing cattle food and is bought in large quantities by European farmers.

The oil made of the kernels is of a better grade than that made from the pulp and is used for food purposes. The oil made from the pulp is used largely in the making of soaps and candles. Quantities are used in the tin-plate industry to prevent the rusting of the plates as they come from the rollers and are waiting to be dipped in the molten tin. Have you ever ridden on a train which has been delayed by a hot box? Palm oil is used by railroad companies for lubricating the axle boxes of the cars. It also enters into the making of glycerin.

Palm oil must always be made where the fruit is grown, for the fresher the fruit the better the oil. The kernels, however, keep well, and the oil which they contain may be extracted in lands far distant from the forests where they were obtained.

Though millions of dollars' worth of palm oil and palm kernels are exported from West Africa to European countries and the United States every year, in the future this amount will be very largely increased. There are large areas where the oil palm grows which are unexplored and undeveloped. As yet few plantations of these trees have been started and few large factories have been built for shelling the nuts or extracting the oil. West Africa is one of those parts of the tropical world which in the future will yield larger and larger quantities not only of palm oil but of many other useful products which will help feed, clothe, and make more comfortable the people of many countries.

The oil palm tree yields other products besides the nuts. The natives make wine from the sap and sponges from the fiber. They use the leaves for thatching their houses and for making mats. They boil and eat as a vegetable the thickened base of the long leaves, known as palm cabbage.

Figure 64. This man will have palm cabbage for dinner. What other useful articles do the natives get from the oil palm tree?

As we go farther north on our trip through Nigeria we come to the little junction town where a branch line runs off to the tin mines in the eastern part of the country. The tin deposits are scattered over a large area.

Some of the richest beds are near the railroad, but other mines lie several days' journey away and are reached only by rough paths. If you were traveling in this part of Nigeria, you would meet long lines of men plodding along in the narrow paths, each with a package of sixty pounds of tin on his head. With this burden they make from twelve to eighteen miles a day. Could you do as well?

The land in northern Nigeria is much higher than that on the coast. The country is flat and open, with low hills and blue mountains rising beyond the plains. We pass many large villages crowded with huts of the "haystack" variety. More people than we have seen in other parts of Nigeria are at work in the fields, bending low over the ground with their short-handled hoes. Some of the fields are separated by thick bushes or straw fences about two feet high. Beyond the cultivated fields large numbers of cattle, sheep, and goats are feeding in the pastures.

Farther on we see in the distance what looks like a gray line of mist. As we approach we discover that it is much more solid than mist, for it is the mud wall which surrounds the great city of Kano.

Kano is the largest native city in Africa north of the equator. Around it for more than eleven miles extends a mud wall forty feet thick at the bottom and more than fifty feet high. We enter through one of the gates by a narrow street which has thick mud walls on either side of it.

Should you like to build a house to live in during

your stay in Kano? You would not have to go out and buy building materials as you would in the United States. You can help yourself to all the mud which you need from the shores of a big shallow pond in the city. The hollow where the water lies has been made by the removal of the earth for housebuilding. There are several such ponds, large and small, in different parts of the city, where people get the mud for building and repairing their houses. The men set the posts and weave the spaces between them with a tough, fibrous bark. Then the women, with their wooden tools, spread the soft mud thickly over the walls and floor. The hot African sun dries out the water and makes the mud

Figure 65. This picture shows you a native building a mud house. His material cost him nothing but his labor, for it came from the hole in the ground where he is standing.

hard and solid. Then the women fill in all the cracks and smooth off the walls as a mason does his plaster. After each rainy season it is necessary to repair the walls which have been softened by the rains.

The Europeans in Kano live in brick houses. These are made with very thick walls which help to keep out the heat, for though we are much higher than the coast lands, the climate is hot.

The street scenes interest us as much as the houses do. Here comes a long line of camels heavily loaded with bundles of hides and skins. Perhaps they have been many weeks on their long journey from some oasis far to the north. Formerly all the foreign goods brought into the Kano market came in this slow way across the desert from the Mediterranean ports. Caravans were from six months to a year on the journey. Now much of this traffic is carried on by rail from Lagos, and Kano has thus been brought much nearer European seaports.

We see many donkeys in the streets loaded with sheepskins and goatskins which have come from farms a considerable distance away. The natives carrying skins on their heads have come in from farms nearer Kano. Some of the skins are of bright colors, for the people have dyed them with native dyes made from the juices of plants. Many of these skins will be manufactured in European cities into belts, satchels, purses, and slippers, or used in the binding of books.

See those donkeys trudging along with heavy bags full of peanuts hanging from either side. The donkeys and their drivers live a hundred miles from Kano and have been several days on their journey here.

The people here are of many different tribes. Some are Fulahs, a strong tribe of the region. Larger numbers are Hausas, who, for centuries, were one of the most powerful of African peoples. They founded the city of Kano and made it the capital of their kingdom. Among the people in the market are many nomads from the desert. They are so tanned from their outdoor life that their skins are very dark. We see other peoples too—Jews, with long black beards, and Arabs from Mediterranean countries.

In front of many of the homes we see women weaving on their homemade looms the cotton cloth which is sold all over this part of Africa. Many natives around Kano raise their cotton, weave it into coarse, strong cloth, and dye it with the juice of the wild indigo plant. Which should you prefer to buy, some of this native cloth or some which was made in English factories? A million yards of foreign made cloth are imported into Nigeria every year, and it is said that half or more of the people who live in the Sudan are clothed in goods bought in the market of Kano.

The Kano market is one of the largest in the world, and several thousand people come here daily. For a thousand years it has been as noisy and dirty as it is today and as crowded with traders from all parts of Africa north of the equator and west of the Nile valley. Many come from Morocco, Algeria, Tunis, and Libya. The wealthy Arabs are beautifully dressed, with turbans of fine cambric or of gold-embroidered cloth. They have come in great caravans across the desert and have brought to the Kano market quantities of European goods to exchange for hides and skins, ostrich feathers, ivory, gums and resins, and nuts and seeds, which they will take back to Mediterranean ports.

Some of the goods are displayed in stalls built of reeds and mud and some are piled on the ground in front of the owner. See the wood carriers coming in from their trip far out on the plains, bringing their bundles of fagots to the stalls where firewood is sold. Here are pillows for sale stuffed with the soft fiber of the silk-cotton tree. There are stalls piled high with leather, and others full of earthen jars and pitchers. Those large crocks are bread jars, not to keep bread in but to bake it in. A fire is made inside the jar, and when it is thoroughly heated the fuel is taken out and thin cakes of dough are stuck on in patches on the inside. The crock is then covered to keep in the heat, and in a few minutes the bread is baked.

It would take a long time to examine all the goods for sale here. There are stalls of the sword makers, the blacksmiths, the basket weavers, and the mat makers. There are booths where sugar, salt, soap, cakes, and sweetmeats are sold. There are others filled with huge piles of kola nuts, of which you will read in another chapter. The animal market is noisier than any other, and we are almost deafened by the bleating of sheep, the braying of donkeys, the lowing of cattle, and the groaning cry of camels. Some of the camels have traveled to the market from their homes in the desert a thousand miles or more away.

Kuka on Lake Chad is, like Kano, an old, important city, once the capital of a strong kingdom whose people became rich and powerful through wars with other tribes and through their trade in slaves, ivory, ostrich feathers, and gold. Today the descendants of these tribes live in their scattered villages, tending their little farms and trading in the products of the land. They raise cotton and have patches of wheat and other grains and groves of banana and coconut trees. The women work in the fields, and the children tend the cattle, sheep, and goats in the pastures.

The market of Kuka is smaller than the one in Kano, but there is much trading going on in similar goods.

When you visit some large city in the United States and see the busy streets, the great factories, and the crowded stores, remember that there are large cities in other parts of the world which, though very different from those to which you are accustomed, are doing a similar work in manufacturing articles, trading, and distributing goods over wide areas of country.

SUGGESTIONS FOR STUDY

I

1. The Niger River and its delta plain.
2. The surface of Nigeria.
3. The port of Lagos.
4. Palm nuts and palm oil.

5. Tin and other minerals.

6. The trade centers of Kano and Kuka.

II

1. What divisions of the continent do we pass on our trip from South Africa to Nigeria? To what nation does each belong?

2. What other nations besides the British have possessions in or on the Gulf of Guinea?

3. Why do these countries near the equator have a heavy rainfall?

4. What rivers of Africa are larger than the Niger? How does the Niger rank among the rivers of the world (see Appendix, page 506)?

5. In a trip up the Niger River, through what divisions of Africa should you pass? What interesting trading center lies near the most northern point of the river?

6. Study the map on page 220 and find how you would go from Kano in Nigeria to Fez in Morocco; to Tripoli; to Khartum.

7. What articles are sold in your grocery store which are made of vegetable oils or fats? Do you use any of these?

III

Make a list of the places mentioned in this chapter. Arrange them by countries, cities, rivers, mountains, etc. From these places select those which you think are so important that you should always be able to locate them and know something about them.

CHAPTER XII
OTHER WEST COAST COLONIES AND ST. HELENA

The Gold Coast and Ashanti

Our next visit in British West Africa will be to the Gold Coast and Ashanti, which you will find on the map a little to the west of Nigeria.

Our landing is very exciting. On account of the pounding surf and the great breakers, our ship anchors a mile or two from shore, and natives row out in small boats to take the passengers and freight to the wharves. The great ocean rollers fling the small boats now up and now down, now away from the ship and now against it. We are lowered to the boats in a kind of basket chair, and we breathe a long sigh of relief when the trip to the shore is over and we feel the solid earth once more beneath our feet.

By looking at the map preceding page 1 you will see that the low coastal plain is much narrower on the Gold Coast than in other parts of West Africa and that the upland areas represented by the light-brown color come nearer to the shore. Therefore the Gold Coast is healthier and somewhat better adapted to development than some other parts of this region. The climate, however, is hot and damp; and, save where human hands have made a clearing, the forest stretches over the land. Every few miles a narrow, shady path, like a tunnel between green walls, opens into a forest-clearing. Around the edges grow the trees on which the natives depend—the banana, the papaw, the coconut, and others. Beyond these are the plantains and the patches of yams. In the center of the clearing, sometimes surrounded by a mud wall, is the village of mud houses roofed with closely woven branches of trees and vines.

There are differences among the people of these villages, as there are differences among the people of your home town or city. The homes of most of the natives are little one-room huts. Some of the more well-to-do, however, have several huts—one for the master and his wives, one for his servants, and one or more storehouses for grain and other supplies. All these may be inclosed by a mud wall similar to that which surrounds the village.

The English have established telegraph lines and built roads and railroads in many parts of this colony. These have been a wonderful help in developing the country. Knowing that they can get their products to the trading centers and the seaports, Englishmen are investing money in great cocoa plantations and are building up a large trade here.

The British waged many wars with the fierce Ashantis before they were conquered. The Ashantis were a powerful, warlike people, and their kingdom covered a wide area. They carried on war with the coast tribes and with those farther inland, made slave raids into the country for many miles around, and were the terror of all their neighbors.

Each year these people are becoming more quiet and industrious. They are beginning to till the soil, produce kola nuts, cocoa beans, and fruits and vegetables. They are obtaining the rich products of the forests which lie all around them—the rubber, palm nuts, gums, and resins. Some of the men work in the mines. The Ashantis can weave good cloth, make earthenware, and do skilled work in gold and silver.

With its high, thick mud wall inclosing its thousands of mud huts, Kumassi looks like an overgrown native village. The building of the railroad from the coast has increased its importance as a trade center, and it is now larger than any of the seaports. The railroads have caused the seaports to grow also, and every year larger and larger quantities of gold, cocoa, palm kernels, palm oil, and kola nuts are brought down by rail to the sea.

Perhaps no part of the west coast has changed hands so many times as has the famous Gold Coast, for many nations have been interested in its gold deposits. The natives first found the precious metal in the sands near the streams and in the river beds. They still obtain some in the old, primitive way, while in other places it is taken from the rivers by dredges.

In the olden days, before the gold was sold to the foreign trader, every village had its goldsmith, who fashioned jewelry, such as rings, bangles, bracelets, chains, and charms, for the native chiefs and kings and for those of the people who could afford such luxuries. Even today the native jewelers are noted for their art in goldbeating.

You have probably read about the production of cocoa in South America and the islands of the West Indies (see Allen's "South America"). Did you know that more cocoa is produced on the coast lands of West Africa and on the islands in the Gulf of Guinea than in any other part of the world?

The people of the Gold Coast raise more cocoa than do those of any other country. Perhaps the natives of this far-away land helped to serve you with the cocoa which you enjoyed with your breakfast this morning, for the United States imports from West Africa large quantities of cocoa beans. In some years more cocoa is sent from West Africa to the United States than to any other country.

Thousands of acres are covered with the trees which yield the cocoa beans. What a good time those workers are having as they squat around the piles of pods, chattering and laughing as they cut them open and scrape out the seeds!

Spread on smooth floors in the hot African sun, the beans soon dry. Then the workmen rake them up, put them into bags, and send them by rail or boat or on the backs of men down to the big warehouses at Sekondi and Akkra. Here they will be loaded on the great ships

Figure 66. These people around the big pile of cocoa pods are breaking them open and scraping out the seeds. What does the text tell you about cocoa production on the Gold Coast? What nation controls this African division?

which will take them to European countries and the United States.

Have you ever visited a cocoa factory? There are many large establishments in the United States. As you approach one you can tell from the smell what is being manufactured there.

In the factory the beans are cleaned and then roasted in huge ovens, some of which may hold a ton. After the nuts are roasted, other machines crush them enough to break the shells, which are blown by a blast of air into large bins. The nuts, partially broken and crushed, are now put into other machines, which grind them into a thick, dark liquid which looks and flows somewhat like cold molasses. This runs into trays and hardens into what we know as cooking chocolate. Sugar is added for the sweet chocolate. To make cocoa much of the rich oil which the chocolate contains, known as cocoa butter, is removed, leaving the fine, dry powder. When you drink a cup of cocoa, nibble a piece of sweet chocolate, or enjoy a piece of chocolate cake, try to count the number of people whose labor has made it possible for you to enjoy this nourishing food.

SIERRA LEONE

Someone has described Sierra Leone as a land of great heat, lofty palm trees, and unclothed natives. All these things are found in the colony, but we shall also find there busy villages, neatly clad natives, valuable products, and Englishmen carrying on important industries.

For many years Sierra Leone was known as the European's grave. The heat is intense and the rainfall heavy, a hundred and sixty inches falling in the course of a year. What is the average rainfall in the part of the country where you live (see Allen's "United States")? The death rate is not so heavy as it formerly was, for foreigners have learned how to live in the tropics, and the government has made better provision for their comfort.

The colony is a little larger than the state of South Carolina and contains nearly as many people. Most of the inhabitants belong to one of the several different tribes. Many of them are descendants of the freed slaves for whom the colony was founded (see page 387). Native African tribesmen also make their homes here, and many languages and dialects can be heard in the streets of Freetown.

All along the coast of West Africa we shall see many representatives of the Kru tribe. The Kru men are fine sailors and handle their boats skillfully in the heavy surf which pounds on the shore. They come out in their small craft to the ocean vessels anchored beyond the breakers and take the freight and passengers to land: They are the coal and cargo carriers, the deck hands, and the firemen of many ships engaged in the West African trade. Most of the Krus are heathen, but many of those who work among the Europeans along the coast are Christians and speak English.

Freetown is one of the oldest and most important ports on the west coast of Africa, and many British ships call here on their way to South Africa. As we approach we see, on the hills around, the forts, the soldiers' barracks, and the government hospital. Down near the wharves are warehouses filled with tropical products.

The harbor is a busy one. Vessels recently arrived are discharging cargoes of cotton goods, iron, lumber, kerosene, hardware, and articles of food and clothing. Workmen are coaling others and loading them with bags of palm kernels, casks of palm oil, bales of ginger root, and bundles of hides and skins. Those steamers which will stop at Lagos are taking on large quantities of

AFRICA, AUSTRALIA, ISLANDS OF PACIFIC

kola nuts which will be sent by train to the great market at Kano. Quantities of piassaba fiber, which comes from a species of palm tree, is also being loaded on English vessels. This stiff fiber is used in cleaning the streets in London and other cities in Europe.

Up on the hills, where the air is not quite so hot as on the lower coast lands, and the ocean breezes make life more comfortable, are the homes of the Europeans who live and work in Freetown. Attractive bungalows with green shrubbery and pretty gardens nestle under feathery palms and long-leaved banana trees, while the tall, graceful oil palm towers over the lower growth.

The street scenes in Freetown are interesting to a stranger. That native policeman looks as trim in his

Figure 67. This girl in Freetown is splitting wood for her fire. Describe her ax. Where is Freetown?

khaki uniform and as dignified as our policemen do. Here comes a European trader on his way to his warehouses, riding in a hammock borne by two natives. Others, who are walking, wear pith helmets and carry white umbrellas. It is unsafe for a European to take any chances with the African sun, for its effects are sudden and often deadly.

Farther down the street come some well-to-do black men riding in rickshaws, each drawn by two native boys. Here are other blacks on their way to the market, carrying in huge baskets on their heads the wares which they have to sell. Those tall men in the long, loose, dark-blue robes are Mohammedans from the Sudan.

From Freetown we can go by rail into the interior of Sierra Leone and see the most important towns and many native villages. While we are away from the seaport we shall not be out of communication with it, for as the train rumbles along we see beside the track the poles carrying the telegraph and telephone wires.

For some miles beyond Freetown we see many large market gardens which supply the port with fresh fruits and vegetables. We pass mud-walled villages with their clustered huts, each with its heavy thatched roof extending nearly to the ground. As the train climbs up to the higher lands of the interior, we ride through deep cuttings and narrow ravines and across bridges spanning swift streams onto the higher inland plains. Here the forests are thinner and more scattered, and the grasslands begin.

At the stations along the way we see casks of palm oil, bags of palm kernels, baskets of kola nuts, and other products of the country. Some are being unloaded from bullock carts, which have come over hard, well-built "feeder" roads which lead back from the railroad to the villages many miles away in the bush. At other stations we see natives bringing heavy loads on their heads or backs.

Did you ever hear of gum copal? It is the sap of a tree which grows in certain hot countries, and hardens on exposure to the air. The natives of Sierra Leone obtain some copal by tapping the trees which produce it, but more is collected from the beds and banks of streams, where for long ages it has been washed by the heavy rains. Because it hardens quickly, gum copal is very valuable in the manufacture of varnish and is used in large quantities for this purpose.

Let us leave the railroad and visit one of the villages from which come the products which we have seen at the stations. There are many villages in the interior of Sierra Leone, and on the roads and paths leading to them we meet heavily loaded bullock carts and natives trudging along with their loads of palm kernels and palm oil, copal, peanuts, rubber, or ginger root.

Outside the village are patches of corn and millet and some plants five or six feet high which we are told are manioc plants, from the root of which the women make flour. Beyond these are tall oil palms, kola-nut trees, and many coconut palms.

See the rice plants drying on those bamboo poles.

Later the women of the village will thrash out the grain and put it into large jars. This rough, brown grain is very different from the white, polished rice which you eat, but in these hot lands the grain keeps much better if the husk is left on. When the women wish to use some rice they pound off the brown husk, which covers the grains, with wooden pestles and boil the rice over their open fires.

Figure 68. These women are pounding rice to get off the brown husks. Can you find out how the rice which you eat is made white and shiny?

Passing through the little patches of grain and vegetables we enter the village itself. The people are busy, but they greet us pleasantly and seem glad to see us. Little children are playing in the sunshine. Some of the women are pounding corn into a coarse meal with a long wooden pestle. For dinner they will make a porridge of rice and fish and thicken it with some of the meal. As we came into the village we saw some patches of peanuts, and here is a woman shelling some. She will put them into her soup or cook them with her fish. Those are plantains lying there by the fire. They look somewhat like bananas, but they are not good to eat raw. See, that woman is peeling them and wrapping them in leaves. Then she puts them in the ashes to bake. With some fish or meat they will make a good meal. Some of the women are cracking palm nuts and making palm oil, others are peeling manioc root. When the roots are about the size of a large sweet potato the women dig them and put them into water. This is to soak out a poisonous matter which some varieties contain. Then they peel the roots and lay them on the roofs of their huts to dry. Sometimes the roots are boiled. When the roots are thoroughly dry the women pound them and sift the coarse grains, and pound and sift again and again until the flour is fine enough to use. This is made into little cakes which take the place of bread. The tapioca which your mother uses for puddings is also a product of the manioc plant. It is interesting to know that we often make use of the same plants on which the natives of distant lands depend.

Let us buy some kola nuts to eat. We have seen these nuts for sale in every market of West Africa which we have visited, we have noticed many donkeys loaded with them, and we have found the people eating them everywhere. In some villages white kola nuts have been given us as a sign of friendship and hospitality. Proposals of marriage, declarations of war, acceptances or refusals of requests and demands, are shown by the sending of kola nuts of the proper color. Like tea and coffee the nuts have a stimulating effect, and the natives ward off fatigue and hunger and even cure some forms of sickness by using them.

Kola trees form a large part of the wealth of the natives in Sierra Leone. Many are employed in gathering the nuts and taking them to the markets or the railroad stations. Between one and two million dollars' worth of these nuts are shipped each year from Sierra Leone and large quantities from other West African ports. Many of the nuts which are bound for inland markets are taken by rail to the seacoast, sent by water to Lagos in Nigeria, and thence by rail to Kano for distribution. Kola nuts are one of the most important articles of trade at Kano, and the prosperity of many traders there depends on a large supply's reaching the market in good condition.

GAMBIA

Little Gambia, the only British possession in West Africa which we have not yet visited, is not quite so large as the state of Connecticut. You will be interested in this little colony, for, next to England, the United States carries on more trade with it than does any other nation. Quantities of tobacco grown on the farms in our country, large amounts of kerosene, and other articles go from our ports to this little division of West Africa.

Like the rest of West Africa, the coast of Gambia is low and damp and covered with mangrove swamps. Beyond the mangroves are forests of other tropical trees.

It is here that the oil palm grows, and in the villages in the clearings we find the people making palm oil and cracking the palm nuts, carrying the bags of nuts to the traders, and rolling heavy casks of oil through the forest paths down to the river.

Most of the people live still farther inland, on the high grassy areas interspersed with groves of trees. The natives here are good farmers, skillful leather workers, and weavers of durable cloth. They produce corn and vegetables for food and raise cattle for their hides. Many of the people keep bees and sell the wax which they make.

Gambia is a prosperous little colony, one of the richest in West Africa. Its prosperity is due largely to the peanuts, which the people raise in larger quantities

Figure 69. This is a peanut plantation. Do you know on what part of the plant peanuts grow? What is the chief use of peanuts?

than any other crop. Several million dollars' worth of peanuts are shipped away every year from Gambia to England and the United States, where the oil which they contain is pressed out.

The Gambia River, which flows through the colony, is of great value to the people, for it furnishes a highway to the eastern boundary. The natives bring their peanuts to the branch streams and sell them to traders who take them down to the main river. Steamers on the Gambia River call at the trading villages and carry the nuts down to Bathurst, the port of the colony. Here are ocean steamers from European countries and the United States which have brought to this colony cargoes of cotton cloth, bags, rice, hardware, tobacco, kerosene, and other articles which the people need. The vessels will be loaded with peanuts, hides, palm kernels, oil, rubber, and wax, which they will carry back to factories in European cities and in different parts of our own country.

Gambia is fortunate in having navigable waterways; but, like the other African colonies, it needs railroads, which will help more than anything else in developing industries and trade.

The Island of St. Helena

There are several groups of islands around Africa which belong to the British Commonwealth. The most famous of them all is St. Helena. It is a little volcanic islet, with an area of less than fifty square miles, lying far out in the Atlantic Ocean, twelve hundred miles from the nearest African port and between seven and eight hundred miles from the nearest land.

Cattle graze in the pastures, and fine crops of flax are raised in the valleys. From the fiber the women spin linen thread, which they use in making lace.

It is not its products or industries, however, which have made St. Helena famous. It is because for six years there lived here a noted man who had been banished from his European home. This man was Napoleon Bonaparte. Who was he? Who banished him? Why was he exiled from Europe? Why do you suppose the island of St. Helena was chosen as his place of exile?

SUGGESTIONS FOR STUDY

I

1. The coast line, surface, and climate of the Gold Coast.
2. Village life in the Gold Coast.
3. Improvements made by the British.
4. The Ashantis.
5. Kumassi and the seaports.
6. Gold deposits.
7. The cocoa industry.
8. The climate of Sierra Leone.
9. Freetown and its trade.

10. A railroad trip through Sierra Leone.

11. Gum copal and kola nuts.

12. An inland village.

13. Our interests in Gambia.

14. People and occupations of Gambia.

15. The island of St. Helena.

II

1. Describe the coast of West Africa.

2. In what colony is the coastal plain widest (see regional map preceding page 1)? Where is it so narrow that it cannot be shown on the map? What effect has its width on the development of the colonies?

3. Sketch the divisions bordering on the Gulf of Guinea. In each one write its name, the name of the nation controlling it, and the places mentioned in the text.

4. In what natural region do most of the people of West Africa live? Why?

5. What are the most important products of British West Africa? For what are they valuable? Of which one do the natives make great use?

6. How has the British Commonwealth improved conditions in its African possessions? What is the greatest hindrance to the development of these lands?

7. Write to the Department of Commerce in Washington asking for statistics on the production of cocoa.

III

Make a list of the places mentioned in this chapter. Arrange them by countries, cities, rivers, mountains, etc. From these places select those which you think are so important that you should always be able to locate them and know something about them.

IV

REVIEW OF THE BRITISH POSSESSIONS

1. Since studying the British possessions what problems have you solved concerning them?

2. Why should Gambia and Sierra Leone be of more value to the British than Somaliland?

3. Why is the Gold Coast a better region for development than the coast of Nigeria?

4. Why are there more towns and cities on the southeastern coast of Africa than on the southwestern coast?

5. Which British possessions are noted for minerals? oil seeds and nuts? Which are great game countries? Which are best suited for light-skinned people? Which one do you think will be of the greatest importance in the future?

CHAPTER XIII

FRENCH POSSESSIONS IN AFRICA

FRANCE controls a very large area in Africa. In the north Algeria, Tunis, and most of Morocco are French possessions. These countries with Libya, an Italian colony, have long been known as the Barbary States. This title comes from the name of the native tribe of the region, the Berbers. When the Arabs from Western Asia invaded the land, they never succeeded in really conquering the Berbers, who fled into the hills and mountains.

South of the Barbary States stretches the Sahara, most of which is in French control. The eastern part of the desert, with some of the Sudan and a large area extending between Nigeria and the Belgian Congo to the Gulf of Guinea, is known as French Equatorial Africa. The western portion of the Sahara and the Sudan, with several smaller divisions on the Gulf of Guinea and the Atlantic, make up the territory known as French West Africa. Togoland and Cameroons were German colonies before the World War. They are now divided between the French and the British, the French having the larger share (see maps on pages 55 and 188).

Figure 70. French possessions in Africa. Write a list of the French possessions in the order of their size (see Appendix, page 500). What is the only possession of France in East Africa? What island belongs to France?

Looking at the map above you will notice that most of the French possessions are in western Africa. The only French colony in the east is Somaliland, a small division near the southern end of the Red Sea, of which you will read in Chapter XXIII. The island of Madagascar and some smaller groups belong to the French.

FRENCH POSSESSIONS IN AFRICA

Along the low coast lands of the French possessions in West Africa are the hot, damp mangrove swamps similar to those which we have seen in the British lands. Beyond the narrow coastal plain, hot and unhealthy, rises a chain of mountains, higher in Cameroons than in any other part of West Africa. Mount Cameroon is the highest peak. Find it on the map which is on page 193.

The rivers, cutting their way from the plateau beyond the mountains to the sea, have their fall line where rapids occur, and are navigable only for a short distance inland. In French Equatorial Africa some of the rivers do not flow into the sea, but into Lake Chad (see map on page 193).

Parts of the deep forests near the coast, though difficult to travel through, are exceedingly beautiful. Wonderful orchids, such as are raised in the United States in conservatories and sold at high prices, grow on some of the trees. Others, covered with ferns, look as if they were draped with delicate green lace. The tree ferns are rightly named, for they are as tall as trees, while other varieties are six feet or more high.

On the higher lands the trees are decorated with trailing gray moss, which hangs in long festoons from their trunks and branches. As we ascend still higher the rich tropical vegetation disappears, and we feel more at home among the cheery dandelion blossoms, the fragrant violets, the tall thistles, and other familiar plants.

Beyond the mountains are the drier, cooler regions of the Sudan. Here the plateaus are from one thousand to four thousand feet high. Owing to the bordering forests, the mountains, and the unnavigable streams, much of this region has not been thoroughly explored. It is here, however, as in the British possessions of West Africa, that the most industrious natives live. They keep cattle and sheep, and raise corn, tobacco, manioc, yams, and other products. The natives of the Sudan have been much influenced by the Arabs from the Mediterranean countries and the Sahara, who have long traded with them and spread among them the Mohammedan religion.

Most of the large plantations of the Europeans are nearer the coast, but as railroads open up the interior more foreigners will settle here and help to increase the products of the Sudan, for the climate and soil are well suited to many crops.

STUDIES ON THE FRENCH POSSESSIONS

1. France is the second greatest colonizing nation in the world. How do her African possessions compare in area with those of the British (see Appendix, pages 499 and 500)? How do they compare with the United States (see Table IV, page 503)?

2. Using the map on page 188, write a list of the French possessions that border on the Mediterranean Sea; on the Atlantic Ocean; on the Gulf of Guinea; on the Red Sea.

3. Which is the largest possession of France in Africa? the most northerly? the most southerly? the most westerly? Which are in the torrid zone (see map preceding page 1)? Which are in the grassland region of Africa (see the map on page 10)? Which are included in the desert? Which contain mountains (see regional map)? Which have swampy coast lands? Which colonies are most like France?

4. What causes a fall line in rivers (see Allen's "North America" and Allen's "United States")?

CHAPTER XIV

FRENCH EQUATORIAL AFRICA

We will begin our explorations in French Equatorial Africa at Duala, near the boundary of Nigeria. Here we find a railroad which will take us some little distance inland, and on this we can make our trip much more comfortably than in any other way.

Duala, the most important seaport on this part of the coast, is in that part of Equatorial Africa known as Cameroons. It is situated at the mouth of the Cameroon River, and behind it rises the dense green mass of the Cameroon Mountains. On market days the beach at Duala is a busy place. Native dugouts loaded with plantains and other articles come from the neighboring villages, and natives from the surrounding country bring in a great variety of wares, which they spread out for sale on mats on the hard sand. All through the morning natives bargain for dried fish, peppers, pineapples, coconuts, yams, and other food.

Duala is an attractive town with modern conveniences and many good houses surrounded by gardens

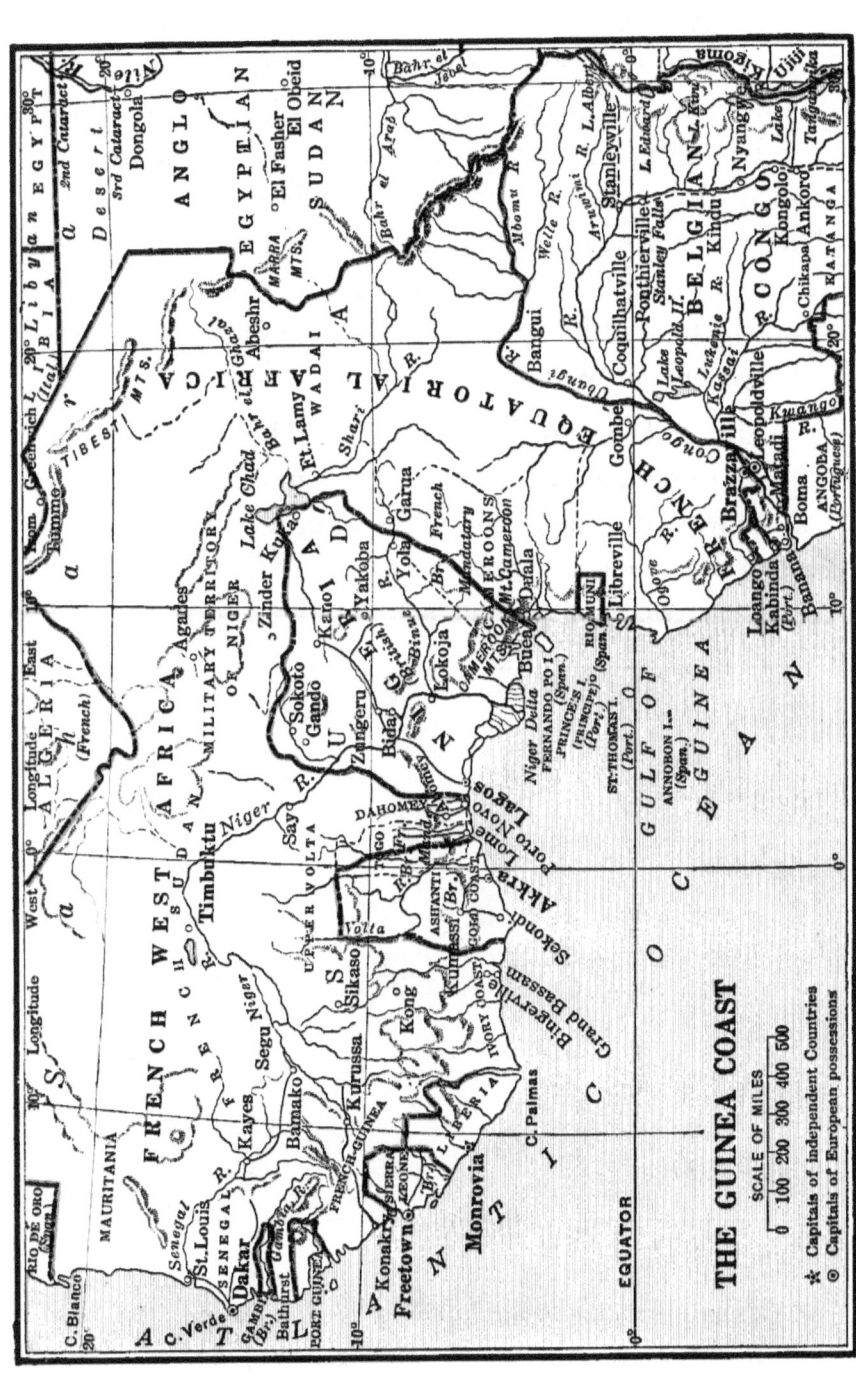

which the heat and rainfall make especially beautiful. Many of the buildings are raised on piles because of the dampness and insects. We see churches and schools, electric lights, uniformed police, a courthouse, a post office, and a railroad station. Yet side by side with all these there are men with huge bags on their heads, little girls carrying baskets of kola nuts, and women, each puffing away at her pipe and carrying a cunning baby tied on her hip with a strip of cotton cloth.

Some of the people here at Duala have come from the Mediterranean countries. They have walked most of the way, and the journey has taken them more than a year. How odd it would seem to us to think of setting out on a two or three years' journey on foot. But did

Figure 71. *The first man in the white robe is the Sultan of Cameroons. The long building is his palace. The roof needs repairing, and he is leaving the palace so that workmen may fix it. Where is Cameroons?*

you ever stop to think how odd the sights in your home town or city would seem to a Kru, a Hausa, or a Bulu? What are some of the things which might astonish them? What might they not like? Perhaps after the noise and confusion of the automobiles and trucks, the street cars and railroad trains, the crowded stores, the hurrying throngs, and the rush hours in the subways they might long for the silence of the desert or the quiet of the little forest-bound village where life is not so strenuous.

Figure 72. This man is dyeing some cloth a dark-blue color. His dyepot is a hole in the ground and his dye was made from a species of bamboo. His wife spun and wove the cloth. He may carry it with other goods to the market at Kano to sell it. Where is Kano?

In the part of the town near the water there are many "factories" (see page 155) where goods are exchanged for native products. As we read the chapter we shall find out what some of these are. Duala is an important trading station, and there are several buildings in some of the compounds here—storehouses for foreign goods and native products, a general store, shipping offices, and comfortable houses for the white manager and his clerks. Back of the compound there is usually a row of little houses which are the homes of the native employees.

Hundreds of miles of good roads have been built in Cameroons to connect the larger trading posts. Motor trucks run on some of these, but in the sections far distant from the larger towns the natives load their little canoes and paddle downstream to the nearest trading station or carry their goods on their heads and backs through the forest paths. When you think that a man can carry only sixty or seventy pounds and travel on an average from twelve to fifteen miles a day, you can realize the blessing that roads and railroads will be to these African colonies. If trains and trucks released hundreds of workers from acting as carriers, so that they might spend their time in cultivating the soil, raising cocoa beans, tapping rubber trees, collecting palm nuts, and doing other useful work, how much greater the products of the country might be.

These tropical countries will produce many useful products if the natives are taught how to cultivate them. In our travels we may chance to see some of the farms where government experts are experimenting in raising cotton, rice, vanilla, spices, and other valuable crops to which the soil and climate are suited.

FRENCH EQUATORIAL AFRICA

On the slopes of the Cameroon Mountains and in other parts of this region we can visit large plantations where hillsides are covered with thousands and even hundreds of thousands of cacao trees, which bear the beans from which cocoa is made. The orchards are splendidly cared for, and the beans are prepared for market by means similar to those on the cacao plantations in Ecuador (see Allen's "South America").

You will be interested also in the rubber plantations here. Formerly the natives obtained all the rubber product from the trees and vines which grew wild in the forest. In the more lonely parts of French Equatorial Africa we shall meet in the forest paths many natives carrying such "wild" rubber to the nearest "factory."

Figure 73. Do you need a pair of shoes? These men can measure your foot and fit you. They travel from place to place making shoes for the people.

Because of the crude methods of tapping, many trees and vines have been killed, and the amount of rubber collected in this way has considerably decreased. Therefore planters have begun the cultivation of rubber on plantations. They have planted thousands of young trees of the best varieties and have trained the natives to care for them. As a consequence the production of rubber has increased until today it is the most important product from parts of French Equatorial Africa.

Most of the rubber and cacao plantations owned by foreigners are near the coast and are connected by good roads. Let us turn off from the main road into one of the paths which will lead us to a village of the Bulus, one of the native tribes. How lovely the forest is! The sun shines hot on the green roof, but few rays penetrate to the brown path at our feet. Huge vines cover the trees. Some of the trees they have choked to death and they are squeezing out the life from many living ones. Long rope-like tendrils, as useful to the natives as manufactured ropes would be, hang from the high branches, while others creep and twist and twine in and out among the trees and vines until the tangle is so thick that it would be impossible to walk anywhere except in the path without cutting our way.

As we come nearer the village we see many oil palm trees, and we stop a minute to watch the men climb them and cut off the bunches of nuts. We see breadfruit trees bearing fruit as big as your head, and plantain trees with their long, drooping leaves. In the cleared spaces some manioc plants are growing, and women are hoeing little patches of rice and corn.

Here we are at last at the village itself. The huts stand in rows on both sides of the long, wide, grassy street, at either end of which is a palaver house where we shall be sure to find many of the men. Here they sit and smoke, talk over the news, and bargain with the trader for his European goods and with one another for goats, dogs, or anything else which they own. While he talks or smokes or trades, each man can keep his eye upon his own house and the doings of his wife and family.

Figure 74. These are street merchants in a village in Cameroons. Should you like some fruit and vegetables, or a piece of juicy sugar cane to suck? Describe the houses in the distance.

The little houses are made of bark with roofs thatched with palm-leaf mats. The natives have no nails, but use the strong vines from the forest for ropes. The saplings, which are used as uprights, are tied together with these bush ropes, the sheets of bark are tied to the saplings, and the mats are fastened to the roof in the same way.

See, that Bulu is inviting us to enter his hut. His wife smiles as if she also were glad to see us. We stoop to enter the low door and step over the high sill onto the mud floor. In one corner is a bed made of split poles laid on two logs. Hanging from the roof there are many bundles done up in plantain leaves. This is the only storehouse the housewife has for her corn, peanuts, manioc roots, dried fish, and other provisions. The fire is built either out of doors or on the floor of the hut, and as there is no chimney everything inside is smoky and dirty.

The schoolhouse in this Bulu village is a bark hut like the rest of the buildings. Here the girls and boys learn to read and write, to work and play, as you do in your school. Near the school is the church. Most of the Bulus are heathen and worship different objects and believe in charms. Many missionaries have gone to Africa, where they are doing a splendid work in teaching the natives about God and showing them better ways of life and work. The school and the church in this village are the results of their teaching.

We have been so interested in the people in this part of Africa that we have said nothing about the animals which live here. On the banks of some of the rivers we may see crocodiles sleeping in the sunshine or catch a glimpse of the awkward hippopotamus in the swampy jungle. Many monkeys in the tree tops chatter with one another or scold at our approach. We may chance to see some of their cousins, the gorillas and chimpanzees. The gorilla is five or six feet tall and larger and stronger than a man. The chimpanzees can make great speed through the forest by swinging themselves with their long, strong arms from branch to branch.

In the forests there are many insects which bite and sting. Large and poisonous serpents also live here. Bright-colored birds flit in the sunshine above the tree tops, and long-legged cranes and pelicans watch for fish along the rivers and lakes. Up in the grasslands there are lions, giraffes, leopards, and many members of the antelope family, large and small, for this higher region is a game country similar to that in East Africa.

SUGGESTIONS FOR STUDY

I

1. The port of Duala.
2. Roads and railroads.
3. The cocoa and rubber industries.
4. A Bulu village.
5. Animals of French Equatorial Africa.

II

1. Using the scale of the map on page 193, estimate the distance from Duala to Garua. To what place would this distance reach from your home? How long would it take you to go to this place by train? How long would it take a carrier traveling fifteen miles a day to bring a load of palm nuts on his back from Duala to Garua?

2. A freight car holds eighty thousand pounds. If a carrier can carry sixty pounds, how many carriers will it take to carry as much as can be taken in a trainload of twenty freight cars?

3. When trains and trucks do the work of all these men, in what occupations can they engage?

III

Make a list of the places mentioned in this chapter. Arrange them by countries, cities, rivers, mountains, etc. From these places select those which you think are so important that you should always be able to locate them and know something about them.

CHAPTER XV

THE FRENCH IN WEST AFRICA

The Ivory Coast and Dahomey

The Ivory Coast and Dahomey are parts of French West Africa. They are very similar to Liberia and the British colonies in West Africa, of which you have already read. Here, as in those regions, we hear the surf pounding on the hard yellow sand, breathe the hot, damp air in the mangrove swamps along the shore, toil through the deep tropical forests farther inland, and come gradually to the hilly stretches and grassy plateaus of the interior. We find little native villages of thatched huts and see men working on the large plantations of the Europeans, carrying to the traders the products of the farms and forests, or idling in the sunshine while Nature and the women supply them with food.

When the natives work, the preparation of palm kernels and the making of palm oil are their most important occupations (see pages 157-159). In Dahomey these products represent nine tenths of all the goods shipped away. Some of the natives in the

AFRICA, AUSTRALIA, ISLANDS OF PACIFIC

Figure 75. This is a village built on the shores of a lake in Dahomey. Who controls this colony? What is its chief product?

forest regions collect rubber; while those who live in the interior grasslands have flocks and herds which furnish hides, skins, and wool.

There are many African mahogany trees scattered through the tropical forests. At present only those are of value which grow near the rivers by which the logs can be floated down to the coast. Natives fell the trees and cut paths to the bank of the river. Using round logs for rollers, they manage to push and pull and roll the heavy logs to the river to float down to the coast. Here they roll and toss and pound one another in the heavy surf. Riding the dancing logs, the men drive spikes into the ends and fasten them together with strong chains. Then the raft, containing from fifty to seventy-five logs, is towed by a puffing tug out to the ship which is waiting beyond the breakers for her cargo.

We certainly expect to see several of the men

drowned before the lumber is loaded. The logs are tossed about by the waves as if they were featherweights instead of ton weights. They pitch and dive in the water, spin round and round like barrels, and smash against one another and the ship with tremendous force; but the Kru boys seem to ride them as easily, one writer says, as if they were wooden horses in a merry-go-round.

Figure 76. This is a section of an African mahogany tree. You can tell how heavy it is from the number of men who are working to roll it down to the river. How many can you count?

Now one of the men knocks out a spike from the end of a dancing log and separates it from the rest of the raft. He hooks big chains around it and fastens them to a strong cable. The winch on board the ship slowly winds up its great cable thread; the heavy log is raised, swung around over the ship, and then lowered into the deep hold.

Firms from England, France, and America have started working the forests of Africa for the valuable woods which they contain, and the lumber which is now exported from African ports is worth several million dollars. But the exports of today are only a "drop in the bucket" compared with the value of future exports. In years to come roads and railroads and modern machinery will make it possible to carry on lumbering in the forests of Africa as easily as in our great Northwest.

SENEGAL, MAURITANIA, AND THE SUDAN

Senegal is one of the oldest and most important of the French colonies. We will land at Dakar and go inland by train and then sail down the Niger River to Timbuktu. From here we will journey across the Sahara Desert to the city of Fez in Morocco. Trace this journey on the map on page 219.

Dakar is an important port. If you will look at a map of the world, you will notice that the distance from here to the eastern point of South America is the shortest route across the Atlantic Ocean. You will notice also that Dakar lies almost in a straight line between Marseille, the great commercial city of southern France, and South American ports. For these and other reasons Dakar is becoming more and more important. The French have improved the harbor, built large docks, and made arrangements whereby goods can be easily transferred from the vessels to trains which will carry them to the

THE FRENCH IN WEST AFRICA

Figure 77. *This is a scene on the docks at Dakar. Where is Dakar? What do you think the barrels and boxes and bags contain?*

interior of Africa. It is hotter here, perhaps, than where you live, but Dakar is as clean, as well laid out, and has as good buildings and as modern improvements and conveniences, such as electric lights, stores, schools, hospitals, churches, etc., as many towns in our country have.

When airplane routes have become more common Dakar will be the "hopping off" station between France and South America. From this town in Senegal to Pernambuco in eastern Brazil the distance is about seventeen hundred miles, and already airplanes have made longer nonstop trips than this.

Senegal is considerably different from the divisions on the shores of the Gulf of Guinea which you have visited. There are no mangrove swamps along its coast, the air is cooler and drier, and the rainy season is much shorter than in the lands nearer the equator. The northern part borders on the desert and is dry and sandy. South of the Senegal River there are forests where natives gather palm nuts and tap the rubber trees and vines. In their villages we shall see them preparing the palm oil, shelling the palm nuts, and smoking the milky juice of the rubber tree.

In nearly every village of Senegal we shall be sure to see patches of ground where peanuts are growing, and find many people tending the crops, pulling the vines, and carrying bags of peanuts to the trading stations. Peanuts are the most important crop of this colony. The best farms are in the fertile valley of the Senegal River, but the nuts are raised everywhere. More than fifty million dollars' worth have been shipped from Senegal in a year.

Mauritania, the colony to the north, has no good port, and the peanuts raised there are brought to Senegal for export. Mauritania lies between the equatorial region of heavy rainfall and the real desert. The Atlas Mountains to the north shut out the moisture borne by the winds from the Mediterranean Sea, and the prevailing northeast trade winds, which have blown for thousands of miles over the deserts of Asia and the great Sahara, have no moisture to give to the land. The little rain which Mauritania receives comes from the local winds which blow in from the Atlantic, but this is not enough to keep the streams flowing throughout the year, and much of the time they are only dry, rocky channels.

Besides the native tribes, we shall find both in Mauritania and Senegal large numbers of Arabs like those who live in the Sahara and the Mediterranean countries. Many of these are nomads moving from place to place to find food and water for their flocks and herds.

Now let us take the train from Dakar for our trip to the interior. As we leave the forested regions near the shore and get up into the higher grasslands we see many cattle feeding in the pastures. Beef hides are already one of the important exports from Dakar, and frozen

Figure 78. Isn't this a pleasant scene? It is a cattle ranch in Senegal. The great pasture lands in Africa and the cattle which will feed on them will be of great importance in supplying crowded European countries with meat and other cattle products.

beef is shipped in considerable quantities. In later years many more cattle will feed on these grasslands, which extend inland for miles.

All the great grassland area stretching from the Desert of Sahara on the north to the tropical forests of the Guinea coast and the Congo Basin on the south, and from the Atlantic Ocean to the Nile River, is known as the Sudan, a word meaning "Land of the Blacks" (see map on page 193). In the Sahara and the Mediterranean countries most of the people are light-skinned, and many of these have spread into that part of the Sudan which lies on the edge of the great desert, but the more southerly part of the Sudan is the true home of the blacks. Here live many tribes who have different customs and languages.

Though we speak of the Sudan as a great grassland area, it is not entirely without trees. There are forests along the rivers and smaller groves elsewhere. A common tree here is the baobab, which is somewhat like a great oak.

The fertile, populous Sudan grasslands are an important part of Africa. For many years they were shut off from the sea and the European nations by mountains and deserts, deep forests and jungles, fever-infested swamps, and unnavigable rivers. As railroads are built farther into the interior the grasslands will gradually become one of the great grazing areas of the world. Millions of Hausas and other native tribes live here, and the products of their flocks and herds will help to feed and clothe many people.

Figure 79. How should you like to go to this Mohammedan school? Your lessons would be from the Koran, the holy book of the Mohammedans, and you would write them on wooden boards. Compare this school with those shown in Figures 26 and 80.

Now we have changed from train to boat and are sailing down the great Niger River. On either side we see many native villages. Camels and donkeys and sheep and cattle are feeding in the pastures, and the crops which are growing on the banks are irrigated by the river water.

On account of the rainfall near its source, the Niger, like the Nile, has its periods of high and low water. In its annual overflow many miles of land on either side are flooded. With great irrigation works, such as have been built on the Nile, the flood waters of the Niger may be saved and used to water large areas of the desert through which it flows.

AFRICA, AUSTRALIA, ISLANDS OF PACIFIC

Figure 80. This is a school in a Sudan city. How many differences can you think of between this school and yours?

Our sail down the Niger River brings us to Timbuktu, an important trading center on the desert edge of the Sudan. For two thousand years or more there has been a market town here. Timbuktu was once the capital of a great black empire, and the Moors from the Mediterranean countries on the north and blacks from the native kingdoms on the south, east, and west brought their wares to its markets. It was a center also for the slave trade.

If you will study the position of Timbuktu, you will understand why a trade center here should have been so important and should have existed for so many years. It is located near the bend in the Niger where the river reaches its most northerly point and where the distance across the Sahara to the Mediterranean countries is shorter than anywhere else. The Senegal River leads in from the west, and the Niger valley opens up the country toward both the southwest and the southeast. Caravan routes from Morocco, Algeria, and Libya meet here at Timbuktu (see map on page 220), and goods which have been brought over the desert are sent from here all over the Sudan.

The low, flat-roofed, windowless houses of the town are built of sundried bricks made of the clayey soil which underlies the sand. Even the ovens are built of clay. See that large oven in the street and the crowd of people before it. Each one has brought a loaf to be baked. The wheat was raised on an oasis in the desert and ground between two stones into a coarse dark flour, but the bread made from it is wholesome and nourishing.

We like to watch the dusty camels come trudging in from their long trip over the desert. Here is a caravan unloading heavy bars of salt. Another has brought large quantities of cloth which was imported into Mediterranean countries from English factories. Tea, sugar, tobacco, hardware, beads, and other articles fill the panniers of other camels. After being unloaded, the tired animals will be sent a few miles out of the town where grass is plentiful to rest and feed for some weeks. Then they will be brought back to Timbuktu and loaded with gums, rubber, oil seeds and nuts, skins, gold, ivory, beeswax, and ostrich feathers, which have been brought here from many places in the Sudan and Central Africa. Then the caravan will start back over the desert for northern cities.

Should you like to send a message from Timbuktu telling your parents that you are safe and well? There is a wireless station here by which you can communicate with friends in Europe or the United States. Is it not wonderful that from this strange trading center on the edge of the great Sahara you can communicate with people in other parts of the world?

Though Timbuktu has long been one of the famous trading centers of Africa, it is now losing much of its importance. In former years all goods for the Sudan were imported into Mediterranean countries and sent southward across the great desert by caravan. All products from the Sudan were exported by the same route. Today goods destined for the Sudan reach there more quickly and cheaply if sent to Senegal and the colonies on the Gulf of Guinea and thence by rail and river into the interior.

In January, 1923, the first caravan of motor trucks to cross the Sahara arrived at Timbuktu. They were twenty one days covering the two thousand miles of desert from Tuggurt in Algeria to Timbuktu. This successful undertaking marks the beginning of motor transportation across the desert.

Slowly but none the less surely motor trucks, roads, railroads, telegraphs, wireless stations, and airplane routes are creeping from the coast regions farther and farther into the interior of Africa; and slowly but surely other improvements are following—schools, churches, just laws, more comfortable homes, better ways of living and working, and all those things which civilized nations enjoy.

SUGGESTIONS FOR STUDY

I

1. The port of Dakar.

2. Occupations and productions of Senegal.

3. The old land of Mauritania.

4. The Sudan.

5. The upper Niger and Timbuktu.

II

1. Describe two routes from Timbuktu to Marseille. Which is shorter in miles? in time?

2. Why is Dakar destined to become an important port?

3. Where will the peanuts raised in West Africa be sent? What use will be made of them (see pages 156 and 182-183)?

4. Trace the journey described on page 206 and estimate the number of miles we shall have traveled when we arrive at Fez.

5. Where is the mouth of the Niger River? Compare the country and occupations along the banks of the river in its upper and lower courses.

6. What countries have possessions in the Sudan?

AFRICA, AUSTRALIA, ISLANDS OF PACIFIC

III

Make a list of places mentioned in this chapter. Arrange them by countries, cities, rivers, mountains, etc. From these places select those which you think are so important that you should always be able to locate them and know something about them.

CHAPTER XVI

ACROSS THE DESERT FROM TIMBUKTU TO FEZ

THE desert of Sahara is as large as the United States. It extends from the southern slopes of the Atlas Mountains to the grasslands of the Sudan and from the Atlantic Ocean to the Red Sea. The southern part of the Barbary States belongs to it and much of Egypt and the Anglo-Egyptian Sudan. The only part of the desert which has a dense, settled population is the Nile valley, where the land is watered by the river floods.

The Sahara is a part of the trade-wind desert, of which you read in Chapter 1. What did you learn on page 12 about the water supply of the Sahara? In many of the oases this supply is permanent. In other places pools are formed in which the water remains for some time before it dries up. These water holes and the grass which springs up around them form the mainstay of many wandering tribes who know their location and the time of the year when they are likely to be of most help.

In recent years the French have dug thousands of

wells. Some of these are around oases, thus enlarging the area of cultivated land; some are in oases where the water supply was failing; while still others have been dug in the desert where no water was available before.

In many places in the desert coarse grass and shrubs grow. On many oases there is not enough food for the camels in the caravans which stop there, and the animals are sent some miles away to feed on this desert growth.

As one would expect from its position and surface the Sahara is very hot in summer. The rays of the sun beat down on the rocks and sand, which often become too hot to touch. How high does the mercury in the thermometer rise where you live? Here in parts of the great desert the thermometer sometimes registers from a hundred and ten or twenty to a hundred and thirty or more. There are no trees to protect one from the fierce heat, and no cooling streams in which to bathe.

After the sun has set, the rocks and sand quickly lose their heat and the nights are often chilly. During the day the rocks expand with the heat, and during the night they contract. This tends to crack them and break them up. The wind blows the smaller particles around, and Mother Nature uses them as cutting tools to grind other particles finer and to wear away the rocks.

We are going to journey from Timbuktu across the great desert through the oases of Tuat and Tafilet into Morocco. All this journey will be in French territory and will take us into the Mediterranean colonies, which we wish to visit. The route which we shall follow is not

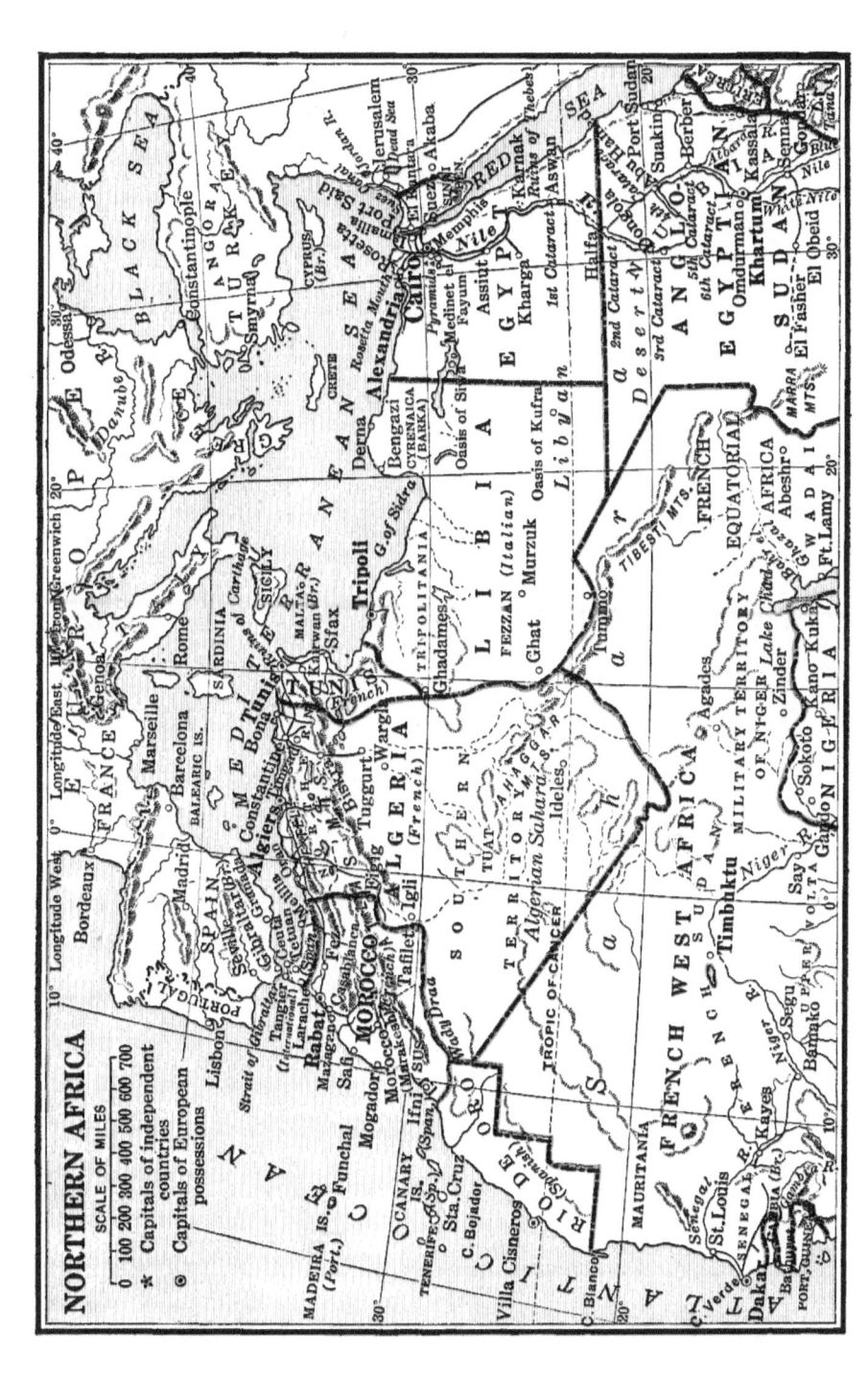

a road or even a path. The Arab sheik who guides our caravan finds his way by the stars and by landmarks known only to himself. Sometimes the way leads up to rocky plateaus and around mountains; sometimes it follows dry, stony river beds; and sometimes the camels plod over rippling sand hills.

Instead of journeying by ourselves we shall find it better to join a large caravan. We shall be less likely to get lost, and there is smaller danger of being attacked by robbers.

At the market in Timbuktu we buy the camels to carry us on our long, hard trip. There is as much difference in camels as there is in horses. The slow, heavy freight camel, the jemal, may be compared to the big, strong draft horse; while the mehari, the tall, swift riding camel, is like the trotter or the saddle

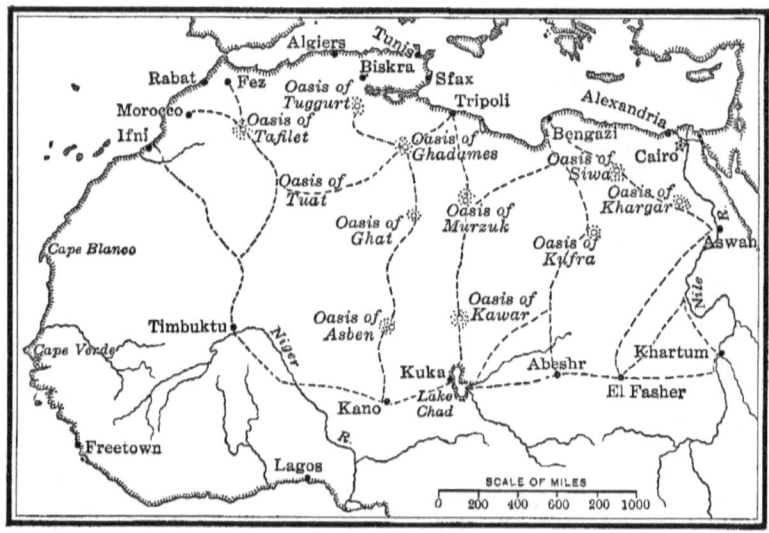

Figure 81. *Some caravan routes across the desert.*

horse. On some of the oases and in the semiarid lands surrounding the desert the Arabs raise many camels of both kinds, and we may chance to meet some of them being driven to an oasis to be sold.

The camel is often called the ship of the desert, and no more appropriate name could possibly have been given it. Its large, flat, padded feet act like snowshoes and prevent it from sinking into the sand. Because of its ability to store up water it can go several days without drinking. From the lump of fat on its back it derives nourishment to live and work with very little food longer than most animals can. When the camel sets out on a long desert journey it is important that the hump be large and firm, but after months of exhausting travel it grows small and flabby.

Mounting our camels, we join the caravan with which we are to travel, and are soon out of sight of Timbuktu. The desert lies all around us; nothing but sand and bare rocks and a few scattering plants and shrubs are in sight. There are hills of sand and valleys of sand. No tree, no path, no object of any kind marks our route. Now we begin to think of the dangers of the trip. We are carrying some water with us in skin bags, but it will not last many days. Suppose we lose our way and miss the wells along the route. Some of them are mere holes dug in the sand; there is nothing to mark them, and we might be only a short distance away and yet not see them.

Suppose a band of robber Tuaregs, the terror of the desert, is hiding behind those rocks and springs out upon us as we pass. Suppose a sand storm arises, and we are suffocated by the cutting, blinding clouds of sand. Comparatively few of the many caravans which cross the desert suffer greatly from these dangers, so we put such thoughts away and enjoy the beauties and the wonders of the trip.

We make our start while the stars are shining. Gradually they grow dimmer as dawn approaches. Soon the sun rises gloriously in the clear blue sky and casts long shadows of men and animals over the glittering sands. Just as the first rays peep over the horizon the caravan stops. The Arabs spread their little rugs on the ground, turn their faces to the holy city of Mekka, and repeat their morning prayers. Wherever he may happen to be at the time of prayer, or whatever he may be doing, a true Mohammedan turns his face toward the birthplace of Mohammed and repeats his prayer to Allah.

As the sun rises higher in the sky and shines hotter and hotter on the rocks and sand, we cover our faces against the blinding glare and heat. We are glad to rest awhile in the middle of the day, and we creep into the shadow of a sand hill, drink a little of the lukewarm water from our skin bags, eat a few dates and some hard bread, and perhaps sleep a little. Soon we are once more on our way, swaying in our seats with the motion of the camel as it plods noiselessly along on its soft, padded feet.

We have been traveling but a short time when the camels begin to appear uneasy; they stop, turn partly

THE DESERT FROM TIMBUKTU TO FEZ

Figure 82. Prayer in the desert.

around, and lie down, with their noses close to the ground. We notice a haze around us and realize that the air has suddenly become very hot. The wind grows stronger and is loaded with sand particles, which cut our faces and blind us so that we cannot keep our eyes open. The dreaded simoom, or sand storm, is upon us. Crouching low in the sand with the camels between us and the wind, we turn our backs to the storm and cover our faces.

Now comes the storm. The wind is as full of sand as the worst blizzard is full of snowflakes. If we dared to uncover our faces and open our eyes, we could see only a foot or two away. Sometimes we have to dig away the sand to prevent being covered.

When at last the storm is over we are nearly buried in sand. The kneeling camels look like sand hills. The desert all around us is changed. Rocks are uncovered, and new hills have grown where none rose before. All the tracks made by the great caravan have been swept away or covered. It is as if nothing had passed this way since the desert was born.

Now the sun is getting lower in the sky. Its heat is not so fierce, and a little cooling breeze has sprung up. As the sun sinks below the horizon wonderful colors appear in the sky and spread over the desert. Soon the stars come out. How low they seem to hang in the sky! The air is so clear and dry that we can see many more than we have ever seen before, and they seem very large and bright.

Now we will start on our travels again. In the silver light of the moon the hills stand out sharp and clear, the black rocks glisten, and the sand is a dazzling white.

How silent the desert is, and how empty! Can you imagine looking off in all directions to where the sky seems to come down to meet the earth and seeing nothing but sand and rocks? Not a living thing is in sight—not a bird or any other animal, not a tree or blade of grass.

There are some animals in the desert, however; and before our trip is ended we may make the acquaintance of some lizards, scorpions, or snakes. We may chance to see an antelope in the distance or hear the sharp barking of foxes and the howling of hyenas. If a camel dies and its body is left behind on the sands, it is not long before a vulture can be seen circling around in the heavens nearer and nearer to the dark spot which the great bird knows will afford it a feast.

Look at those figures coming over the hill off there to our right. Now there is a long line of camels looming

Figure 83. Which animal should you choose for a ride?

black against the sky. It is a caravan making its way toward the oasis which we have just left. The camels trudge slowly along under their heavy loads. Many of them are carrying bars of salt, each about a yard long and weighing sixty pounds. These will be sold in the market at Timbuktu and taken from there to trading centers in the Sudan.

Though the Sahara has long been a highway of trade between the lands on its northern and southern borders, salt and dates are the only export products of great value which are produced on the desert itself. Salt has accumulated in great quantities in those places where once lay salt lakes and arms of the ocean, and in such areas there are seemingly inexhaustible amounts.

On many oases the date palms are the only means of income of the people, and a man's wealth is often reckoned by the number of trees he owns. The date palm is queen of the desert. The Arabs say that it must have its head in the sunshine and its feet in the water. They lead the water in trenches from the wells to the trees, and in the moist patches around the palms they raise grain and vegetables.

Millions of pounds of dates are sent by caravans from the oases of the Sahara to be consumed in the countries to the north and south. Should you like to live on an oasis and help in harvesting the dates? When the fruit is ripe the Arabs climb the tall trees and cut off the heavy bunches. The women pick the dates from the bunches and spread them out to dry. They turn them over and over so that the sunshine may get to all parts of the fruit.

THE DESERT FROM TIMBUKTU TO FEZ

The picking, the sorting, the drying, and the packing keep the village people very busy, and during the harvest season many nomads come in from the desert to help gather the dates and to obtain a supply for themselves. Soon caravans from nearly every oasis on the desert are loaded with the fruit and are making their way to trading centers and shipping ports or to railway termini on the borders of the desert.

There are many varieties of dates. Some are sweet and juicy, and some are hard and dry. These latter keep much better than the moist varieties, and the natives use them as food. In some parts of the desert dates are the chief food not only of the people but of the animals as well. Horses, cows, and goats are often fed with them. The caravan drivers carry dates with them on their long journeys across the desert. They are crushed into balls or pounded into a solid mass and sewed up in matting. When the driver wishes to feed them to his camels he has to pound them loose with a stone.

You might not like these dry, hard dates as well as the kind which you buy in the stores, but they are very nourishing and serve the Arab well. His life on the desert would be even harder than it is were it not for the dates, which he can so easily carry with him on the march.

The Department of Agriculture at Washington is constantly trying to introduce new products adapted to the soil and climate in different parts of our country. Which one was spoken of on page 135? In some of our Western states conditions are like those in the arid and semiarid regions of Eastern lands where dates are grown. Experts have gone to Africa and Asia to study the date industry and to bring back to this country some of the best varieties of fruit. These have been planted in parts of Arizona and California where the sun is hot, the air dry, and plenty of water for irrigation can be obtained. The date industry is growing here, as the fig and lemon industries have grown, and in the future we may expect that large quantities of dates will be produced.

The third day after leaving our last oasis the camels suddenly lift their heads and sniff the air. Then they begin to walk faster than before. We can see nothing, but the camels have smelled water and know that an oasis is near.

Perhaps you are thinking, as many people do, that an oasis is a small place with one or two wells or springs, a few trees growing, and a few people living on it. It is true that there are many small oases in the desert, but there are many also which cover an area as large as your home town or city. Others, much larger, contain hundreds of native villages and millions of palm trees.

The arrival at an oasis of a large caravan like the one with which we are traveling is known for long distances; and soon after our arrival nomads begin to come in to trade, bringing with them salt or dates, which they exchange for supplies which the caravans carry.

Should you like to live as the nomads of the desert do, staying in one place a short time and then finding a new home where the grass is green and the water more

THE DESERT FROM TIMBUKTU TO FEZ

Figure 84. These desert nomads have no settled homes. They pitch their tents where grass and water are found, live there for a few weeks, and then move on to another oasis. What things do you think these nomads must carry with them in their travels?

plentiful? It is true that the Arabs love their wandering life, but they live in this way from necessity rather than from choice. Their lives depend on their flocks and herds, and these in turn depend on grass and water, which must be sought for in different places at different times of the year.

Therefore a nomad can have no settled home and can live in no permanent village or town. He can accumulate no property except his animals. In his travels he can carry little with him but the barest necessities of life—leather skins to hold water, skin bags for his clothing and that of his family, mats and goat's-hair rope with which to make his tent, rugs to furnish beds and seats, and coconut shells and gourd shells to hold milk.

When we are rather more than halfway through our trip from Timbuktu to Morocco we come to the great oasis of Tuat. There are hundreds of wells here, supporting a population of fifty thousand people, who live in villages of flat-roofed mud houses. The people are Arabs, with one or two hundred Europeans and some natives. The cultivation of dates is the chief occupation here, and many thousand bags of them are sold.

The French officials here at Tuat make our stay as pleasant and restful as possible. French officials are stationed at many of the wells and oases. In some cases they may be the only European residents within hundreds of miles. Like the other nations that have possessions in Africa, the French have done many things to improve their territory. They have established schools,—the best thing a nation can do for its people,—and today thousands of boys and some girls are studying in schools in French Africa. Post offices have been established also, roads and railroads have been built, thousands of wells have been dug, and the natives have been introduced to many new methods of working and better ways of living.

When we reach the great oasis of Tafilet we feel that our journey is nearly completed, for we are only about two hundred miles from the city of Fez. This seems a short distance compared with the many hundreds which we have already traveled from Timbuktu. Tafilet is the principal trading station between Morocco and the Sudan, and caravans starting southward provide themselves here with their final supplies of food, water, and other necessities.

The narrow, crooked streets are bordered on either side by the mud walls of the houses. Few strangers ever see more of the houses than the blank street walls. Like the Mohammedans in other parts of the world, these people keep their family life from the eyes of the public. We see many men in the bazaars and coffeehouses, and we meet some veiled women in the streets; but the life in the low mud houses and the open courts behind them is for the family alone.

The oasis of Tafilet owes its life to two rivers which flow down the southern slopes of the Atlas range. These are fed by the melting snows on the mountains and, unlike many other streams in the desert which dry up in the hot sunshine, furnish water during the entire year. Were it not for these streams the thousands of palm trees which surround the villages, and the delicious dates for which the oasis is famous, would not be possible.

In many lands which we have visited we have seen what a friend to man Mother Nature is. She provides him with great rivers, deep forests, fertile soil, abundant rain, and other resources, and in many ways helps to make his life comfortable and happy. It is in such lands as the great Sahara that Nature appears more in the light of an enemy to man, handicaps him in many ways, and makes his life a hard one. Here, on large areas, she withholds her life-giving rains, she supplies no great rivers, no green grass, no deep forests, and but few of the other materials on which man in other countries has learned to depend. He lives in the desert not because of Nature's gifts but in spite of the lack of them.

Hard as their life is, the desert people love the clear, dry air, the brilliant sunshine, the blue sky, the bright stars, and the freedom of the open spaces. If we lived in the desert we should love it, too, for then it would be our home. Everywhere, in every country all over this wide world, whether people live on mountain or valley, on plain or plateau, in desert regions or on fertile farmlands, they love their homeland and are happier there than anywhere else.

SUGGESTIONS FOR STUDY

I

1. The Sahara Desert.
2. Water in the desert.
3. Trip across the Sahara.
4. A sand storm.
5. Products of the desert.
6. The date industry.
7. Oases and nomads.
8. Tuat and Tafilet.

II

THE DESERT FROM TIMBUKTU TO FEZ

1. Sketch an outline map of North Africa. Trace on it the route we have followed from the Atlantic Ocean to the Mediterranean Sea. Write on your map the names of the places mentioned.

2. Why do we build houses with slant roofs, while the people of the desert live in homes that have flat roofs?

3. Why should there be deserts in the trade-wind belt?

4. What are the two chief products of the Sahara?

III

Make a list of the places mentioned in this chapter. Arrange them by countries, cities, rivers, mountains, etc. From these places select those which you think are so important that you should always be able to locate them and know something about them.

CHAPTER XVII

IN THE LAND OF THE MOORS

For many years Morocco was one of the few independent countries of Africa. It occupies an important position at the mouth of the Mediterranean Sea and helps to guard the entrance to its waters. In 1912 an agreement was made among European powers that Tangier, an important port at the very mouth of the Mediterranean, and an area of about a hundred and forty square miles around it should be made an international zone. South of Tangier an area of about 18,000 square miles, more than twice the size of Massachusetts, was put under the control of Spain, and all the rest of the country was made a protectorate of France (see map on page 219).

The Sultan, the Moorish ruler, still holds his court and issues his laws, but France is represented in the country by a Resident General, whose advice in all important matters must be followed.

In the old days, when the Sultan ruled supreme, he held court and had palaces in several Moorish

IN THE LAND OF THE MOORS

cities—Fez, Tafilet, Marakesh (Morocco), and Rabat. Now he has appointed three khalifas, or governors, who live in Fez, Tafilet, and Marakesh, each having charge of that part of the country in which his city is located. The French governor general and the Sultan have established their headquarters at Rabat, which is today the real capital. Find these places on the map on page 219. Which of them is the largest (see Appendix, page 501)?

Figure 85. The man on horseback is the Sultan of Morocco. Where does he live? Whose advice must he follow in important matters? Over what part of Morocco has he no control?

Did you ever see a peacock with his brilliant tail outspread? An old Arab proverb says that the earth is a peacock, and Morocco is its tail. This is a fanciful Arab way of saying that Morocco is the gayest, most beautiful part of the world. Its northern shores are washed by the blue Mediterranean, and the Atlantic rolls along its western coast. The Atlas Mountains, which stretch across the country in several parallel ranges, raise their snowy heads from green palm groves. The desert in the south is beautiful, too, with its wonderfully colored sunsets and sunrises, its clear, dry air, its deep-blue sky, and the shimmer of its yellow sands in the sunshine.

Roughly speaking, the Atlas Mountains are the boundary between the desert regions to the south and the more fertile northern lands stretching down to the Mediterranean Sea. The mountains are a great wall over which the winds from the Mediterranean blow, leaving most of their moisture on the northern slopes and the tops. It is the streams fed by the melting snows of the mountains which make life possible in the drier regions of the south.

Figure 86. It is very convenient to go to our faucets for a drink of water. In most places in Morocco you would get it from the water carrier, who pours it lukewarm from a skin bag.

The people of Morocco are often called Moors, though this is a very general name, and it would be more correct to classify them as Berbers, Arabs, and Moors, the last term meaning people of mixed Arab and Berber blood. What was said about the Berbers on page 187?

The Berber villages in the hills and mountains are surrounded by mud walls, and all their houses are high

IN THE LAND OF THE MOORS

and strong. We shall recognize the men by their fierce, muscular appearance and by their cloaks of goat's hair, each with its patch of red or yellow.

Most of the towns and cities of Morocco lie north of the Atlas Mountains, and most of the people live in that part of the country. A large part of southern Morocco is known as the Sus (South) and is inhabited chiefly by wandering people who live in rude tent villages. They move from place to place to find food and water for their flocks and herds.

The Sus contains many mineral deposits, and some day these will yield immense wealth to the people who develop them, but it will take great courage and a large amount of money to undertake such a task in such a region. At present most of the people in the Sus are far away from the improvements which the French are making in the northern part of the country. Until more railroads are built, they must travel by caravan, stop at oases for food and water, and rest in tents during the heat of the day just as we have done in our trip through the Sahara.

The Arabs call their country El-Maghrib-el-Aksa, which means "the Farthest West," and the city which we know as Morocco they call Marakesh. In this book we shall call it Marakesh in order to avoid confusion between the names of the city and country. Marakesh is a great market place and trading center. To it come the chiefs and wild tribesmen of the mountains, the nomads of the Sus, and the slow caravans from Timbuktu and the Sudan.

All these people mingle in the crowded bazaars. Here the narrow lanes are roofed over with rushes to keep out the heat of the sun, and the little shops are so small that they remind us of huge packing cases standing on end. In each one sits the merchant among his wares, with everything within reach of his hand. There is no room inside for the customer. He sits on the threshold, with his feet in the street, and bargains for everything he buys. Usually he offers about half what the merchant asks. Then the merchant lowers his price a little, and the buyer raises his bid a trifle, until finally a bargain is struck. Shopping in the bazaars of Morocco takes time. In fact, nothing in this country is done in a hurry. An old Moorish proverb says that it is better to walk than to run, better to stand still than to walk, better to lie down than to stand, and when lying

Figure 87. Here we are in an old street in Fez. How many differences do you notice between this street and the one in front of your schoolhouse?

down it is better to close one's eyes than to keep them open. What changes do you think would take place in our country if we practiced this Moorish proverb?

In the bazaars we wander through the lane of the cloth sellers and through the street of the leather merchants. We see tiny shops with scores of red slippers for the women and yellow ones for the men. In the booths of one alley are the dealers in pottery, where the people buy vessels for grain and jars for carrying water. The lanes of the brassworkers and coppersmiths are noisy ones, for the workmen are hammering on sheets of metal, shaping them into dishes of all kinds. On other streets silversmiths and goldsmiths are making bracelets, anklets, necklaces, and rings.

All around us is a babel of tongues and languages. Donkey drivers shout to their slow steeds; merchants cry their wares; sellers of sticky sweets, of fruits, and of vegetables call to the people at the tops of their voices; filthy beggars urge us to help them; bread boys shout at one another in a medley of tongues; and water carriers, loaded with their skin bags, jingle their bells as they force their way through the crowds. A clatter of hoofs and some louder shouting announce the passing of some donkeys loaded with brush for firewood. Their loads nearly fill the narrow street. To avoid being scratched we make ourselves as flat as possible and nearly fall into one of the little shops which line the streets.

Look at the people! They are of all complexions —white, black, and bronze. Some are dressed in white

Figure 88. This picture shows you the size of the shops in the bazaars. These men sell leather goods. If you stopped to buy something, the man would probably offer you some coffee from the pot in front of the shop.

robes and wear yellow slippers with no heels. Some are wrapped in ragged brown cloaks. Those weather-beaten-looking men with the bright patch on the back of their cloaks are Berbers from the mountains. Those blacks carrying such heavy burdens on their backs are slaves from the Sudan. Here come some Jews in their long, dark robes. The Jews in North Africa are merchants, traders, bankers, and money changers, and have little to do with the Arabs and Berbers.

We know from the green turban which that Moor is wearing that he has made a pilgrimage to Mekka and now has the honor of being addressed as Hadji, which means "pilgrim." Every Mohammedan wishes more than anything else to make a pilgrimage to Mekka, the birthplace of Mohammed, and he will make great sacrifices to accomplish it. Then he can wear the green turban, have the title Hadji, and be sure, so he thinks, of reaching heaven.

Not all the people in the bazaars have come to trade. Some have come to meet friends or to hear the latest news. There are few roads, railroads, telegraphs, or telephones in the country, and news is carried slowly from place to place. Here, in the bazaars, people have come from so many different regions and from such great distances that one is sure to hear everything of interest.

Many have come also to be entertained. The snake charmer is always sure of an audience. The snakes twine

Figure 89. Snake charmers are among the attractions in the bazaars.

themselves around his neck, and one even puts its head into his mouth. They are poisonous snakes, but their fangs have probably been removed so that the one who handles them so freely is in no great danger.

See the crowd gathered around that story-teller, who is just beginning a story of some hero in Mohammedan history. The crowd is as interested as we should be in hearing some talented speaker tell the story of Paul Revere or Nathan Hale or some tale of George Washington or Abraham Lincoln. See how excited the story-teller is! He waves his arms, and his eyes flash. Now he has come to the most thrilling part of the story, and his audience is worked up to a great pitch of excitement and feels that it must know what happens next. But see, the story-teller stops and takes up a collection among the crowd. If his hearers are not liberal, he may not continue. Surely it is worth a few coppers to hear the rest of such a thrilling tale.

There are few large cities in Morocco. Most of the people live in the country regions, where they till their little farms and raise cattle, sheep, and goats. Farming is carried on in the valleys between the mountains, and on the plains near them, but the best farming lands of Morocco lie in the great rolling plains of the west. Let us leave the great city and go out into the country and visit some of the farms and villages. Traveling here will be much easier than it was across the desert in the Sus, for the French have built roads from Marakesh to the west and north.

The first village which we see is made up of tents

covered with coarse cloth woven from goat's hair. In places where the villages are permanent the houses are made of mud. The tents are arranged in a circle, with the openings toward the center. Around the circle is a high, thick hedge of thorn shrubs. This is as good a protection as a strong wall would be. As we approach we see out on the plain some boys tending the sheep and goats. At night they will drive the animals inside the thorn hedge and put the thorn door in place so that the animals will be safe.

If we wish to watch the women as they begin the day's work, see the flocks before they are driven out to the pastures, and hear the news and gossip of the village, we must go to the well. Without the wells no life would be possible here. When the water dries up, the people must move to another place. The tents must be taken down, and the bags and baskets of grain, the water jars, the mats, and other household possessions loaded on the backs of donkeys and women. The men and boys drive the flocks and herds, and thus the entire village journeys over the land to some place where water and grass can be found. Here they live for some months and then move on to a new home.

At present there seems to be plenty of water in the well. With their fiber ropes the women let down the goatskin buckets and fill the clay troughs where the animals drink. Then they fill their jars, swing them onto their heads, and return to their work in the tents while the men thresh the grain which has just been harvested.

The threshing floor is a yard where the earth has

been beaten hard and flat. The grain has been spread out on the ground, and the donkeys walk round and round upon it, treading out the seeds. Then the farmers toss the grain high in the air on their wooden shovels, and the wind blows away the lighter chaff and straw. The women grind the grain for their bread between two stones.

The people of Morocco raise corn, wheat, barley, and other grains. They have large olive and fig orchards and many vineyards. They raise almonds and other nuts and many dates. They gather seeds, too, which are valuable for the oil which they contain. All these products are useful to the French people. There are so many large cities and so many people in France that large quantities of food products must be imported. This is why the French colonies in Africa are of such great value to the mother country.

On the other hand, the people of Africa need the cotton cloth, the boots and shoes, the flour and other foodstuffs, the manufactures of iron and steel, and many other products from French mills, factories, and foundries. So a great and increasing amount of commerce is carried on each year between the seaports of France and Morocco.

Look at the map on page 219 and find the names of the seaports on the western coast of Morocco. Since the French took possession of the country all these seaports have been greatly changed. Breakwaters, piers, wharves, and warehouses have been built and other improvements made by which vessels are loaded and

IN THE LAND OF THE MOORS

unloaded more easily, quickly, and cheaply.

So many Europeans have come to live in the seaports that many things have been done for their welfare. On the streets we see poles with telegraph, telephone, and electric light wires. Many houses like those to which the French are accustomed in their own country have been built; so that today the coast towns, and the larger interior cities as well, are divided into two parts. There is the old Moorish city, with its narrow, crooked streets lined by mud walls, its flat-roofed mud houses, its bazaars, its veiled women, and its long-robed men. In another section the houses are modern, and the streets are wider, lighted and drained, and filled with well-dressed people similar to those whom you might meet in any city of France.

Of all the Moorish ports on the Atlantic, Casablanca is the most important. Miles of new streets have been

Figure 90. This is the garden of a wealthy gentleman in Casablanca. How interested the family is in the baby!

built here, stores, hotels, banks, schools, and other public buildings have been erected, a sewage system and an electric light plant have been installed, and industrial plants have been started in the more modern parts of the city, where more than fifty thousand Europeans live.

From Casablanca we can take a train to Rabat, farther north. About ten thousand people live here, in the new European section, which is as different from the Arab Rabat as Peking is different from New York City. What was said about Rabat on page 235?

Figure 91. This is the veranda of a gentleman's home in Rabat. It does not open on the street as ours usually do, but on a court behind the house.

From Rabat we can go by rail to Fez, the second largest city of Morocco. For many centuries Fez has been a center of Arab art and learning and the pride of the empire. To it in former days large numbers of students came to study in the libraries and colleges connected with its mosques. Its fame as a seat of learning has largely departed, and the number of its students is smaller than in the old days, but it is still the university town of Morocco.

From the hills around Fez a fine view of the city may be had. In one part we see a jumble of green roofs and the tall minarets of many mosques gleaming above the low gray walls of the houses. This is the Kasbah, the fortified place such as is found in every Moorish city. The Kasbah at Fez is very large and is entered through several strong gates. Within its walls are beautiful mosques, the Sultan's palace and castle, and the government buildings. Not far away is the Mellah, the section where the Jews live.

The old business part of the city is called the Medina. Here some of the narrow streets are covered from roof to roof with vines and rushes. Someone has called the Medina a human beehive, with each bee sitting in his own little cell, while thousands are constantly flitting to and fro gathering honey. In the bazaars there is as much noise and confusion as there was in those of Marakesh. Here, as there, are the little packing-box shops lining the lanes of the coppersmiths, silversmiths, and goldsmiths, the pottery sellers, and the rug merchants. Here are the charcoal burners, the leather workers, the slipper makers, and scores of others. We see and hear the water carriers, the beggars, the snake charmers, the story-tellers, the crowds of Arabs, the black-robed Jews, and the green-turbaned Hadji with his followers. Not far away are the markets where horses and mules, cattle, grain, and fuel are sold.

In several parts of the city there are smaller markets where the people buy their everyday necessities, but it is only in the great bazaar that there is such a large collection of all kinds of wares and so much noise and confusion.

In the summer the weather is very hot. The people do their work early in the morning and then rest from before noontime until four or five o'clock. The evening hours on the roofs are the time that the women love best. You would like it, too, if you had been shut in the house all day long. Each roof has a low wall around it, and it is not considered polite to look over it onto your neighbor's roof. Sometimes the women make calls on one another on the roofs when they are sure no men are around.

From Fez we will take the train to Tangier. What was said about this city on page 234? Tangier has long been a gateway for travelers into Morocco and in many ways it is more like European cities than like those in Africa. To be sure, we shall find here dark-complexioned men in gowns and turbans, water carriers with their goatskin bags, Moorish women with veiled faces, and crowded bazaars. But we shall see also many people in European clothes, and we shall find many shops with signs in English, French, and Spanish. So many tourists visit Tangier on their way into the country that there are more hotels, guides, curio shops, and such things than there are in the cities which are located farther toward the south.

The situation of Tangier destines it to be one of the great shipping and coaling ports of the world. You can see by looking at the map opposite page 189 that it is the nearest to Europe of all African ports. You will notice, too, that it is as much a gateway to the Mediterranean as is the stronghold of Gibraltar on the southern shore of Spain, and it is easily accessible to all vessels entering and leaving the great sea.

Figure 92. Tangier is an ancient city. This gate and wall have been here hundreds of years. Why is Tangier an important place?

With railroad connection with the interior of Morocco and with Algeria, Tangier will some day become the terminus of a great transportation system. Already millions of dollars' worth of goods enter and leave her harbor every year, and this is only the beginning of a vastly greater trade which will come with

Figure 93. This is one of the business streets in Tangier. Notice the costumes of the people. Can you see any men who may have come from Europe or the United States?

the development of the countries of northern Africa.

The United States is interested in Morocco, as it is today in all countries of the world. From it we import large quantities of gums, and nuts and seeds valuable for the oil which they contain, and many thousand dollars' worth of sheepskins and goatskins, which are made into leather in our tanneries and manufactured into shoes in our factories. Perhaps the leather in your shoes may have come from some sheep or goat which once fed in the pastures of Morocco. In return we send to these African neighbors of ours kerosene, tobacco, dried fruits, some iron and steel, and foodstuffs, such as salted meats and canned goods. As Morocco develops and the needs of the people increase we shall send larger quantities of farming tools and implements, machinery, hardware, pumps, roofing, paints, and many other articles. The better acquainted we are with the customs, desires, and needs of the people, the faster we shall be able to increase our trade with them.

SUGGESTIONS FOR STUDY

I

1. Position of Morocco.

2. Divisions and government.

3. Surface and population.

4. Changes and improvements.

5. In the bazaars.

6. Village life.

7. Marakesh and Fez.

8. The internationalized city of Tangier.

9. Our interests in Morocco.

II

1. What differences can you think of between Marakesh and your home city?

2. Why should there be a larger proportion of Europeans in Casablanca than in Fez or Marakesh?

3. Why is Tangier sure to become a city of great importance?

AFRICA, AUSTRALIA, ISLANDS OF PACIFIC

4. Who controls Gibraltar? Why should this nation be interested in the control of Tangier?

5. How was Morocco divided by the treaty of 1912?

III

Make a list of the places mentioned in this chapter. Arrange them by countries, cities, rivers, mountains, etc. From these places select those which you think are so important that you should always be able to locate them and know something about them.

CHAPTER XVIII

IN ALGERIA, THE MOST IMPORTANT COLONY OF FRANCE

From Tangier, our last stopping place, we will go by train through northern Algeria to the great city of Algiers. The railroad runs between the blue Mediterranean on the north and the Atlas Mountains on the south. These mountains divide Morocco, Algeria, and Tunis into three sections (see map on page 254). Along the coast is the Tell, through which we are traveling. This coastland region is the best-watered, the most fertile, and consequently the most important part of the Barbary States. Here are the best farms, the largest cities, and most of the people.

By looking again at the map you will see that between the ranges of the Atlas Mountains there is a wide plateau. Beyond the southern, higher range, which shuts out the moisture of the Mediterranean from the interior, the desert begins, and much of Algeria belongs to this desert region.

In our ride through the Tell we see great vineyards

Figure 94. What lies between the northern range of the Atlas Mountains and the sea? What lies between the ranges? What lies south of the mountains?

which remind us of southern France, groves of olive trees which are like those across the water in Spain, and groves of orange and lemon trees similar to those in southern Italy. Many of these industries are in the hands of Europeans who have settled in Africa. Surely all this Mediterranean coast land is more like southern Europe than it is like the part of Africa south of the Atlas Mountains.

Wheat, barley, and corn have been raised by the natives in the Tell for centuries, and this region furnished large amounts of food supplies for the great city of ancient Rome. In some regions, where little rain falls, irrigation is necessary, and we see here the ruins of irrigating works which carried water to the fields two thousand years ago.

Our first stop is in Oran, an important port in western Algeria. One of the products which we see here on the wharves in large quantities is esparto, or alfa, grass which is used in England for the manufacture

ALGERIA

of paper. For centuries the Arabs have used the fiber of this grass, which they call alfa, for making rope, baskets, muzzles for camels, coverings for the camels' humps, and mats to be used as sieves in the olive presses. The grass is one of the important products of both Tunis and Libya.

The esparto leaves are from two to three feet long. In the heat of the summer they turn brown and wither in a long, tight roll. The natives pull the leaves from the stalks and tie them up in bundles. They load so many of these bundles on their small donkeys that all we can see of the little animals is four brown legs underneath. In some sections camels are used instead of donkeys. The animals carry the esparto to some city or town where it is graded according to quality and pressed into bales,

Figure 95. This is a scene in the Tell. Where is this region? Notice the great vineyards in the picture.

and then sent to Oran, whence it is shipped to England.

In our eastward trip we pass several mining regions, where we see great heaps of red rock, and low buildings which cover yawning holes in the mountain sides. Deep in the earth, blasting, loading, and hoisting the iron ore, are Arabs, Moors, Kabyles, Spaniards, Italians, and Frenchmen. Algeria is rich in mineral wealth, and the iron industry is becoming more and more important every year. In other parts of the country zinc, lead, and other minerals are obtained. Algeria is one of the countries where quantities of phosphate rock are mined. Phosphorus is a valuable plant food and is much used in fertilizers. The phosphate mines in Algeria are very valuable to the farmers of France, who need great quantities of fertilizer.

Figure 96. The picture shows one of the many fine roads which the French have built in Algeria. Why should France spend so much money in Algeria for roads, railroads, bridges, etc.?

Now we are riding past forests of cork oak where the workmen are stripping the bark from the trees. This is piled up and left for some days in the forests to dry. After this it is taken to stations where it is boiled in large vats to loosen the woody matter, which can then be scraped off.

What have you ever seen which is made of cork? It is used for the stoppers of bottles, life preservers, inner soles, bicycle handles, and penholders. Cork paper is used for cigarette tips. Cork dust, shavings, and the small waste pieces are used in making linoleums, table mats, and mattresses, and in packing fruit (see Allen's "New Europe").

The city of Algiers is the capital, the largest city, and the most important port of Algeria. The harbor seems full of craft, from coal barges and tooting tugs to big ocean liners. Away to the south we can see the Atlas Mountains, some of them purple in the distance and some white with snow. Between the purple and white mountains and the blue sea the white city of Algiers rises in terraces to the green hills behind. Here a tall minaret of a mosque rises above the low houses; there a cluster of palm trees makes a splash of green on the white picture.

In the old Arab city on the slopes of the hills the streets are just wide enough for two horsemen to meet each other, and in places the old houses meet overhead. The bare mud walls on either side are broken only here and there by a heavy door or a small barred window. Sometimes we climb steep places where the streets are like flights of stairs. Sometimes a little alley leads into

Figure 97. This is a street in the old Arab quarter of Algiers. What things which seem to you peculiar do you notice in the picture?

a small bazaar where the merchant squats among his wares. But why have wide streets when narrow ones keep out the fierce heat of the sun much better and when loads are carried only on the backs of men and animals? Why have front yards and windows when the women of the family must always stay in back rooms, hidden from the eyes of the passers-by?

The part of Algiers which lies near the water is more like a city of France than of Africa. Here the streets are wide, the buildings modern, and the hotels large and comfortable. The open-air cafes are like those of Paris, and Frenchmen and other Europeans sit at the tables sipping their wine and coffee while they chat with friends or watch the sights in the streets.

There are many French ships in the harbor. We see also several flying the English jack and the flags of other European countries. There are some from China and Japan, from South American countries, and from the United States. These have brought to Algeria machinery, tools, and other iron and steel goods, cotton cloth, sugar, coffee, boots and shoes, and quantities of coal. Can you tell why large amounts of such goods are needed?

Ships from Algiers carry across the Mediterranean to the French port of Marseille quantities of wine from Algerian vineyards, grain from the farms in the fertile Tell, and phosphates to fertilize French farms. There are sent also to French factories wool and hides and skins from the plateau regions, cork from the forests, and esparto for making paper. Tobacco products and iron, zinc, and lead ores also help to fill the vessels.

All these things are very valuable to France, and she is trying each year to enlarge the farms in Algeria, improve the breeds of animals, develop the minerals, and extend the roads and railroads so that the products may the more easily be brought to the large centers and the seaports. Already France has built more roads and railroads and introduced more modern improvements in Algeria than in any other of her colonies.

Some of the ships in the harbor of Algiers will sail for ports in the United States. Among other things they will bring us quantities of cork bark. Perhaps the cork which was used in making the linoleum on your floor came from Africa. Some of the cream of tartar which your mother uses may have been the product of some Algerian vineyard. Cream of tartar is made from a powder which forms on the sides of the vats in which grape juice ferments. From what other countries do you think that we may buy much of this product (see Allen's "New Europe")?

We import from Algeria many thousand dollars' worth of brierwood for pipes. Dates, figs, sheepskins and goatskins, cattle hides, and iron ore are loaded at the wharves of Algiers and Oran on vessels which are bound for New York City or some other seaport of the United States.

Leaving Algiers we run swiftly by the white villas and lovely gardens outside the city and past the truck farms owned by thrifty Frenchmen who supply the city with fresh vegetables and fruits. Farther out we see acres of vineyards. The vines are pruned back to a height of three or four feet and tied to stakes as they are in the vineyards of France.

The farms which are owned by the Arabs and Moors are not so large and thrifty-looking as those which are owned by the French. Many of the Arabs still cling to the old time methods of their ancestors. Their crops are small, for they use no fertilizer; and their little wooden plow, made of a crooked stick tipped with iron, just scrapes the surface of the ground. Many improvements are taking place, but it takes a long time to change the habits of a people who have lived and worked in the same way for thousands of years.

We pass many groves of gray old olive trees. Millions of these trees grow in Algeria, and every year Europeans are planting more. Large quantities of olive oil are used

Figure 98. Here are some Algerian farmers hauling their products to market. What do you think may make up the load on the wagon?

by the Algerians, but so much is made that several thousand tons are exported, some of it to Tunis and Morocco, but by far the most of it to France. Most of the oil presses owned by the natives are run by water power or horse power, while the larger proportion owned by Europeans are now run by steam or electricity.

Soon the train begins to climb, and we catch sight of the mountain villages of the Kabyles and see the stone houses clinging close to the rocky slopes. We are in the land of Kabylia, the home of the tribes of mountain shepherds who have inhabited the land for centuries. These people are of the same ancestry as the Berbers, whom we saw in Morocco, but here in Algeria they are known as the Kabyles. They have maintained their independent ways of life against Romans, Arabs, Turks, and other invaders. Now they have accepted the rule of the French and are turning to more peaceful occupations.

Wars with other tribes are less frequent now than in the past, and the men spend much of their time working on their farms raising grain and vegetables, caring for their fig and olive groves, and tending their sheep and goats. When there is little to do at home they often go down to the cities and towns to earn money or work on the large farms in the Tell. The Kabyle woman is the sole wife of her husband and eats her meals with him instead of waiting until he has finished, as the Arab woman does. She does not veil her face and live in privacy, but works hard in the fields with the men and animals.

Many roads and paths wind up the steep slopes to

the Kabyle villages. We see some Kabyle women doing the family wash beside a gurgling brook. Some boys are driving in the flocks from the pastures. The goats and sheep, headed by a small donkey, come pushing and crowding up the steep path. The low stone houses have neither windows nor chimneys. All the smoke from the little charcoal fire which cannot get through the door or through the small hole which is left in the roof for that purpose stays in the room. Consequently everything is black and dirty. If we stayed to dinner the people would offer us some couscous, a common dish in Algeria, made of dough thoroughly steamed and served with meat, vegetables, and gravy.

Leaving the Kabyle village we go down the steep path and take the train to continue our journey. The scenery is beautiful. Violet peaks rise against the sky, little Kabyle villages high on the slopes gleam in the sunshine, sheep and goats graze in the high pastures, fields of wheat and barley surrounded by thorn hedges wave in green valleys, olive groves cast their deep shadows, and the long leaves of corn rustle in the breeze. Now and then the railroad runs parallel with a fine road on which workmen are making repairs. The stone crusher which is grinding up the rock, and the steam roller which is rolling it smooth, make as much noise as such machines do on our city streets.

We stop for a while at Constantine, an ancient city and an important trade center. It is a wonderful place. Think of a city of over seventy-five thousand people built on a high rock and surrounded on all sides by a narrow gorge nearly a thousand feet deep. If your

Figure 99. What a lovely ride it must be through this gorge in Algeria with the green mountains topped with fleecy clouds on either side.

schoolhouse were set in the bottom of the gorge, how high would it reach on the sides? Through this deep gorge rushes a swift river. Only in one place is the rock on which the city stands connected with the mainland by a natural rock bridge. In other places iron bridges have now been built.

Can you imagine a better situation for a fortress? There is an old saying in the country that he who would rule Algeria must hold Constantine. Because of its commanding position and of the fertility of the surrounding lands, the city has been besieged by Carthaginians, Romans, Arabs, and Turks. Today it is an important commercial center for this part of Algeria. All around is a rich grain-growing country, and each summer hundreds of Kabyles come down from the mountains to help in the harvest.

Along the route southward from Constantine there are many ruins of Roman cities. The most interesting of these are at Timgad, a city built about a hundred years after the birth of Christ. How old is it? At the time of the Arab invasion in 692 it was destroyed, and it has never since been inhabited, except by the panther and the jackal. Now a road leads to the ancient city, and men are working in the ruins to learn what this old center of life may tell us.

We look about at the pillars and pedestals which mark the site of the ancient forum and try to imagine the crowds gathered there and the addresses and discussions which took place. Behind the forum is the circle showing where stood the colosseum, or theater.

Figure 100. These are the ruins of the city of Timgad. How long have these buildings been here? Who built them?

Most remarkable of all the ruins are the remains of the public library. In little recesses or niches on the walls were kept the rolls of papyrus, which were the books of these days. There were benches for the readers and decorations of carvings and statues. A tablet dug out of the city tells us that the library was presented to the city by Marcus Julius Quintianus Flavius Rogatianus. Though the name sounds different, it all seems very much like the present custom whereby wealthy men present gifts to their home cities or towns and have their names inscribed on tablets.

On we go, southward bound, through a country of cultivated fields and then over stretches of sandy wastes. Soon after this there rises before us a rocky mountain range which shuts out the scenes beyond. Just as we

ALGERIA

begin to wonder how we can get through the mountain mass, we see a great gash in the rocks and through it catch a glimpse of the sky beyond. This great gorge of El Kantara, cut by a mountain river, is from three to four hundred feet wide and four hundred feet high. The Arabs call it the mouth of the Sahara, and as we pass through we see a typical oasis, with its wells and palm trees. Straight south, out into the Sahara, the railroad takes us to the great oasis of Biskra, Queen of the Desert.

Figure 101. There is a fine highway leading south through El Kantara. It looks here as if the mountain blocked the road, but the gorge makes an opening out into the desert.

Biskra consists of several villages, each built around the well which makes it possible. Here is also the government headquarters of the Algerian Sahara. Many French officials live here, and a French garrison is stationed here.

Figure 102. This is a street in Biskra. Describe it.

ALGERIA

The railroad has brought many changes to Biskra. It has built the modern French town where are the wide, paved streets, the pretty parks, the stores, and the hotels, and it has brought the many tourists who come here from different countries for a glimpse of the real desert.

Biskra is a center of caravan trade. Always there are camels coming in from the desert, resting outside the walls of the town, or kneeling to be loaded with freight for the people far out on distant oases.

The chief business of Biskra is buying and selling dates. Great quantities are gathered from the thousands of palm trees here, and large amounts are brought in by trucks, carts, mules, donkeys, and camels from other oases. These will be sent northward to Algiers and loaded on vessels bound for many parts of the world. What did you read about the date industry on pages 226-228?

If we wished, we could continue our trip by rail still farther south through the desert to Tuggurt. You will find this place on the map on page 219. This is another important oasis, whose green palms, white domes and minarets, and mud houses seem to rise out of the desert sands which surround them on all sides. The houses are built of reddish sun-baked earth, and arcades cover the narrow streets and keep out the fierce heat of the sun.

In and around Tuggurt there are hundreds of thousands of palm trees watered by hundreds of wells. When the French first penetrated this region many of the trees were dying because of the lack of water. In spite of the efforts of the people, the desert sands were slowly

Figure 103. Here is a well in another street in Biskra. The water flows away in a little brook and will be used in many ways before it loses itself in the sand.

but surely covering the native wells. Much to the joy of the natives, the French have driven many artesian wells here. Water has become more plentiful, the number of palm trees has increased, and the poverty of the people has been removed. Do you suppose that any of the dates which you see in the stores or which you may eat with your Christmas dinner have come from this lonely oasis of Tuggurt far out in the desert of Sahara?

There is one more French colony bordering on the Mediterranean Sea which we have not yet visited. This is Tunis. By looking on the map on page 219, or on the one preceding page 1, you will see that Tunis is the most northern country of Africa. Let us leave the desert and the life on the oases and turn our faces northward once more to see what interesting sights await us in this ancient land.

SUGGESTIONS FOR STUDY

I

1. Physical divisions of the Barbary States.
2. Occupations and productions.
3. The port of Oran and the esparto trade.
4. Mineral wealth of Algeria.
5. The city of Algiers.
6. Farms and villages.
7. Kabyles and Kabylia.
8. The city of Constantine.
9. Roman ruins.
10. Biskra and Tuggurt.

II

1. Write to the Department of Commerce at Washington requesting, for school use, information concerning the exports and imports of Algeria and the countries receiving and sending them. What articles come from the United States? How much greater than those of all other countries are the imports from France? Why should this be so? Does the list of exports from

AFRICA, AUSTRALIA, ISLANDS OF PACIFIC

Algeria help you in solving the problem on Algeria given on page 397?

2. Sketch a map of Algeria. Show on it the two chief seaports, the surrounding countries, and enough of the Mediterranean to include Marseille.

III

Make a list of all the places mentioned in this chapter. Arrange them by countries, cities, rivers, mountains, etc. From the list select those which you think are so important that you should always be able to locate them and know something about them.

CHAPTER XIX

TUNIS, THE MOST NORTHERLY COUNTRY OF AFRICA

Look at the position of Tunis on the map on page 219 and see how near it lies to Sicily and the toe of Italy. Notice also how these lands divide the Mediterranean Sea into two great basins. Tunis is an important country; and the city of Tunis, at the narrowest point of the Mediterranean, has grown to be one of the largest cities of Africa. Positions like this which control commercial routes always make places important. Can you think of any other places similarly situated?

The surface of Tunis, rising from the low Tell to plateaus and mountains, and with hot, dry lands in the south, gives the country a wide range of climate, which results in a great variety of products. This is another reason for the importance of the colony.

As in the other countries of North Africa the rainfall is limited. Only two small rivers have sufficient flow of water to last throughout the year. Yet, though thus handicapped, little Tunis is important in international trade and ships large quantities of its products, its surplus crops, and its minerals to foreign countries.

As we travel through northern Africa we become more and more accustomed to the sight of long-robed Arabs, mountain Berbers, bearded Turks, black-robed Jews, and blacks whose original home was in the Sudan. There are other peoples here in Tunis of whom we have seen but few representatives in other countries—Maltese from the island of Malta, swarthy Sicilians, some Greeks, and many Italians. Some of these are fishermen, some work in mines, and others work on farms and in the cities. Of course there are many Frenchmen in Tunis. Some are officials in the government or soldiers in the army. Others have taken up large areas of land for farms.

A boundary stone tells us when we pass from Algeria to Tunis, but the sights from the car windows remain about the same. We still run by fields of wheat and barley, past groves of fig and olive trees, and near orange and lemon groves. In the higher lands there are forests of the cork oak where men are stripping the bark from the trees. We pass large, prosperous-looking farms owned by Europeans, where the work is carried on much as it is in our country. Some of the plows, harvesters, and other implements used on these farms came from the United States. We notice that the farms owned by the Arabs are usually small ones; and we are sure that no factory in America ever made the little wooden plow, drawn by a moth-eaten-looking camel, which that Arab in the field yonder is using.

Now the train runs by some large vineyards owned by Frenchmen who understand well the cultivation of the grape. How heavily loaded the little vines are and how flourishing they look! You can imagine how many vineyards there must be in Tunis when you see on the wharves at the seaports the long rows of wine casks and learn that millions of gallons of wine are produced here every year.

The wharves and docks in the city of Tunis are busy places. Men as black as coal, Berbers in loose brown robes, Arabs in white with richly colored turbans, Jews in black, and Maltese and Sicilians, working, loafing, crying their wares, and acting as baggagemen, porters, and longshoremen, make a picture of life and color. See the casks of olive oil and wine and the bags filled with wheat and barley. Those piles of boxes contain dates from many oases, and those bales are esparto, of which you read on pages 254 and 255. There are bundles of hides, bales of cork bark, bags of almonds, and boxes of oranges and lemons. Large quantities of minerals also—iron ore, lead, zinc, and manganese—will help to make up the cargoes of the many vessels which leave this busy port.

If we could examine the contents of those bags and bales and boxes which the men are unloading from the steamers at the wharves, we should find large quantities of cotton cloth, white and colored and plain and figured. There is woolen cloth too, and men's clothing. There are many articles of iron and steel—nails, screws, tools, and machinery. There are drugs and medicines and chemicals. There are canned goods of many kinds—meats and fruits and condensed milk. There are dried beans and peas and great quantities of sugar. There are paper, leather, matches, and thousands of tons of coal. In fact, there is everything that people need who live in a land where little or no manufacturing is carried on, and where over a wide area few food products can be raised.

Some of the goods which we see on the wharves have come from the United States. There is not a country on earth which does not receive something from our fields or factories. From every land there come to us also some articles which our world neighbors have produced. Here at Tunis are bags of corn and wheat which were raised on our Central Plains, machinery from our foundries, petroleum from our wells, meats from our stockyards, cotton-seed oil from the mills in our Southern states, shoes from our factories, condensed milk from our dairies, and farm machinery from our great manufacturing establishments.

The ships in the harbor of Tunis will bring to us sponges, olive oil, ores, dried fish, leather, carpets, some native pottery, and small amounts of other goods.

All Frenchmen love Paris. When they settle in other countries, they like to make the cities there as much like their beloved Paris as possible. So in the newer parts of Tunis, as in other cities of these North African lands, the French have built wide, tree-lined boulevards, modern hotels, shops, and open-air cafés, and they live and work there in very much the same manner as was their custom in the homeland of France.

If we once get into the crowded alleys of the native quarter where the bazaars are, we shall soon forget all about the newer part of the city, with its avenues, stores, banks, hotels, and theaters, and remember only that we are in an Arab city, a city which had existed for centuries before anything was known of America and other Western lands, a city where life flows on in the same slow, noisy, crowded way that it has for some thousand years.

Figure 104. Freight and passenger transportation in the old city of Tunis.

The Arabs, in their long robes, sit in their little shops waiting till Allah sends them a customer. If no customer appears and no goods are sold, it is the will of Allah, who rules all things, and so why worry or complain? Not so the Jews and Sicilians and Maltese. They cry their wares continually and beseech us to buy, each one insisting that his goods are cheaper than those of the other merchants.

Rugs and leather are two of the most important articles manufactured in Tunis. Some of the rugs in the bazaar are finely woven and beautifully colored. We should like to buy one of them and also some cushion covers, card-cases, bags, and other articles made of leather decorated and embroidered in lovely colors, but we have not time to bargain until the merchants will accept a reasonable price.

When you notice how near to Italy the country of Tunis is situated you will not be surprised to learn that there are more Roman ruins here than in any other

Figure 105. These are the ruins of Carthage. What do you know about this ancient city?

part of North Africa. Among them are the remains of Carthage, once an important city as large as St. Louis is today. Before the time when Rome rose to its greatest power, even before the time of Christ, the Carthaginians were the greatest nation of the world. They controlled all of northern Africa and had a large army and a great fleet which helped them in extending their trade and influence.

All this time the Roman Empire across the Mediterranean was growing more and more powerful. The two nations were rivals, and each realized that the other might prevent both the increase of its territory and the growth of its commerce. So they quarreled and fought for many years. These conflicts were known as the Punic Wars. In high school you will read in your ancient history lessons and your Latin about these wars and the doings of some of the famous Roman and Carthaginian generals.

These old Romans, who lived so long ago and left their ruins in so many parts of the world, have taught us many things—not only love of country, but how to build good roads and bridges and strong, beautiful buildings. Many of our laws and forms of government date back to Roman times. Many of our words are derived from the Latin language, which they used. The thing of which a Roman was the proudest was that he was a citizen of Rome. It mattered little what might happen to him personally if his country might be benefited. Do you think that we are as patriotic citizens as these old Romans were?

Now we are on our way to Sfax, the second largest city of Tunis. We ride by many large olive groves where the gnarled, twisted trees are loaded with fruit. We should like to be here in the harvest season and watch the Arabs gather the fruit and carry it to the olive presses. The first pressing of the fruit makes the best oil. The pulp is pressed again several times, each pressing resulting in a poorer grade of oil. The last oil produced is not fit for food, but is used in the making of soap.

Millions of gallons of olive oil are exported from both Tunis and Sfax, and large quantities are consumed in the country.

As we ride southward we see here and there large groves of almond trees. Should you not like to have a nut-gathering picnic here and race with the Arab boys and girls to see who could gather the most nuts?

In the pastures large flocks of sheep and goats are tended by shepherds in long cloaks. Both the flocks and the shepherds look as flocks and shepherds in this country have looked for three thousand years. Farther on we pass a party of Bedouins, with their camels and donkeys, seeking new homes and pastures, as Bedouins here have done for centuries.

As we approach Sfax we see hundreds of camels feeding on the coarse grass. They have brought from the little oasis towns far out on the desert great quantities of dates which will be shipped from the seaport. The camels are resting and feeding here before they begin their long, tiresome journey back to the people farther south, who will buy the cotton cloth, food products, saddles, and other goods which will fill the panniers.

Still nearer Sfax the air grows sweet with the perfumes from great gardens filled with orange trees, rosebushes, narcissus, jasmine, verbena, and other plants which bear sweet-scented flowers. Eastern peoples are fond of perfumes, and quantities are made and sold in the bazaars.

Soon we see the walls and towers of Sfax and catch a glimpse of the harbor dotted with fishing boats and

Figure 106. In this town in Tunis the people have built their stone houses around the ruins of the old Roman colosseum, or theater. Notice how the walls line the streets and are pierced with doors leading into the houses.

larger vessels. Down by the water swarthy Greeks and Italians, bronzed Sicilians with gold rings in their ears, and Arabs in ragged gowns are busy cleaning their boats and nets and preparing for the next day's trip to the fishing grounds.

Perhaps you would like to go out with one of the sponge fishermen and watch them pull the sponges from the rocks to which they cling. There are fishermen also who go after tunny, sardines, anchovies, lobsters, shrimps, and other creatures of the sea. Altogether the fisheries of Tunis are a very valuable industry. They furnish many of the people with food, and the fish and sponges shipped annually from the country are worth several million dollars.

AFRICA, AUSTRALIA, ISLANDS OF PACIFIC

Figure 107. This is the busy port of Sfax. See the fishing boats moored to the docks and the steamers farther out.

One of the products which has helped, perhaps more than any other, to increase the importance of Sfax is the phosphate which is shipped from its harbor. What was said about phosphate on page 256? The phosphate rock in Tunis is more valuable than any other mineral. The largest company in the country operates several mines and employs hundreds of Frenchmen and thousands of Italians. Some of them work in surface mines, and others go down in cages through shafts and mine the rock hundreds of feet underground. They blast out the phosphate rock, break it up, and carry it to the drying grounds. After it is thoroughly dried, it is loaded on cars which carry it to Sfax, where it is shipped to European countries. There the grain, the grapes, the sugar beets, and other crops grow better because of this plant food. Look closely at those locomotives and freight cars on the siding and you will find on them the names of firms in the United States.

We wish that we had time to see more of this interesting country. We should like to visit the oases in the south, some of them the richest and greenest in all North Africa, on which grow wheat and barley, fine vegetables, and orchards of many fruits. We should like to explore those odd towns where the troglodytes live in their cave houses in the rocks. We should like to join the pilgrims on their way to Kairwan, a holy city of the Mohammedans, visit the mosques there, and walk through the courtyards paved with tiles and decorated with marble columns into the interior, where Moors in their long white robes and rich turbans kneel in prayer on the tiled floor. We have not time for a longer visit in Tunis, but must take a peep at the island of Madagascar and then begin our trips into the colonies of other nations.

SUGGESTIONS FOR STUDY

I

1. Position and importance of Tunis.

2. Occupations and productions.

3. The city of Tunis.

4. Commercial interests of the United States.

5. Carthage and Carthaginians.

6. Sfax and its commerce.

7. Phosphate mining.

II

1. How many countries the size of Tunis would Algeria make? Compare the number of people in these two French colonies (see Appendix, page 500).

2. What African cities are larger than the city of Tunis (see Appendix, page 501)?

3. Why should there be more Sicilians, Maltese, and Italians in Tunis than in other countries of North Africa?

4. Why do the people of Tunis use francs instead of quarters, as we do, or shillings, as the English do? What is the value of a franc?

5. Sketch a map of Tunis. Show on it the places mentioned in the text. Show the Mediterranean Sea, Italy, Greece, and the islands of Sicily and Malta.

III

Make a list of the places mentioned in this chapter. Arrange them by countries, cities, rivers, mountains, etc. From the list select those places which you think are so important that you should always be able to locate them and know something about them.

CHAPTER XX
THE ISLAND OF MADAGASCAR

MADAGASCAR is one of the large islands of the world. In her wonderful storybook Nature tells us that it was once joined to Africa, but this must have been ages and ages ago, for no lions, tigers, giraffes, or any of the other great animals which live on the continent are found on the island.

The people too are different from those on the mainland. With their straight black hair and yellowish skins, these tribes in Madagascar remind us of the Chinese and of the people on the islands of the East Indies..

On the coast the air is hot and damp, for we are in the torrid zone and in the path of the trade winds, which blow in, full of moisture, from the Indian Ocean. Most of the rain falls on the eastern slopes of the mountain ranges, and west of the highlands there are brown grassy areas very different from the green jungle forests in the east.

How green the rice fields are! Every village is surrounded by them and by garden patches where manioc is growing. Manioc is used by the natives for making flour, and some is sent to France for the manufacture of tapioca. What was said about manioc on page 180?

We will take the train which runs from Tamatave on the coast to Tananarivo, the capital. From the car windows we see large fields of cotton and big coffee plantations. Farther on we run so near a grove of cacao trees that we can see the big yellowish-brown fruit which contains the cocoa beans hanging from the trunks and limbs. Once in a while we catch sight of fields of sugar cane and tobacco, and here and there we see people at work on clove plantations, such as we saw in Zanzibar.

Off in the forests we might find some natives collecting the pods from the vanilla vine, gathering the milky juice of the rubber plant, or cutting the leaves of a kind of palm tree to obtain the fiber called raffia. Have you ever made any baskets from raffia fiber?

Near some of the villages we see women at work in fields where lima beans are growing. Later they will shell the beans and sell them to the trader, who comes to the village to buy them. In the southwestern part of the island we should see larger fields of beans and greater quantities of them being shelled in the villages. During the rainy season the rivers in this part of Madagascar rush down the steep slopes of the mountains, overflow their banks, and spread out over the fields, leaving a rich coating of soil behind as the water subsides. After the rains are over, the natives, who have been tending their cattle on the hillsides during the wet months, come down to the lower lands and plant their beans. At the harvest time they pick the pods, shell the beans, and pack them in raffia baskets. The women hang a basket at either end of a bamboo pole balanced across their shoulders, and start out on a walk of perhaps several miles to the nearest trader's station.

Farther up the slopes, where the air is cooler and drier, are pasture lands where cattle, sheep, and goats are feeding. Many hides and skins are exported from Madagascar, and there are some establishments here for preparing canned, salted, and frozen meats. Canned beef from Madagascar has appeared on the shelves in our grocery stores, and Madagascar hides and skins are used in our shoe factories. You may be sure that some of the cotton cloth in which the people on the island are dressed came from our mills. They use also petroleum, machinery, and tools from the United States.

Another product which we import from Madagascar is graphite. When you studied Asia (see Allen's "Asia") do you remember reading about the production of graphite in Ceylon and its importance in making lubricating greases and stove blacking? Mixed with fine clay it forms the lead in your pencils. Formerly Ceylon produced nearly all the graphite used in the world. Now the mineral is worked in several other places, Madagascar among them. The graphite here is found near the surface and can be worked more cheaply than in deep mines.

As we approach Tananarivo the villages grow larger and more numerous. Green rice fields lie in every valley, and grassy pastures on every hillside. The capital stands on a rocky hill, and the rows of houses rise one above another. Topping all are the roofs of the government buildings. Some of the slopes are too steep for streets, and stone stairways have been built instead. These cross fine streets which run around the hill.

Long before the French took control of Madagascar, Tananarivo was the principal village of the Hovas, the chief tribe of the island. They conquered other tribes and built their capital here in the highlands, with their palace on its highest point. The pleasant, modern capital city of today is very different from the old native city.

SUGGESTIONS FOR STUDY

I

1. People and animals of Madagascar.

2. Improvements made by the French.

3. Climate and surface.

4. Products of Madagascar.

5. Tananarivo, the capital.

II

1. How does the population of Madagascar compare with that of New York City (see Appendix, pages 500 and 504)?

2. What islands of the world are larger than Madagascar (see Appendix, page 505)?

3. Why does more rain fall on the eastern side of the island than in the western part?

4. What is said of graphite and diamonds on page 112?

5. What facts have you found in the chapter which will help you in solving the problem on Madagascar given on page 397?

III

REVIEW OF THE FRENCH POSSESSIONS

1. Since studying the French possessions what problems have you solved concerning them?

2. In what ways do you think that the people are better off than they were before they came under the control of France?

3. With which colonies do you connect the following: camels and caravans, esparto, phosphates, vineyards, peanuts, olive oil, sponges, mahogany, grain, dates, Roman ruins, Berbers, Kabyles?

4. Where is there an internationalized zone? What were some of the reasons for internationalizing this area?

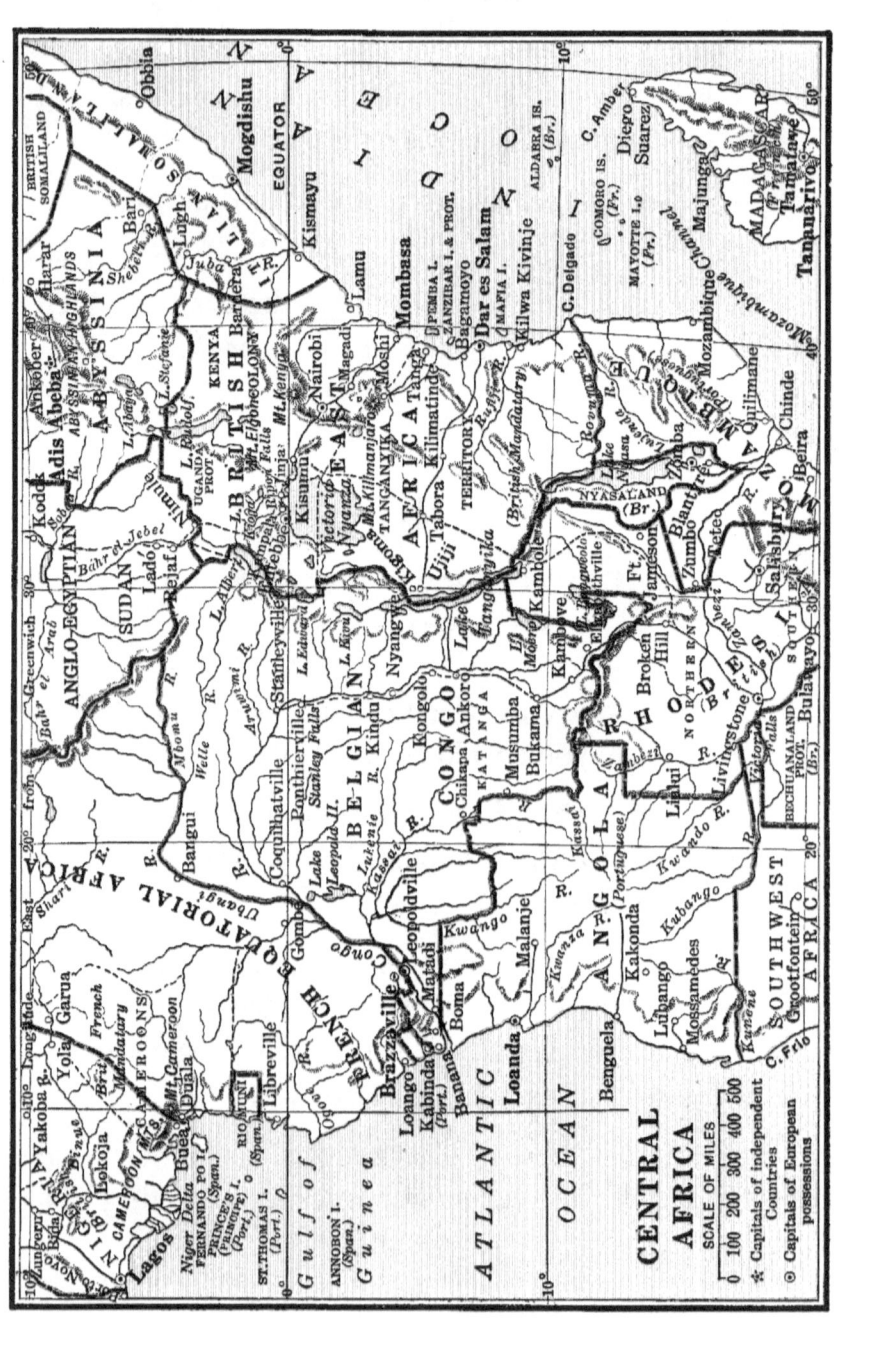

CHAPTER XXI

A HOT JOURNEY THROUGH BELGIAN CONGO

Our next trip will take us into the Belgian Congo in the valley of the Congo River. This great river basin is surrounded on all sides by higher plateaus and mountains. On the east are lofty highlands from ten to fifteen thousand feet high; on the south are grassy plateaus; on the north a still lower watershed separates the branches of the Nile and the Congo; and on the west is the rugged plateau through which the river has cut its way to the sea (see regional map on the opposite page).

The higher regions around the Congo Basin are cooler and healthier than the lowlands. In the east especially there are splendid pasture lands where, in the future, prosperous farms and ranches will furnish fresh meat, milk, and butter to many parts of the colony.

If we could read the story of the Congo Basin in Nature's storybook, we should learn that long, long ages ago this great area was filled with an enormous lake about six times the size of our Great Lakes. After many centuries, and perhaps helped by some volcanic eruption, the waters of this inland sea broke through the highland on the west, and a great river flowed out to the Atlantic, cutting its path deeper and deeper as the centuries passed, until, in time, the basin was drained of its water. This river was the Congo, one of the greatest waterways of the world. Its basin is half as large as the United States, and on the rivers which drain it we might sail more than half the distance around the world. In canoes and steam launches we could travel twice as far.

Where the Congo has cut its way through the rocky highlands, falls and rapids occur. Those in the western plateau are less than a hundred miles from the ocean. No boats can navigate the river here, and thus for years explorers were kept out of the heart of Africa. Today a railroad two hundred and fifty miles long runs around

Figure 108. Here you get a glimpse of the Congo River at Stanley Falls. In the foreground you see the fish pounds and nets of the natives.

the rapids from Matadi to Leopoldville (see map on page 290).

From Leopoldville the great, muddy, forest-bordered stream, several miles wide, is navigable for about twelve hundred miles to Stanley Falls. Here the river has cut its way through some of the eastern highlands, and navigation is again interrupted by several stretches of rapids and falls. Above Stanley Falls steamers built for shallow waters can sail several hundred miles farther.

If you were coming to this part of Africa from some European port, you would probably stop at Banana. It has one of the best harbors on the coast of West Africa, and for this reason has grown to be a port of considerable importance. There are large warehouses near the water and many vessels at the wharves. In our journey through the country we shall find out what goods are contained in the bags, barrels, and bales which are being loaded here.

The real entrance to the Congo River is at Boma, the capital of Belgian Congo. Here lives the governor general, who represents the king of Belgium and who has charge of this colony, which is about a third as large as the United States.

What a change has come to Africa since the time when Boma was the center of the slave trade of the region, when men and women were taken from their homes in the interior, loaded with ivory tusks, and marched in gangs to the port, where they were put on ships and sent far over the water to work in cotton fields or on sugar plantations! Now the Belgian government has built many miles of road and railroad in the colony, established steamer traffic on the rivers, set up radio stations, and started airplane service to carry mail across the country. Boma is the headquarters of a civilized government and the home of consuls from different nations, who have stopped the slave trade, punished the cannibal tribes who used to cook and eat the captives taken in tribal wars, forbidden other cruel customs, and sent out missionaries to teach the natives who live in this part of Africa better ways of life.

In the section of Boma where the Europeans live we should hardly know that we were in Africa except for the tropical heat. The government headquarters are well built, the homes of the Europeans are pleasant, the streets are well laid out and cared for, and the water, lights, and other conveniences are as well arranged as in many cities and towns in Europe and America.

The farther up the Congo River we go, the more wonderful it seems to us. In places it is so wide that we see no shores on either side, and it seems as if we were sailing on an island-dotted lake. The tropical forest borders the river on either side. In one of his descriptions of Central Africa, Henry M. Stanley, the explorer, tells us to imagine this area crowded with great trees from one to five feet in diameter and two hundred feet high, with their thick, glossy foliage so interlaced that the hot, glaring sun of the tropics is quite shut out. Each tree is lashed to the others by numberless vine cables, ranging from the tender threadlike creeper to the thickness of a big cable on a battleship.

Beneath the thick shade is the impenetrable undergrowth, appearing so thick and firm that one fancies that he could travel on it more easily than through it. Imagine the forks of each tree crowded with little conservatories of orchids and ferns, and the great horizontal limbs burdened with big gray-green lichens. Drooping growths of air plants, with their hosts of tendrils, swing ceaselessly about. Here and there are great, swaying walls of vines covered with flowers, on which the wild bees hum, the fierce wasps dart, and the brilliant butterflies sail in myriads.

Let the ground, Stanley tells us, be moist and black like rich hothouse soil, let the vines be of the greenest, and the wrinkled bark of the giant trees be of the grayest. Let the air be hot; let the murmur of the insects above, below, and around be heard, indicative of the seething life that exists in the hot, damp shades. Then imagine yourself dazed and mazed in this weird shadow land and marching from dawn till dark in a perpetual duskiness, lit at rare intervals by a little ray of sunlight, and you have a dim idea of the great jungle forest of Africa.

Figure 109. Imagine yourself walking through this forest path shut in on either side by the green wall of the jungle forest.

We must try to imagine this great forest tract peopled with tribes of natives dwelling in villages from ten to thirty miles apart, in ignorance of any world but their own. Of course today many of these Africans have seen and worked for foreigners, but there are even now many miles of forest where no foreigner has ever trod and hundreds of villages which no European has ever visited.

In traveling through Central Africa we must keep all clothing and other articles in metal cases, for the white ants will destroy anything made of fiber or wood. Railroad sleepers and telephone poles must be of iron if they are to last any length of time. There are big red ants which bite and sting; there are small black ants which cover food if it is not well protected; there are ants which build nests a foot or two high over which we may stumble in the dusky paths; and there are others which build their hills from fifteen to twenty feet high or even more.

Figure 110. Judging from the height of the people how tall do you think this ant hill is?

We hope that we may not encounter the driver ants. They move in great swarms from place to place in regular beaten tracks like little roads. They eat everything in their path. Natives desert their homes when they hear of the approach of an army of driver ants, and any insects or mice or reptiles which do not get out of their way are quickly eaten. Even the larger animals, such as elephants, lions, and leopards, give them a wide berth.

Another pest is the tsetse fly. The bite of one variety poisons horses and cattle, and none can be kept or raised where this is found. Another variety is responsible for the scourge of sleeping sickness among the people.

In the eastern sections of the Belgian Congo the people look as much like Arabs as they do like blacks. They dress like Arabs, wear the Arab turban on their heads, and are followers of Mohammed. For centuries this part of Africa has been under the influence of people from Arabia, who controlled the slave traffic and the ivory trade.

Have you ever read about the little people, the pygmies, whom the explorers found living here in Central Africa? Many of the women are less than four feet in height, and the men are but little taller. They live in huts made of boughs stuck into the ground, bent over, and tied together at the top. They eat the flesh of animals, the wild honey from the woods, the fungi which grow in the damp forests, and the seeds and roots of plants. They gather bananas from the trees and use the oil of the palm nut. They dig pitfalls and set traps to catch the wild animals and shoot them with poisoned arrows. Though the pygmies are so small, they do not hesitate to attack the elephant, largest of animals. They are wonderfully quick with their weapons and can shoot two or three arrows from their bow before the first one falls to the ground.

In some of the villages of the Belgian Congo we shall find the natives living in round houses with thatched roofs. In other settlements the houses are square; in others, oblong. We shall see villages of grass huts with nearly flat roofs. We shall find houses raised on piles, and others squat on the ground, with earth floors. In one part of the country the people live in caves hollowed out of the rocks. Some tribes build their houses of clay, some of bark, and some of poles. In one section the houses are built on immense ant hills which have been leveled off.

Figure 111. The worker is making runs in the bark of the rubber tree so that the juice will flow down to the cup which he will hang to catch it.

The villages on the river are inclosed on all sides save one by the green wall of the forest. Narrow, winding paths lead off through the forest to other villages far away from any stream. In many parts of Central Africa such paths are the only highways, and they have been worn hard by the barefooted natives, who have traveled over them for centuries.

Here come some men through one of these paths to the river village. They walk in single file, each one carrying a heavy bundle on his back. They are bringing palm nuts, ivory, rubber, peanuts, gum copal, and other products of the region to the trader at the village.

In the chapter on Sierra Leone you read about the gathering of gum copal in that section of Africa (see page 178). This gum is a very important product of the Belgian Congo also. The natives pack the copal into strong baskets which the women have made from some forest fiber, and if their village is far from a stream they swing the heavy loads onto their backs and trudge away through the path on a journey of perhaps several days. Do you suppose that the varnish on your schoolroom furniture was made from African copal?

Gum copal is only one of the many products which in the future will come in increasing quantities from tropical regions. We use today a large quantity of the splendid hard woods which tropical forests yield, but there are still many other varieties just as fine in quality which are not known commercially. Besides lumber there are other forest products, such as saps, gums, seeds, fruits, roots, leaves, and bark, of whose value and uses we know little or nothing. Some day large amounts of these will be used in drugs and medicines, in the fine arts, and in manufacturing. Much exploration must yet be done, and scientists must experiment with many products to find their uses. I wonder if any child who reads this book will some day explore the tropical forests of South America or Africa, or experiment in a laboratory with the products from these regions until he or she finally gives to the world some new and useful substance.

There has been a great change in recent years in the rubber industry of the world. Formerly all the rubber we used came from the forests of Brazil and the vines in the jungles of Africa. It took a great deal of time to collect this wild rubber, trees and vines were killed by careless tapping, and the distance between the source of supply and the nearest stream or station became so great that rubber grew more and more expensive.

With the introduction of automobiles and the increased use of electricity the demand for rubber

Figure 112. This is a rubber plantation in Central Africa. What advantages are there in cultivating rubber trees on a plantation over collecting the juice from wild trees in the forest?

became so great that it could not be supplied from the wild plants, and men began planting rubber trees on large plantations. Millions are cultivated in southern Asia and the East Indies, and today most of the world's supply comes from these countries.

The forests of Brazil still supply considerable quantities of rubber, and native gatherers still collect enough juice from the trees and vines in the Congo to make rubber an important export. Rubber plantations have been started here and in other parts of tropical Africa and will prove of increasing value as the years go by.

Figure 113. These natives are boiling the juice or latex to cause the rubber to harden.

Among the newer industries of the Belgian Congo is the cultivation of cocoa. Europeans have started many plantations, which produce so many beans that they form one of the four chief exports. Rubber, palm nuts and oil, and copal are the other three.

Figure 114. These workers are carrying rolls of rubber from the plantation down to the coast to be shipped away.

Many natives of the Belgian Congo work in cotton fields, such as we have in our Southern states. You have read descriptions of our cotton fields, of the fluffy, white bolls of fiber, of the pickers, and of the ginning mills and oil mills where the seeds are extracted from the fiber and crushed for the oil which they contain (see Allen's "North America" and Allen's "United States").

There are parts of the Belgian Congo where we might see similar scenes. The Belgian government has started several experimental plantations, and some of the natives grow cotton on their farms. As the years go by and more roads and railroads open up the country, cotton will be one of the important crops.

See those piles of palm nuts which the men have brought in from the forest. In scores of villages here the women make the oil and shell the kernels as they do in West Africa (see pages 156-160). Then the men take them to the station on the river and sell them to the trader there.

Let us follow some of the natives who have come to the river station back to their village homes and see how they live. They treat us kindly and hospitably and offer us the best that their modest homes afford. The grass-thatched houses of the village are arranged on either side of an open space like a street, which, with the passing of many feet, has been trodden free of grass. The chief's house is situated at the head of the street and is larger than the others. A woman in one of the low doorways beckons us to enter.

There is little furniture in the hut. A mat made of leaves or fibers spread over some smooth logs forms the bed. Around the room are jars for holding water, some made of clay and some of fiber, so closely woven that they are water-tight. There are baskets for carrying things to and from the market and the garden patches. We see several dishes made from gourd shells. These vegetables are somewhat like pumpkins, with smoother, harder shells. They are used for bowls, drinking cups, and other purposes. These gourd shells, a few wooden or earthenware plates and dishes, and one or two knives for cutting up meat make up the kitchen equipment. A stool or two, mere sections of solid tree trunks, are the only chairs. The natives seldom use them, as they usually sit on the ground. The smoke from the open fire burning on the earth floor makes things dirty, but it is useful in keeping away the mosquitoes.

The woman who invited us to enter her hut has just returned from the stream close by, where she filled her water jars, exchanged the news and gossip of the village with her neighbors, and had a bath in the warm water.

The women plant and cultivate the patches of rice and corn, the beans and peas, the peanuts, the sugar cane, and the manioc plants. They use no fertilizer, and when the soil in one place becomes exhausted they clear another place close by and plant their little gardens there.

They have few tools to work with except a short-handled hoe and a two-pronged rake, which the village blacksmith made. The blacksmith is a busy man, and his work is of great importance to the people. He makes the hoes, knives, axes, spearheads, hooks for catching crocodiles, lances for killing hippopotamuses, and many other articles which the people need. Some of the tribes who live in the parts of Central Africa where foreigners have traveled use tools brought from European countries. In such villages the blacksmith's work has become less important.

See that woman squatting over a little open fire in front of her hut. She has mixed some manioc flour with water and kneaded it into a stiff dough. Now she breaks off a piece of the dough, rolls it up in a ball, wraps it in a banana leaf, and puts it into her iron kettle to boil. Another woman is baking some manioc bread in the hot ashes. Among some tribes the dough is fried in palm oil or even eaten raw. We sample some of the bread; but it has a sour, gluey taste that we do not like. But perhaps Lelo and Kumbi and Koso and other African boys and girls would not like some of our food any better than we like theirs.

When the sun gets low the women begin to prepare the food for the chief meal of the day. They have brought the firewood from the forest in baskets on their backs. The corn has been ground between two stones, and the manioc root has been made into flour. Perhaps some of the women may boil some of the manioc leaves for a vegetable, for they are as tender as spinach.

The men may bring home with them some fish which they have caught. While they were in the woods they may have heard the call of the honey bird and followed it to a "bee tree," where they found a nest. They know how to smoke out the bees with a smudge fire and get the honey. If they have killed an antelope or a monkey, they will be sure of meat for supper. When they kill an elephant there is great rejoicing, for its ivory tusks are very valuable and its flesh will furnish food for some days.

See the little child with her large dark eyes. When she was a small baby she spent her time riding on her mother's hip. When her mother was at work in the field Lelo slept close by in the shade of a tree. When she is a little older she will have a doll made of a stick, a root, or a corncob. She will tie it on her hip with a piece of cloth, so that the doll may ride as comfortably as Lelo herself used to ride on her mother's side. When her baby is sleeping Lelo will take the little basket which her mother has given her and fill it with twigs and carry it on her back just as her mother carries her firewood basket. Perhaps she will play "make believe grown-up," as you have often done, and will carry her tiny sticks of firewood to her little make-believe hut and cook a make-believe dinner over a make-believe fire.

The boys have other games. They often have sham fights, using wooden knives and basket-work shields which they have made. When quite young the boys and girls learn a great deal about the deep forest in which they live. They know the names and habits of many of the animals and birds and can pick out the trees and vines which yield good fibers and dyes and medicines.

Figure 115. This is a native village in the Belgian Congo. What other kinds of villages are spoken of on page 298?

Our visit to the native village has been interesting, but the life there represents in many of its features the Congo of yesterday. We are more concerned with the Congo of today and tomorrow.

Besides its forests and grasslands and rich soils and other resources, the Belgian Congo has valuable mineral deposits which will grow more and more valuable as time goes on. The region contains deposits of lead, coal, tin, iron, petroleum, diamonds, ores from which radium can be obtained, and very rich beds of gold and copper.

When you started to visit the Belgian Congo you probably expected to see forests and jungles, native villages, piles of ivory, rolls of rubber, and bags of palm nuts. All these are very common there. But did you expect to see American locomotives, railroad rails, jitneys, motor trucks, listen to American banter and slang, watch American steam shovels biting out great mouthfuls of ore, smell the sulphurous fumes of copper smelters, eat griddlecakes covered with Vermont maple sirup, and see the stars and stripes of Old Glory waving

Figure 116. In many parts of Africa railroads are being opened, bridges constructed, and roads built. Notice here in the picture the thick jungle on either side of the track.

amid the trees of the jungle? Yet you may see, hear, smell, and taste all these things if you visit the diamond fields and copper mines of the colony.

Figure 117. In the ovens which you can see behind the freight car, coal is being changed into coke. This is used in smelting the copper from the Katanga mines. Why is coke better than coal?

We will sail several hundred miles up the Kassai River, a mighty branch of the Congo, and then journey through the forest to Chikapa, the American headquarters of the diamond industry (see map on page 290). We pinch ourselves to make sure that we are not dreaming. We hear Americans chattering and laughing; we see American women working in their neat little homes and American children playing on the shaded piazzas. Thousands of natives are employed here also. They have brought along their wives and children, and keep house in the villages which the company has built just as they did in their old homes in the forest.

The diamond mines of the Belgian Congo are very different from those in South Africa, where the precious stones are found deep in the hard blue clay pipes. There may be such pipes here in the Congo, but at present the diamonds are found near the surface of the earth in old creeks and river beds.

More important even than gold and diamonds is the copper in the district of Katanga. The deposits there are so rich that one writer calls Katanga a great copper mine. These mines are being developed by Englishmen and Belgians, but there are many skilled American workmen here as well as American trucks, tools, and machinery.

For a trip into this famous copper region we can go by river and rail the entire distance from Boma, at the mouth of the Congo River, to Elizabethville, the capital of the province of Katanga and the center of the copper industry.

Elizabethville was named for the queen of the Belgians. Not many years ago it was a part of the African jungle, and its inhabitants were chiefly ants which lived in hills from twenty to thirty feet high. It seems as if Aladdin must have been here with his magic-working lamp. Now people from England, Belgium, and America live in brick houses facing electrically lighted streets, ride in motor cars, and play tennis and golf and other games, all very much as they would in Europe and America.

Unless you prefer to go on a bicycle, we will go in an automobile to the mines. We will visit the Star of the

Congo, one of the most wonderful mines in the Katanga district, about eight miles from Elizabethville, and then go on to Kambove, a mountain of copper. The steam shovels rattle and bang as they bite great mouthfuls of the ore from the hillsides. The concentrating works, the smelters, the loaded cars, and the bustle and hustle make it very easy for us to imagine that we are in the copper regions of Montana or Arizona.

Iron and lime, both necessary for smelting, are found in the vicinity. The rivers furnish water power for generating electricity, and so rich are the mineral deposits that it seems as if the remark made by an official might be true when he said, "God made this country to produce copper." Hundreds of foreigners and thousands of natives are working in these mines, which are fast making the Belgian Congo one of the great copper-producing countries of the world.

SUGGESTIONS FOR STUDY

I

1. Situation and climate of the Belgian Congo.
2. The Congo River and its basin.
3. Banana and Boma.
4. The African forest.
5. Ants and tsetse flies.
6. People and villages.

7. Occupations and products.

8. Diamond mining.

9. The Katanga district and copper.

II

1. From the description given on pages 294 and 295 describe the tropical forest through which the Congo River flows.

2. What grasslands border the tropical forest of Africa? of South America (see Allen's "South America")?

3. Tell Nature's story of the Congo Basin.

4. Compare the area of Belgium with that of her colony in Africa (see Appendix, page 500). How many people on the average live on each square mile in Belgium? in the Belgian Congo? Account for the difference.

5. Of what future importance do you think that the Belgian Congo will be to the world?

6. How has the Belgian government helped to develop the colony?

7. What changes have taken place in rubber production?

8. What rivers are longer than the Congo (see Appendix, page 506)?

9. For whom was Leopoldville named? Stanleyville?

III

Make a list of the places mentioned in this chapter. Arrange them by countries, cities, rivers, mountains, etc. From the list select those places which you think are so important that you should always be able to locate them and know something about them.

CHAPTER XXII

ITALIAN AFRICA AND A TRIP THROUGH LIBYA

ITALY is not a great colonizing nation and she has few possessions scattered throughout the world. Her colonies consist chiefly of islands in the Mediterranean and three divisions of Africa, the country of Libya, formerly known as Tripoli, in the north, and Eritrea and Italian Somaliland in the east. Of these three Libya is by far the largest and the most important.

The area of the Italian colonies in Africa is small when compared with that of the British and French possessions. These colonies also are among the thinly peopled parts of the continent. What you will read about them will help you to understand why so few people live in them.

The Arabs have described Libya as a land with her feet in the blue Mediterranean, her head in the fire of heaven, and her back against the silence of the Sahara. This is a true though fanciful way of describing the surface of the country. Along the Mediterranean shores lies a low coastal plain. Near its southern edge hills and mountains lift their heads toward the blazing sun, while still farther south stretches the great, silent desert, traversed only by caravans and peopled only in the oases.

Notice on the map on page 219 how the coast of Africa bends southward along the shores of Libya. You can see that because of this bend the distance from the city of Tripoli across the great desert is shorter than from any other of the Mediterranean seaports. For this reason the caravan trade of Tripoli has been important for centuries, and the city is often called the Gateway to the Sahara.

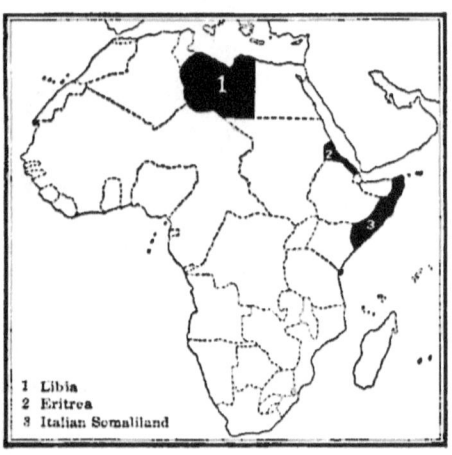

Figure 118. Italian possessions in Africa. What are the names of the Italian possessions? Which one is the largest? Which one borders on the Red Sea? Where is the Somali coast? What nations control it?

On one side of Tripoli, far out beyond the fringe of palm trees, stretches the yellow desert; on the other side lies the blue Mediterranean. Between the desert and the coast is the city, glistening white in the bright sunshine, with green, feathery palms casting dark shadows on the flat roofs.

The flags of the different nations flying from the

consulate buildings make a touch of color in the white picture. Among them we see the Stars and Stripes. Even in this distant region we are not out of touch with our homeland. Our consul here will give us much information about the country and will help us if we get into any trouble.

In one section of the city are the modern houses where the Europeans live. In the old, native city many of the narrow streets are roofed with matting or spanned with arches. These arches help to support the walls on either side and also, like the matting, give shade from the hot sun. Here comes a line of loaded camels, and there go some little donkeys covered with huge panniers bulging out on either side. In and out of the shadows we watch the people moving, turbaned Moors, camel men from the desert, water carriers, beggars, and strong native porters with great bales and boxes on their backs. On certain days of the week we might see many women, hidden under long cloaks and veils, on their way to the baths. Each one is accompanied by a native woman, who carries on her head a basket filled with soaps, oils, and perfumes.

The harbor of Tripoli is dotted with vessels, which fly the flags of many nations. Near the wharves are the smaller fishing craft and the boats of the Greek sponge gatherers.

The three most important industries of Libya are esparto picking and shipping, the caravan trade, and sponge gathering. Someone has said that the esparto picker works in his waving sea of grass, the caravan driver on his shifting sea of sand, and the sponge gatherer on his restless sea of brine.

See the quantities of sponges! They are stored in the warehouses, piled on the wharves, tied in long strings to the rigging of boats, and packed in boxes on the vessels.

Many of the sponges gathered in the Mediterranean Sea come from waters near Libya. If we sail out a few miles, we shall probably find the Greek sponge fleet at work. Nearer the shore we may happen to see some men in small boats pulling up sponges with a sort of long-handled fork, but many more are obtained in deeper waters by divers.

Most of the divers wear diving suits and stay down in the water for an hour or two, being supplied with fresh air by the men at the pumps on the ship. With heavy weights on his feet a diver sinks through the water until he reaches the bottom of the sea. Then he walks slowly along until he locates a colony of sponges, from which he gathers the best ones. When his bag is full he signals to be pulled up. The sailors empty the bag and tread out the ooze and slime with their bare feet. Then they string the sponges on lines and hang them over the ship's side, where they trail in the water overnight. The bits of shell and rock which are still in them are beaten out with sticks, and the sponges are again well soaked in the sea.

Some of the sponges are taken to Tripoli, and some go to the Greek islands in the Mediterranean, where the people know how to prepare them and put them into condition for European markets.

Some of the great warehouses in Tripoli are full of esparto, for this industry is as important here in Libya as in the French possessions farther west (see pages 254-255 and 275).

We are fortunate to get the permission of an English merchant in Tripoli to visit his warehouse. As we enter, the odor is like that of a well-filled hay barn. Could you walk as straight as those men do with such a huge bundle balanced on your head? They are carrying the bundles of esparto to the baling machine. This presses the leaves into a compact mass, around which it clamps strong iron bands. The bales are stored with others until they are loaded on a vessel which will carry them to an English port. From here they are taken to English mills, where the leaves are put through the processes necessary to convert them into paper.

As we turn to leave the warehouse we find the great yard full of camels loaded with esparto. The leaves are stuffed into coarse-meshed rope bags made of esparto fiber. These bags are twelve feet long and four feet wide, and one of them full of esparto leaves makes a big load.

On the beach, a little way out of Tripoli, are the great markets. Quantities of fruit, grain, vegetables, and other articles have been brought here by caravans of donkeys and camels, many of which carried not only the bags of grain or other products but their owner as well. The shepherds who have driven their flocks in from distant pastures are gray with the dust raised by the scores of little hoofs.

Wandering in and out among the piles of goods are blacks, Arab farmers from the oases, sunburned caravan drivers, camel raisers from the esparto-covered plateau, Jews with long beards, Turks with red fezzes on their heads, and Italians in European dress.

Figure 119. We should think this a very crude motion-picture machine, but the Arab looking at the pictures thinks it is very wonderful.

As in other markets which we have visited, the place swarms with story-tellers, beggars, snake charmers, water carriers, and venders of candy, fruit, and a score of other things. Here the wool merchants are hanging up skeins of wool fresh from the dye pots; there the carpet weavers are working at their looms. The leather workers are making dainty slippers and fine saddles and bridles. The silversmith and goldsmith are hammering out articles of jewelry, and the stalls of the perfume sellers scent the air around.

In the animal market there are goats and sheep, donkeys and mules, and horses and camels, big and little, swift and slow, fat and lean. Buyers and sellers walk among them, bargaining and haggling until a price is reached which is satisfactory to both.

The camel market is very large, for many caravans are fitted out here. If you walk among the camels which are lying down, take care that one does not bite you, for their jaws are strong and their teeth are sharp. If the camels are standing, you must watch both "heads and tails," for an ugly camel will kick as well as bite.

Kipling says of the camel, "He's a devil an' a ostrich an' a orphan child in one." In the narrow streets it gives no warning of its approach, and suddenly its scornful face with its curling underlip is thrust over your shoulder. You do not stop to argue with it as to the right of way, but jump hastily aside.

On the map on page 220 you can find the caravan routes that lead south from Tripoli across the desert. Enormous wealth has been carried over these desert routes between Tripoli and the Sudan. Sometimes a caravan loaded with hundreds of thousands of dollars' worth of goods of some Tripoli merchant disappears into the desert. Nothing is heard from it for months, perhaps even for years. Even the owner, who has risked everything he owned in the venture, gives up all hope of its return. Finally the thin, weary camels and the tired, sunburned drivers are sighted, and hundreds of people

Figure 120. These camels were raised on an oasis far away and have been brought to the market at this oasis to be sold.

go out to meet them, to celebrate their return, and to hear of the dangers which they have encountered in their long, hard journey across the desert.

The larger caravans sometimes consist of ten thousand camels, and their size is often increased by smaller caravans whose leaders feel safer from desert thieves if they travel in company with a larger band. After months of travel the caravan arrives at Kuka on Lake Chad. Here the camels must feed and rest for weeks before they can begin the homeward journey, while the goods must be disposed of and others bought to be carried north. Among these are ostrich plumes, skins of wild animals, goatskins from the dye pits of Kano, tusks of ivory, gold from the sands of tropical rivers, wax from the Sudan forests, and many gums and nuts and seeds.

Many camels die on such a long journey; desert thieves may attack the caravan, stampede some of the camels, kill the drivers, and steal the goods; some wells may be found with no water; a sand storm may hide every sign of the trail and nearly bury animals and men, but in spite of these and other dangers the caravan creeps on over the burning wastes, day by day and week by week lessening the distance between them and the busy city for which they are bound.

Surely these caravan drivers are worthy of our respect. Faithful to their trust, honest when they have pledged their word, brave in the face of many dangers, tireless in their endurance, these white-robed Arabs

Figure 121. This is an oasis. You can see flat-topped mud houses and the thousands of palm trees around the village. Of what use are these palms to the natives?

have carried on for centuries a great commerce in this region and have kept alive a knowledge of the needs of the people of the Sudan.

Today the European nations are reaching the Sudanese by other routes (see page 163). Fewer large caravans like the one described now travel over the desert, and the great inland trade of Tripoli is slowly but surely decreasing.

On the oases in southern Libya are representatives of every tribe from the Mediterranean to Lake Chad and from the Atlantic to the Red Sea. Most of the people, however, are Arabs, Tuaregs, and Berbers. They live in palm-leaf huts and spend their time in caring for their olive and fig trees and their almond groves. They raise a little wheat and barley in the cooler season and endure as best they can the terrific heat of the hotter months.

The Tuaregs are an offshoot of the liberty-loving Berbers. When the conquerors overran the country the Berbers took to the mountains in order to maintain their independence. For the same reason the Tuaregs retreated into the desert. Here they have built their towns under the shadow of the palms on the oases. In parts of the desert every traveler through their territory must pay a tax to these lords of the sand. Every southbound caravan from Tripoli passes through territory ruled by the Tuaregs, and many a caravan has been looted of its wealth, especially if the Arab sheik who led it refused to pay tribute.

On the other hand, a Tuareg is often found in charge of a caravan, and woe be to anyone who dares to attack it. The leader has made his compact with the owner over the bread and salt, and the life and property of one who has eaten with a Tuareg is absolutely safe from harm while the compact lasts. This is the law of the desert.

The Bedawi are more peaceful inhabitants of the desert. Near some oasis where there is plenty of water and grass they pitch their tents, sow their corn, and remain until they harvest it. When the grass and water give out, the Bedawi strike their tents and move to another oasis. When they camp near a city or town they trade the articles which they make—the baskets, the pottery, the homespun cloth for their long robes, and the coarser material for the tents—for the things which they need in their wandering life.

The oases of Ghadames, Ghat, and Murzuk (see map on page 219) have been very important places in the history of the caravan trade, and their chief business for centuries has been in caring for the men and animals who cross the great desert. At each of these places and at other oases there are large fonduks, where caravans may be accommodated. A fonduk is a rectangular building surrounding an open space. The entrance from the outside is protected by a heavy door, which is closed and barred at night. Enormous wealth has often been stored in the fonduks, while the hundreds of camels which carried it fed in the pastures on the borders of the oasis or feasted on straw and dates in the inclosure.

During the centuries that Libya was under the control of Turkey little or nothing was done to increase products, to improve agriculture, to extend irrigation, to develop industries, or to foster trade. The Italians are doing many things which will add to the health, the beauty, and the importance of the city of Tripoli and will benefit the country. New buildings, new streets, a new European quarter, a better water supply and drainage system, larger docks and wharves, large warehouses, and modern machinery for loading and unloading ships are changing Tripoli as they have changed the cities in the colonies of other nations.

Figure 122. This looks up-to-date, doesn't it, even if it is Africa? This tractor was made in the United States.

There are as yet few railroads in Libya. Short ones connect Tripoli with other coast towns and extend a little way into the interior. Gradually, however, they will follow the telegraph lines to the oases, suitable roads

ITALIAN AFRICA AND LIBYA

for motor trucks will be built, new wells will enlarge the area where crops can be produced, and more and better animals will be raised on the pasture lands.

Our interest in the country of Libya began soon after our Revolutionary War. Libya, like the other Barbary States, was a stronghold of pirates who were working havoc with the commerce of our new little republic. Some of our ships were captured, and the officers and sailors cruelly treated. In 1804 we sent a fleet to Tripoli to blockade the harbor and bombard the city. The pasha was forced to pay for some of the damage which his pirates had done to our fleet and to sign a treaty of peace. Eleven years later, in 1815, Lieutenant Decatur was sent to Algeria on account of her raids on our vessels.

Our relations today with Libya are friendly ones. Our trade is less important than it is with the other Barbary States; but as the country develops and new ways take the place of old methods of work, we shall find that the people of Libya will use more and more of our tools and implements and other manufactures.

SUGGESTIONS FOR STUDY

I

1. Surface and coast line.
2. The city of Tripoli.
3. The sponge industry.

4. Gathering and shipping esparto.

5. The caravan trade.

6. Southern Libya and its oases.

7. Development of Libya.

II

1. Name the four Barbary States. What nations control them? What are the chief cities of each? Which country is the most developed?

2. Into what surface divisions do the Atlas Mountains divide this region? How has the surface affected the occupations of the people?

3. Who are the people of the Barbary States?

4. Sketch a map to show the chief caravan routes across the Sahara. Write the names of the important places on these routes. What goods are carried over them?

5. Why is the caravan trade across the Sahara decreasing?

III

Make a list of the places mentioned in this chapter. Arrange them by countries, cities, rivers, mountains, etc. From the list select those places which you think are so important that you should always be able to locate them and know something about them.

CHAPTER XXIII

ERITREA AND THE SOMALI COAST

Eritrea

We shall make but a short visit to the Italian possessions in East Africa, for they are less important than many other divisions of the continent.

Eritrea is both hot and dry, and few crops can be raised without irrigation. Most of the people, however, do not care about raising large crops. They are content if they can find grass and water for their camels, oxen, sheep, and goats. These are their chief wealth and furnish them with meat and milk for food.

In the low, hot coast region there is very little rainfall, and few people live in this part of the country. The regional map preceding page 1 shows you that part of Eritrea is included in the Abyssinian Highlands. The climate here is pleasanter than on the coast, and the air is cool enough to chill the trade winds and cause them to drop some of their moisture, thus giving more rain than the coast lands receive.

Look again at the map, and you will see that Eritrea lies between northern Abyssinia and the sea. Therefore the trade of this part of inland Abyssinia passes through it. The caravans coming from Abyssinia to the border of Eritrea bring many tons of hides and skins, products of the herds of the Abyssinians. They bring, too, oil seeds and nuts from the forests, honey and wax which the natives have gathered from the bees' nests, and some grain which they have been able to raise on their little farms.

Figure 123. Much of the coast region of Eritrea is a desert. The man shown in the picture has been with his camel and donkeys into the interior to get brushwood for fuel.

At the border of Eritrea these products are loaded on motor trucks or slower ox wagons and brought over the roads which the Italian government has built through the colony to the railroad. This now extends from the coast to some distance beyond the capital,

Asmara, and it will not be long before it reaches the Abyssinian border and penetrates that country.

Goods are also carried to the railroad on the backs of mules and camels from those parts of Eritrea and Abyssinia where no roads have yet been built. Asmara is a center of this caravan trade, and many of the animals rest and feed here before they begin their homeward trip.

Many of the people of Eritrea are Abyssinians, and if we should follow the trucks and wagons or the pack animals back over the plateau, we should pass many of their odd little "toadstool" villages, which are described in Chapter XXVIII. In regions where there is rain enough for crops the villages are permanent ones. Many of the people of Eritrea, however, are nomads who follow the rains from place to place, driving their flocks and herds before them and carrying with them all their household goods. If you had to move several times a year and take with you, loaded on donkeys and camels, everything that you own, how much do you think that you should have to throw away?

We will take the train from Asmara to Massaua, the chief port of Eritrea and one of the most important shipping centers of the Red Sea. Though we are thousands of miles away from home, the steel rails over which we ride were made in a United States foundry. The trains which run over these rails carry to the people of Eritrea and Abyssinia many things, some of which have come from the United States. We send them hardware, macaroni, soap, cloth for their dresses, kerosene for their lamps, and galvanized-iron sheeting for their buildings.

At the docks of Massaua modern traveling cranes lift the freight from the holds of large ocean vessels and deposit it on the wharves. Besides these ocean-going ships, there are many coasting vessels here which carry freight through the Red Sea to Aden, where it is reloaded on vessels bound for England.

Those native boats with the colored sails have just come in from the pearl-fishing grounds. The shells which the divers bring up contain comparatively few pearls, but they are valuable for their beautiful colored lining of mother-of-pearl. This is an important export from Massaua, and several thousand dollars' worth comes each year to the United States. We use also considerable quantities of beeswax and gum arabic from both Eritrea and Abyssinia.

The vegetable-ivory nuts of which you read in the chapter on the Anglo-Egyptian Sudan (page 61) are found also in Eritrea, and many of the people find employment in gathering them. What are they used for?

Many of the natives of Eritrea are employed in the industries which have been mentioned, but far more of them spend their time in raising cattle, goats, sheep, mules, and camels. There are more sheep and goats raised than any other animals, but there are many thousand cattle also, mostly of the humpbacked breed. Their flesh makes good beef, and their hides are exported. Sheepskins and goatskins from the herds of the natives and also from Abyssinia make a valuable export. We buy some of these skins to use in our shoe factories. Do you suppose that the leather in your shoes came from the skin of some animal which fed in the pastures of Eritrea and was watched and tended and driven into the thorn-protected inclosure at night by some native boy or girl?

The Somali Coast

South of Eritrea lies the Somali coast, divided among the Italians, British, and French. On account of its shape this part of Africa is sometimes called the Eastern Horn. On the tip end of the horn is Cape Guardafui, the most easterly point of the continent. The face of this cape is a vertical wall of rock rising from the water for nearly a thousand feet. How high would your schoolhouse reach beside this great cliff?

Until we have rounded the cape we may have an unpleasant voyage, for on this part of the coast the winds are strong and the currents swift. Most of the coast is rock-bound and desolate, and we see few good harbors and few settlements along the shore.

Somaliland consists chiefly of a barren lowland near the coast, rising into a plateau in the interior. Much of the plateau is covered with a tall coarse grass. There are few trees, but there are thickets of thorn bush which the natives use for fences. Along the rivers there are dense beds of reeds twice as high as your heads. In these thickets and in the tall grasses hide many wild animals such as you saw in British East Africa. What are some of them?

We should find a trip into Somaliland very tiresome because of the hot desert belt along the coast. The only railroad runs from Jibuti in French Somaliland to the capital of Abyssinia (see map on page 68). In any other part of the country one must travel on muleback or by slow caravans. How should you like to ride all day, and day after day, with the temperature ranging around a hundred and ten degrees in the shade and more in the sunshine? In places the ground is covered with large boulders, and with thorny bushes which would tear our clothes and scratch our flesh. We should have to climb ranges of rugged, stony hills, traverse dry, gravelly river beds, and cross hot, parched plains.

On a trip inland we should pass villages surrounded by thorn fences inside of which are little huts covered with skins or with mats made of grass or bark; we should meet flocks of sheep and goats, and camels loaded with all the possessions of some Somali tribe who are making their way over the rocky trail toward some oasis which will furnish them grass and water; we should see caravans carrying ivory, bundles of hides and skins, bags of coffee, and gums and resins down to the coast. We might meet also native carriers with heavy packs on their backs and shoulders making their way to the coast, to some village from which the goods can be taken by caravan to the seaports, or to some station on the railroad. What seaports do you find in the three colonies of Somaliland (see map on page 68)?

The Somalis are fighters, and the men like nothing better than to make a raid on a neighboring tribe and drive off some of their animals. Conditions are slowly changing here, however, as they are in most parts of Africa, and some of the men today spend their time gathering gums, resins, and saps from the trees and shrubs. You have heard of myrrh, frankincense, and balm of Gilead. These and similar products useful in medicines, drugs, soaps, and perfumes are found in Somaliland.

Figure 124. From what you have read in the chapter what do you think these camels are carrying from the interior of Somaliland down to the coast?

The people on the grassy plateaus raise cattle, sheep, and goats, and, in parts of the country, camels. These people have no settled homes, but follow the rains to find food and water for their flocks and herds. The women do much of the hard work. They weave the mats with which their huts are covered and the cloth for their long loose garments. On the march they carry the heaviest loads. They tend the animals, prepare the food, and, where crops are raised, do the work in the fields.

Marco Polo, that famous traveler who in 1271 started from his home in Italy for China and other countries of the East, speaks of stopping at Mogdishu in Italian Somaliland and calls it a large city. Another writer in the fourteenth century describes the city as immense. Mogdishu is no longer a large, flourishing city. It has been but little developed and has few modern conveniences. The house of the Italian governor stands between two native villages, with their thickly clustered huts, while in and around the town are ruins which remind us of its great age.

The most fertile part of Italian Somaliland lies near the Juba River (see map on page 68). In its upper valley there are splendid pasture lands, and nearer the mouth

Figure 125. Salt making on the shores of the Red Sea. The mills which are shown in Figure 123 pump up the salt water into these ponds. The water evaporates in the hot sunshine, and men rake up the salt in piles.

there are fertile plains where many of the people live in settled homes and raise corn, rice, and cotton.

If we are to realize the importance of the Somali coast we must look, as we have done in other parts of Africa, to the future rather than to the past or the present. We must try to imagine the time when the cotton product of the Juba valley will be an important export to the manufacturing countries of Europe. We must think of the millions of cattle, sheep, and goats which will sometime feed on the grasses of the plateau, and of the greatly increased amounts of hides, skins, and meat which will be sent out of the country to thickly settled lands. The products of gums and resins will be increased also and used in a thousand ways to benefit mankind. Irrigation systems will be planned to provide for larger crops and a greater variety of products. Roads and railroads will be built, and as the years go by a larger proportion of the natives will engage in useful work and live in permanent homes.

You and I may not live to see the kind of country which all these changes will produce, for they will come slowly in Somaliland and other regions which are of small importance. But it is pleasant to think of the better conditions which will sometime make the life of the people who live in such places easier and more enjoyable, and their work of more benefit to the rest of the world.

SUGGESTIONS FOR STUDY

I

1. Position and climate of Eritrea.

2. People and villages in Eritrea.

3. The capital and seaport of Eritrea.

4. Products of Eritrea.

5. Cape Guardafui and the Somali coast.

6. Surface and climate of Somaliland.

7. Life and occupations in Somaliland.

8. Seaports of Somaliland.

9. A glimpse of the future.

II

1. What three nations control the Somaliland coast? Which colony is the largest? the smallest?

2. Through which colony in Somaliland are many products of Abyssinia carried? From what port on the Red Sea are they shipped?

3. How does Eritrea compare in size with the state in which you live?

4. On what waters will a vessel sail in going from Jibuti to Marseille? to London? What goods will such a vessel carry?

5. Many goods are taken on small vessels from Jibuti to the British port at the southern end of the Red Sea and there reloaded on ocean vessels bound for England. What is this port? Why is it important?

6. In what year did Marco Polo visit Mogdishu and find it a large, flourishing city? What were the conditions in America at that time?

7. Sketch the Eastern Horn of Africa. Show the colonies into which it is divided. Write in each one the name of the nation which controls it and the chief seaport. What is exported from these ports?

III

Make a list of the places mentioned in this chapter. Arrange them by countries, cities, rivers, mountains, etc. From the list select those places which you think are so important that you should always be able to locate them and know something about them.

IV

REVIEW OF THE ITALIAN POSSESSIONS

1. Compare the area of the Italian possessions in Africa with that of the British and French (see maps on pages 55, 188, and 314 and see also Appendix, pages 499 and 500).

AFRICA, AUSTRALIA, ISLANDS OF PACIFIC

2. Which Italian colony is located mostly in the temperate zone? Which lies partly in the Sahara Desert? Which is partly in the Abyssinian Highlands? Which is an outlet for the products of an inland country? Which one has esparto fields? Where is sponge fishing important?

3. Why has the city of Tripoli been such an important center for caravan trade? What goods are carried southward over the desert? What are taken northward from the Sudan? What trading centers in the Sudan may be reached by caravans from the north? Why is the caravan trade declining?

4. Why is Italian Somaliland a less important colony than Eritrea?

5. If you lived in Italian Africa should you prefer to be a Somali, a Tuareg, a Greek sponge diver, or a caravaneer? Write a description of your life as one of these people.

8. What interests has the United States in Italian Africa?

CHAPTER XXIV

ANGOLA, THE LARGEST COLONY OF PORTUGAL

Now let us take a trip through the African possessions of Portugal. This little European country, somewhat larger than the state of Maine, was once rich and powerful, famous for her explorers, who sailed on long voyages to all parts of the world, and proud of her colonies in every continent and ocean. The great country of Brazil was under her control, and many products from her possessions in the Eastern Hemisphere added to her wealth.

Portugal long since lost her colonies in the Western Hemisphere, and Brazil has been for years an independent republic. The Portuguese possessions in Africa and Asia cover an area about a third as large as the United States. Most of these colonies are in Africa.

Angola, in southwest Africa, is the largest Portuguese colony. Mozambique, on the eastern coast, is one of the oldest European colonies on the continent. Portuguese Guinea is a low, hot region, the delta plain of many small rivers which are connected with one another by smaller streams and shallow lagoons and which are useful for getting into the country, for there are no roads or railroads here. In Portuguese Guinea we should see natives gathering oil seeds and tapping the rubber trees and vines. Farther inland we should find them raising peanuts for export, cultivating rice and millet, and hunting the elephant for its ivory tusks. All these products are very similar to those which are produced in neighboring countries.

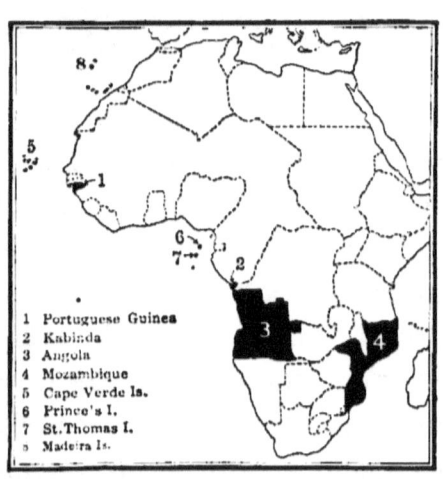

Figure 126.

Portuguese possessions in Africa. On page 500 of the Appendix find the area of the Portuguese possessions in Africa. With what state or states in our country do they compare in size?

The Portuguese were among the earliest explorers of Africa, and Angola is one of the oldest colonies on the west coast. Out of the four million people who live here, only about twelve thousand are light-skinned. Most of these are Portuguese. In years to come, when roads and railroads have opened up the cool, healthy plateau regions back of the low, hot coast lands, doubtless more Europeans will settle here and carry on farming and stock raising. Comparatively little has been done as yet in developing the industries of the colony, and Angola

ANGOLA

today is more backward than some of the younger colonies of European nations.

Let us study the regional map preceding page 1 and see what it tells us about Angola. You will notice that the country lies well within the torrid zone, that the northern part is in the lowland valley of the Congo River Basin, and that the northeastern portion stretches into the grassland area. These facts tell you that the climate and vegetation are much like the adjoining parts of the Belgian Congo. Picture the same damp, dense forests, the tangled jungles with their innumerable vines and creepers, the tall ferns, the many insects, the crocodiles on the banks of the streams, and the paths of the hippopotamuses through the thickets. Picture, too, the little native villages in the clearings and on the

Figure 127. In many parts of Africa bridges such as we have are unknown. The one in the picture is made of bamboo fastened together with strong fibers. No nails or hammers were used in its construction.

banks of the streams. As in other parts of West Africa, you might meet in the forest paths men bending under loads of palm nuts, palm oil, or rubber, or paddling their canoes loaded with these and other forest products down to the nearest trader.

For many years rubber has been the most important product of Angola, and it is still a very important export. Careless methods of smoking the rubber affect its quality, and ignorance of the best ways of tapping has killed many trees and vines. Each year the rubber gatherers have to go farther and farther away from paths and streams and traders' factories in order to obtain their supply. Some rubber plantations have been started in the colony; and in time these, and others which may be planted, will help to increase the rubber exports, for the soil and climate are well suited to this product.

The coastal plain around the old port of Loanda is very fertile. Millions of oil palms grow here, and large cotton and sugar plantations have been started. Notice on your map the river just south of Loanda. What is its name (see map on page 290)? It is a small river, but it has been of great use to traders in getting goods from the interior of the country to the seaport. Caravans of porters from native inland villages bring to the river loads of rubber, coffee, cotton, palm oil, tobacco, wax, ivory, nuts and gums, and hides and skins. These are taken down in boats to Loanda and there shipped to Europe. Many products are now carried on the railroad which leads from the interior down to the coast. Can you find this on the map?

The importance of Angola and its seaports is increased by the fact that the colony is a gateway to the Belgian Congo, and each year the railroads are helping to carry increasingly large quantities of freight in and out of that country.

About midway of the thousand-mile coast of Angola is the port of Benguela. Like Loanda the importance of this seaport is linked up with interior Africa. The shortest and easiest route between the Katanga copper district of the Belgian Congo and the ocean leads through Benguela, and the railroad which will connect these two regions will be one of the most important on the continent.

Not all the minerals which will pass over this railroad will come from the Belgian Congo. Within the borders of Angola copper, iron, petroleum, salt, and gold have already been found; and rich deposits of malachite, that rock of beautiful, mottled green, occur here also. Have you ever seen any table top, lamp base, paper weight, or other article made of malachite?

On the railroad trip inland from Benguela we realize more and more the great future value of Angola to Portugal and the world. The land grows higher, and the air correspondingly cooler. The rainfall here is light, for we are nearly on the border of the equatorial rain belt, and we are too far from the east coast of Africa to receive the moisture which the easterly trade winds bring in from the Indian Ocean. In the rainy season large quantities of water from the rivers which flow down the slopes from the plateau run to waste. The farmers use some of this for irrigation; and as settlers take up the land, more and more of it will be stored in reservoirs and used to water fields of growing crops.

We pass large fields of sugar cane and see other lands suitable to its growth. New mills for crushing the cane and extracting the juice are being built, and Portugal plans to depend on her African colonies in the future for a large amount of her sugar.

Cotton is another product which the Portuguese government is desirous of increasing, and in the villages through which we pass we see many fields of this valuable crop. The government is furnishing the natives with seed and is introducing cotton gins for extracting the seeds, and baling presses for the fiber.

Figure 128. This is Mossamedes, a town on the coast of Angola. Can you find it on the map? The large building is the house where the governor of this part of the colony lives.

ANGOLA

We have already read about the production of cotton in other parts of Africa, and from the soil and climate we know that some day cotton will be of very great importance here, even though in some colonies, as in Angola, the industry grows but slowly.

The train climbs from the low plain along the coast up through a hilly, rocky region to the higher plateau which occupies most of interior Angola. Here, because of the lack of rain, there are few forests, and we see instead wide areas covered with tall grass. You could easily get lost here, for the waving brown grass is taller than you are.

We see corn growing around nearly every village, for it is one of the principal articles of food. The women are hoeing it with little short-handled hoes which have blades only about a quarter as large as those which we use. With the use of modern methods and tools large quantities of corn might be cultivated on the plateau back of Benguela, for the climate is favorable and the soil somewhat like that of our prairies.

Farther up on the plateau the natives raise cattle and sheep. Sometimes they pay their taxes with these animals. The wool and hides and skins are sent to the manufacturing countries of Europe and America, and the meat is shipped to more populous parts of West Africa.

As we ride over the Angolan plateau we see some natives returning from an elephant hunt. They look happy, for they are bringing back some large tusks. The ivory is valuable, and the trader will give them a good price for it. With the money they will buy some bright-colored cotton cloth, some tools and dishes, and some beads or other ornaments for the people in their village.

Like rubber, ivory has long been a valuable product of Angola. The elephants have been hunted so ruthlessly for their tusks that their numbers have decreased, and the Portuguese have now made laws regulating their slaughter.

When the elephant hunters reach their village of grass thatched huts the people come out to welcome them. They dance and sing when they see the huge tusks. The men have brought back some of the elephant meat, and the women prepare a feast which will last all night. Everybody will eat so much that few if any of them will do any work for some days.

Here come some men bringing in baskets of coffee berries, which they have gathered from the wild coffee trees in the forest. Some of the natives work for European companies who control great areas of land where the coffee trees grow, and others gather the berries from the trees which grow near their villages. There are few modern coffee plantations in Angola, yet so much is obtained from the trees which grow wild there that coffee is one of the most important products of the colony.

Those odd-looking beehives in the trees which shade the village are thatched over with grass to keep off the rain. The men get large quantities of honey and wax from these nests and collect a good deal also from the hives of the wild bees in the woods. They eat the honey and sell the wax to the trader, who sends it down to the coast to be shipped away.

Figure 129. *What do you think of this—an American sewing machine in Angola! You would find manufactures from our country in many parts of Africa. What do we receive in return?*

As we have traveled in Angola we have noticed here and there articles which have come from the United States. Now it was some cans of petroleum marked with the familiar name of an American corporation; now a windmill which had on one of its blades "Made in U.S.A." In one of the business offices of Loanda we noticed a native stenographer working with an American typewriter, on an office desk which was made in a city of our Middle West. On one of the sugar plantations we saw a sugar mill made in the United States, and in some of the stores in the seaports we found hardware, tools, beds, fountain pens, cash registers, and various other articles bearing the names of American manufacturers.

Our trade with Angola is not large, but we have some commercial interests here, as we do in every country on earth. The better we know the people here, the more we learn of their country, their lives, and their occupations, the greater our trade with them will be.

SUGGESTIONS FOR STUDY

I

1. Former possessions of Portugal.

2. Portuguese Guinea.

3. Surface and products.

4. Loanda and Benguela.

5. Village life in Angola.

6. Our interests in Angola.

II

1. How far south of Angola is the boundary of the torrid zone? What lands in the Western Hemisphere are in about the same latitude?

2. Why is the rainfall of Angola lighter than that of Mozambique? What effect does this rainfall have on the occupations of Angola?

3. Why is the output of coffee, rubber, cocoa, and other plantations likely to be of more value than the wild products?

4. Why is the port of Benguela likely to increase in importance?

ANGOLA

5. What goods from the Belgian Congo will form much of the west-bound freight to Benguela? What articles needed in the Katanga district will go eastward over this route?

6. Why are the people of European countries especially interested in increasing the production of cotton in their colonies?

III

Make a list of the places mentioned in this chapter. Arrange them by countries, cities, rivers, mountains, etc. From the list select those places which you think are so important that you should always be able to locate them and know something about them.

CHAPTER XXV

ON THE PLANTATIONS OF MOZAMBIQUE

In some geographies the province of Mozambique is called Portuguese East Africa. It is one of the oldest of European possessions in Africa and one of the richest in possibilities for the future. It has a rich soil, good harbors, and valuable resources; it contains no desert, no large swamps, and no impenetrable jungles.

Look at the map on page 93 and find the city of Lourenço Marques. This seaport has one of the best harbors on the east coast of Africa. Find on the map the railroad which runs from Lourenço Marques to Johannesburg in the Transvaal and notice how short it is compared with any road which runs between Johannesburg and a British port. What is the nearest British port to Johannesburg?

The greater part of the freight which enters and leaves Lourenço Marques is bound for or comes from the Transvaal. Gold from the rich mines near Johannesburg is shipped from this Portuguese seaport, and food and clothing materials, chemicals, mining machinery, tools, and other articles which such a newly

PLANTATIONS OF MOZAMBIQUE

developed mining country needs are shipped through Lourenço Marques into the interior.

Thousands of the natives of Mozambique work in the mines of the Transvaal. They are well paid and well cared for and learn many of the foreigners' ways. For these reasons the custom is a good one; but it has its disadvantages in causing a shortage of workmen in Mozambique.

Figure 130. This looks like some port or freight yard in the United States. It is really Lourenço Marques. Why is this port an important one?

About five hundred miles north of Lourenço Marques is the port of Beira, also important as an outlet to the British possessions. Beira is the gateway to Rhodesia, and a railroad runs from this port across Mozambique to the English town of Salisbury (see map on page 93). From Beira, also, copper from the

AFRICA, AUSTRALIA, ISLANDS OF PACIFIC

Katanga district of the Belgian Congo is sent to Europe. What other route is convenient for the shipping of this mineral (see page 343)?

Aside from the trade which passes through Beira from the English and Belgian colonies, large amounts of freight from Mozambique are exported from here, for the port is surrounded by a region which is rich in mineral and agricultural resources. Some gold and copper mines are already worked here, and it is asserted that the country is rich in other minerals.

The products of the soil, however, are much more important than the minerals: Let us make a visit to Beira and by talking with some of the people there learn something about the products and resources of Mozambique.

We are on a low, sandy coast in the torrid zone. The weather is hot, and the glare of the sand is trying. We are glad that we have become acquainted on the boat with a Portuguese gentleman who invites us to rest at his home while he tells us about the place.

We ride to his house in his private car. No; it is not

Figure 131. These men are trying to get this automobile across the Zambezi River. The use of automobiles will hasten road building in many parts of Africa.

PLANTATIONS OF MOZAMBIQUE

an automobile. In the street there are narrow tracks extending from one end of the town to the other, with branches running into yards of shops and private houses. We look around for the trolley poles and wires, but find that the power to run the cars, which are little more than wide chairs, is supplied by two natives who push them from behind. There are no public electric cars in Beira. Most of the foreigners own their little chair cars and hire natives to push them.

Our Portuguese friend is the owner of a large sugarcane plantation a few miles away. He tells us that sugar is one of the most important products of Mozambique and one which is sure to increase in the future. On his plantation there are hundreds of workmen, and the cultivation of the cane and the extraction of the

Figure 132. See the big pile of coconuts! The natives who are having their pictures taken will cut them open and dry the meat. This will be sent to Europe, where the oil is extracted.

AFRICA, AUSTRALIA, ISLANDS OF PACIFIC

sugar are carried on in as scientific a way as on a sugar plantation in Louisiana (see Allen's "North America" and "United States").

While we are resting, our host tells us something about the mangrove-bark industry. Mangrove forests such as we saw on the west coast of Africa are found also on the low coastal plain of Mozambique. Natives strip off the bark, load it into their boats, and paddle along the shore to the nearest harbor. Here they reload the bark onto larger craft, which take it to ports where it is again loaded on ocean going vessels. Thousands of tons of bark are sent every year from this colony to Europe to be used in tanning leather.

Our friend tells us that some natives of Mozambique spend their time in tapping the rubber trees and vines in the forests. Planters have started rubber plantations, but as yet the industry has not become of great importance. Cotton also grows well in this warm, moist land, and exports of cotton fiber are expected to increase. We learn, too, that Mozambique, like other warm parts of Africa, is rich in oil nuts and seeds, and great quantities of these and the oil which they produce are exported. Especially important are the coconut oil and the peanut oil, of which hundreds of thousands of tons are shipped away.

Ivory has long been an important export from Mozambique. In many villages in the province there is great excitement when the men go off on an elephant hunt and much rejoicing when they return with the long ivory tusks and loads of meat for feasting.

PLANTATIONS OF MOZAMBIQUE

Figure 133. For many years natives have brought ivory tusks from the interior to Mozambique to be shipped away. In former years the black carriers were sent to other countries as slaves.

Going north from Beira we pass the broad delta mouth of the Zambezi River. You will notice on the map that the Zambezi crosses Mozambique and thus affords a means of getting into the interior. On a sail up the river we should see natives loading their dugout canoes with rubber, nuts and seeds, and mangrove bark, and meet others paddling down to the nearest trading station.

Still farther north, on a small coral island about a mile from the coast, is the old city of Mozambique. It was founded in 1508, and for many years was a large, flourishing city. In the days of the slave trade it was one of the important slave markets of the continent.

From the sea Mozambique looks today like a large city. Houses and palaces built by Arab merchants who became rich and powerful in the slave trade stand along the water front. The great castle, dating from the early part of the sixteenth century, is built of stones brought in the small vessels of that time from Portugal, thousands of miles away. Some of the streets are paved with blocks of black and white stone and remind us of immense checkerboards.

Probably no town in Africa has altered less in appearance in four hundred years. Yet few people today walk over the checkerboard pavements; few live in the great houses, loiter in the courtyards of the palaces, or worship in the gray churches. The part of the country around the old city is fertile and capable of producing good crops. The time is coming when the great houses will again be occupied by prosperous merchants, and the old fortresses filled, not with prisoners and slaves, but with grain, ivory, nuts and seeds, mangrove bark, rubber, sugar, and cotton. The harbor will again be crowded with vessels waiting to be loaded with useful products for the mills, factories, and homes in many lands.

SUGGESTIONS FOR STUDY

I

1. Advantages for the development of Mozambique.
2. Relations of Mozambique with the Transvaal.

3. Lourenço Marques and Beira.

4. Industries and products of the colony.

5. The old city of Mozambique.

II

1. Describe the mangrove swamps of West Africa (see pages 151-152).

2. How old is the city of Mozambique? How does its age compare with that of the oldest city in the United States?

3. What effect will the development of Rhodesia have on the ports of Mozambique?

4. In what zones is Mozambique? How do you know?

5. How does Mozambique compare in size with Angola (see Appendix, page 500)? Which colony receives the most rain? Why?

III

Make a list of the places mentioned in this chapter. Arrange them by countries, cities, rivers, mountains, etc. From the list select those places which you think are so important that you should always be able to locate them and know something about them.

CHAPTER XXVI

ISLAND POSSESSIONS OF PORTUGAL

BESIDES her colonies on the mainland Portugal has several island possessions around Africa. Among these are the Azores Islands, the Madeira Islands, and the Cape Verde Islands.

Like the other island groups northwest of Africa, the Azores have been built by volcanic action. If you could drain the ocean dry, you could see the tall cones, of which the islands are the peaks, towering from the ocean bed into the air for thousands of feet. The hot springs which are found in many places, and the many earthquakes which have visited the islands, sometimes burying whole towns, tell us that Nature is still busy here in her underground workshops.

In the summer, when the northeast trades blow off the continent of Europe, there is little rain; but in the winter, when the sun has moved south, the moist, westerly winds move south also far enough to bring rain to the Azores and Madeira islands. The Canaries are so far south that the moist westerlies do not reach them, and their climate is much drier than the more northerly groups.

Some of the people on the Azores Islands are fishermen. Some go on long voyages for the sperm whale, the oil from which is so valuable. Some are engaged in bottling and shipping away the water of the mineral springs. Many tourists and people in search of health come here to bathe in the springs or drink the water as medicine.

Figure 134. If you visited the Azores Islands you would probably land here. Where are the Azores Islands? What should you see in a tour through them?

Many of the people on the islands raise grapes, which they make into wine, some have orange groves, and others cultivate pineapples. Perhaps you have heard how fast the pineapple industry on the Hawaiian Islands has grown; people on the Azores Islands also have found that the cultivation of this fruit is profitable and are producing increasing quantities each year.

THE MADEIRA ISLANDS

The Madeira Islands are the most beautiful of Portugal's island possessions. The group consists of the island of Madeira, on which most of the people live, and several smaller islets.

The city of Funchal is an attractive place, with its fine hotels and lovely houses surrounded by tropical gardens brilliant with blossoms. Back of the city the land rises into hills, behind which green mountains rise still higher. The terraces are covered with flowers, and on the slopes there are many country houses owned by wealthy people.

Figure 135. Should you like a ride in a bullock sledge? You would surely ride in a team like the one in the picture if you visited the Madeira Islands.

ISLAND POSSESSIONS OF PORTUGAL

Thousands of tourists visit the Madeira Islands every year, attracted by their balmy climate, their beautiful scenery, and their interesting sights and scenes. The temperature throughout the year is from about sixty to seventy degrees, never very hot or very cold. The scenery is magnificent. Dark cliffs hundreds of feet high rise from the water, and deep ravines into which leap sparkling streams lie between green mountain slopes.

There is little level land on the island. So steep are the hills and so deep the valleys that in order to have any farms at all the natives have terraced the hillsides with stone walls to prevent the soil from being washed away in the rainy season. Some of these terraced farms remind us of those in Germany and France, for in both places vineyards cover the ground (see Allen's "New Europe"). The grapes are used for making the wine for which Madeira has long been famous and which has been exported for five hundred years.

Have you ever seen for sale in the stores underwear, doilies, table covers and napkins, and other linens decorated with Madeira embroidery? Doing embroidery is the most important industry in Madeira, and thousands of the women spend their time in such work. They make beautiful lace also and do other fine handwork. We buy large quantities of these goods, and many are sold to tourists. The men make baskets and articles of carved wood which are very popular in the tourist trade. What should you like to carry home from Madeira?

The Cape Verde Islands

Farther south and nearer the coast of Africa are the Cape Verde Islands, another group of volcanic mountains whose tops reach above the surface of the ocean. They consist of ten principal islands and four rocky, unoccupied islets.

This group is both hotter and drier than those farther north, and little can be raised without irrigation. In places the coffee tree grows well, and coffee is the chief export. Some of the natives raise cattle on the grasslands, and the hides are exported.

It is not their exports which have made these islands important, but their location on the ocean route between western Europe and South Africa. Because of this position they have become an important coaling station. Large quantities of coal are stored near the wharves of the little seaport, and many vessels stop here to renew their supply.

St. Thomas and Prince's Island

Before we leave the Portuguese possessions we will sail southward from the Cape Verde Islands and follow the coast of Africa into the Gulf of Guinea. Here we will visit the two little volcanic islands of St. Thomas and Prince's Island. These islands lie very near the equator and in the equatorial rain belt. They are hot and damp, with torrents of rain in the wet season and heavy mists at other times of the year. Deep mosses and ferns, tropical forests, and tangled jungles formerly covered the valleys and slopes.

Many thousand acres, especially in St. Thomas, have now been cleared, and more than half that island is covered with cacao plantations. Other products besides cocoa are raised to some extent,—coffee, rubber, and the cinchona tree, from the bark of which quinine is made,—but the cocoa is worth more than all these put together.

The workers on the cocoa plantations gather and cut open the big pods, take out the beans, heap them up in great piles, where they sweat and ferment, and then rake them over on the cement drying grounds with a skill and care unexcelled in any cocoa-producing region of the world. A railroad leads a few miles into the interior, and the larger plantations have short railroads which connect with this line or with the seaport. On other plantations the beans are carried in carts drawn by bullocks or mules.

SUGGESTIONS FOR STUDY

I

1. Nature's work in the Azores.
2. Occupations and productions in the Azores Islands.
3. Attractions for tourists in the Madeira Islands.

4. Madeira embroidery.

5. Position and importance of the Cape Verde Islands.

6. The cocoa industry on the island of St. Thomas.

II

1. Which group of islands mentioned in this chapter is not a Portuguese possession? To what nation does it belong?

2. How have these island groups been formed? For what are they valuable?

3. Why do the Canary Islands receive less rainfall than the other groups?

4. What countries of the world produce large amounts of cocoa (see Allen's "South America," also pamphlets from the Department of Commerce)? Why should cocoa be an important product on St. Thomas and not on the Cape Verde Islands?

5. In what kind of regions do you find terraced farms?

III

Make a list of the places mentioned in this chapter. Arrange them by countries, cities, rivers, mountains, etc. From the list select those places which you think are so important that you should always be able to locate them and know something about them.

ISLAND POSSESSIONS OF PORTUGAL

IV

Review of the Portuguese Possessions in Africa

1. Sketch an outline map of Africa and show on it the Portuguese possessions. Write their names and the names of their chief cities. Show the railroads mentioned in the text.

2. Which is the largest colony? Which is on the west coast? on the east coast? Which lie in the torrid zone? What island groups belong to Portugal?

3. Which Portuguese colonies are included in the low coast lands of Africa (see regional map)? Which lie on the plateau? How does the position in these regions affect the occupations and products of the people?

4. Which colony shall you remember for its cocoa? its tourists? its rubber? its sugar? its embroidery? Which ones are outlets for products from territory of another nation?

5. How many times the size of Portugal are its African possessions? How do the populations compare (see Appendix, page 500)?

CHAPTER XXVII

SPANISH POSSESSIONS IN AFRICA

LIKE Portugal, Spain has been very famous in exploration and colonization. At one time all the South American countries except Brazil were Spanish colonies. The rich silver mines of Mexico and the Andean countries brought great wealth to the Spanish treasury, and Spanish galleons sailed from ports on the Caribbean shores laden with gold and silver torn from the Aztec temples or wrung from the Indian rulers of these lands.

Spain has lost her great colonial empire. Today there is nothing left to her of the vast lands which she once controlled except a few small colonies in Africa and some islands near it, of which you will read in this chapter. These cover a smaller area and are less important than the African colonies of any other nation.

You have already read of the French in Morocco and about the agreement of 1912, which gave to the Spanish a small area in the northern part of that country (see map on page 219). This extends from

SPANISH POSSESSIONS IN AFRICA

Ceuta, opposite Gibraltar, to the boundary of Algeria. Tangier, you remember, is not a Spanish port, but an internationalized city.

Spanish Morocco is not well developed. Much of the region is hilly and rugged and fit only for pasture land, and the good farming lands lie in the east and west. Here we see vineyards like those in French Morocco where grapes are raised and made into wine. The people raise also some grain, vegetables, and fruits, but they give these crops little care. They sow the grain broadcast, use no fertilizers, and do little or no weeding and cultivating from the time of planting until the harvesting.

Figure 136. Spanish possessions in Africa. Read the chapter and decide which one you should most like to visit.

Northern Morocco is an old country which has been known for centuries. It was a part of the great granary of northern Africa from which ancient Rome received much of its food supply. Barbary pirates put out from its ports and scoured the sea for ships which they might capture and whose officers and crews they might hold for ransom or sell for slaves. Even in recent years bandits have captured travelers and held them for ransom.

About seven hundred years after the birth of Christ, Moors and Arabs from northern Morocco crossed the Strait of Gibraltar and conquered much of southern Spain. In Granada, Seville, Cordoba, and other Spanish cities we can see today beautiful palaces and mosques built by the Moors. The Alhambra in Granada is the most beautiful of these buildings. After looking at

Figure 137. This is the Court of the Lions, in the Alhambra. Notice the beautiful arches and decorations. In what city of Spain is the Alhambra? Who built it?

pictures of its courts and pillars, its arches and fountains, you can better appreciate the art and talent of the Moors.

The Spaniards finally succeeded in driving the Moors out of their country, and for many years, since about the time of the discovery of America, Spain has held possession of some of the coast towns of Morocco. Tetuan is one of the oldest of these. We can still see here the old mines—with their stone slides for hoisting the ore, and the piles of refuse rock at the mouths of the tunnels—from which the Roman general Cæsar obtained supplies of copper for Rome. Can you find out when Cæsar lived?

The thirty thousand people who live in Tetuan are nearly equally divided between Moors and Jews. A few thousand Europeans live here also. Much trade is carried on with towns around, and its markets are busy places.

Tetuan is well known for its manufacture of Morocco leather. See how soft and fine those pieces of red and yellow leather are. The yellow skin will be used for the heelless slippers which the men wear, and the red for women's slippers. These and other colors—black, white, brown, green, and blue—are used not only for slippers but for bags, cushions, bookbindings, etc.

Making pottery is as common an occupation for the women in Spanish Morocco as sewing is for your mother. A Moorish woman digs her clay, carries it home, and in her spare hours shapes and molds her jars for cooking and holding water and grain just as your mother fills her spare time with her sewing and mending.

The people of Tetuan use the clay around the city for making tiles also. The work is carried on in caves just as it has been for centuries, and the processes which produce the wonderful glaze which has lasted for hundreds of years are still a secret. The floors and courtyards in the better houses in Moorish cities are paved with tiles, and more beautiful ones ornament the mosques.

Figure 138. This woman is making some couscous for dinner. What is couscous (see page 263)?

On the west coast of Morocco you will find the Spanish colony of Ifni, not as large as Rhode Island. In the coast villages many men are fishermen. Others cultivate date palms, sell dates, and raise grain and vegetables.

SPANISH POSSESSIONS IN AFRICA

Rio de Oro, farther south, is the largest of the Spanish colonies. The Portuguese were the first people to visit this region, as well as many other parts of the African coast. They found the natives in possession of considerable quantities of gold. Thinking that the little bay on the coast near the capital was the mouth of a river, and that the gold had been obtained in its sands, they named the region Rio d'Ouro—in Spanish, Rio de Oro, which means "river of gold."

There is little gold or any other product of any great value in this Spanish colony. Like the rest of the Sahara, of which it forms a part, Rio de Oro is nearly waterless. The few mixed tribes of Mohammedans and Berbers who live here are nomads who raise cattle and sheep and go from one oasis to another for grass and water.

Figure 139. *This is a desert scene near Cape Blanco. Where is this cape? It is near the boundary between what two African divisions?*

The coast waters abound in fish, and quantities of cod and other varieties are caught here, as on the coast of Ifni. Vessels from the Canary Islands and some manned by French sailors come here in the fishing season.

Fernando Po is the largest island in the Gulf of Guinea. The success of the cocoa industry in St. Thomas and of sugar and coffee and other crops on the mainland have led white men to start plantations for the production of these crops on Fernando Po. Many natives from the mainland are employed on the large island farms. It is difficult to induce the native islanders to work steadily. They like better to hunt the gazelles and monkeys in the forests or gather turtle eggs on the shore. Like other tribes they pick bananas and palm nuts and raise in their little garden patches the yams, rice, and vegetables which they need.

Figure 140. This man with his nets and his boat fishes off the coasts of Rio de Oro and Mauritania. To whom do these colonies belong?

In the densest parts of the forest on Fernando Po are native villages so well concealed that it is often difficult to find the entrance. These people wear little clothing except broad-brimmed hats made of palm leaves and a coating of clay to protect their bodies from the mosquitoes and other insects. They wear armlets made of ivory and beads, and in holes which they make in their ears they hang large pieces of wood.

These Spanish islands in the Gulf of Guinea are under the control of a governor general, who lives at Santa Isabel, the chief town of Rio Muni on the mainland.

From what you have read of other colonies along the coast of the Gulf of Guinea you know that Rio Muni is a hot, damp region of dense forests and jungles, changing along its eastern border to a higher, drier country.

All the rivers flowing from the tableland to the coastal plain have rapids and falls in their courses, and most of them have sand bars at their mouths. The Muni River, for which the land is named, is the largest and most useful of these streams.

Rio Muni has no good harbors, no fine seaports, and no rivers navigable for vessels of any size. A few European settlements are scattered along the coast, backed by plantations where cocoa, coffee, and sugar are raised. In the forests the natives gather the palm nuts and the juice from the rubber vines and trees and bring them to the "factories" of the traders on the coast.

The Canary Islands

The Canary Islands lie near the ocean route between European ports and South Africa, and many vessels stop to take on island products or to leave freight and passengers. Most of the people who land here are tourists who have come to enjoy the climate and the lovely scenery.

The cone-shaped mountain of Tenerife is the tallest of the volcanic range which form the Canary Islands. In 1909 an eruption of Tenerife took place, and great lava streams poured down its slopes. Fortunately the eruption ceased, and the lava cooled enough to stop its flow before it reached any towns.

The volcanic rock of which the islands are composed has crumbled into a fertile soil. Unfortunately the rainfall is light, and hot, drying winds often blow in from the Sahara, making irrigation necessary for most of the crops. The low coastal plain looks much like the tropical regions of the mainland. The date palm flourishes, and sugar cane and bananas are raised. The banana plantations have increased greatly in recent years, and the fruit is now the most valuable crop on the islands. See the long line of women coming toward the packing house, each carrying on her head a heavy bunch of green bananas. These will be loaded on high two-wheeled carts drawn by bullocks and taken to the seaport, where they will be put on the vessels northward bound to European countries.

Higher on the slopes of the hills, where the air is cooler, other crops are grown—olives, grapes, oranges, and grains such as we might see in the Mediterranean countries. Years ago grapes and wine were the most important products in the Canaries. Later there was a great demand for the red dye made from the cochineal insect. When this industry began to decline, because of the manufacture of dyes from coal tar, the people on the lowlands turned their attention to raising bananas, and those in the cooler, higher zone to the cultivation of tomatoes and onions. In a trip through the islands we pass field after field where the tomato vines are trained on supports to keep the fruit from the ground. On our ride we learn that several million dollars' worth of tomatoes are exported every year.

The onion fields are immense. Many of these vegetables are raised for their seed, which are considered excellent for planting. Most of the onions are sent to the West Indies, while the larger part of the seed comes to the United States. Can you find out if any onions are grown near your home from seed produced in the Canary Islands?

The women in the Canary Islands make beautiful embroidery, drawn work, and fine lace. Agents from European countries supply them with the cloth and thread and sometimes with the designs to be made. Many tons of these articles are shipped annually to Europe and America and play a large part in the Christmas trade, though they may be bought at any time of the year.

SUGGESTIONS FOR STUDY

I

1. Former and present colonies of Spain.

2. Spanish Morocco and the old city of Tetuan.

3. The Moorish invasion of Spain.

4. Making pottery and tiles.

5. The Spanish colony of Ifni.

6. Rio de Oro.

7. The island of Fernando Po.

8. Rio Muni.

9. The Canary Islands.

II

1. Sketch a map of Africa and show on it the Spanish possessions.

2. Write the names of the Spanish colonies in the order of their size (see Appendix, page 501). Beside the name of each colony write two words which you think best describe it.

3. Which colony is most like southern Spain? Which is important because of its position? Which is famous for its tomatoes and onions? Which is inappropriately named? Which is most like the island of St. Thomas?

SPANISH POSSESSIONS IN AFRICA

4. Compare the area of Spanish Africa with that of the Portuguese possessions (see Appendix, pages 500 and 501).

5. How was Morocco divided by the treaty of 1912?

6. Sketch a map of the western Mediterranean, including Spain and Morocco. Show on the map the places mentioned in the text.

III

Make a list of the places mentioned in this chapter. Arrange them by countries, cities, rivers, mountains, etc. From the list select those places which you think are so important that you should always be able to locate them and know something about them.

CHAPTER XXVIII

THE ABYSSINIAN PLATEAU

Ever since we left Egypt we have been traveling in the possessions of European nations. In Abyssinia, however, we shall find ourselves in another independent country. Like little Switzerland in Europe, Abyssinia owes its independence largely to its surface. It is mainly a high plateau in which rivers have cut deep gorges and from which high mountains rise. Such a surface makes communication difficult with lands around it, and it is due largely to this reason and to the warlike character of its people that the country has retained its independence for centuries.

Through long ages the Blue Nile, hurrying down from the great Abyssinian Highland, has carried northward in its waters the rich soil which has made Egypt the fertile land that it is. Other rivers wash quantities of silt into the valleys of Abyssinia, where the fine, rich soil is hundreds of feet deep.

In the latter years of the nineteenth century the emperor Menelik II, a ruler stronger and wiser than those before him, succeeded in uniting the wild tribes of the region into one empire. This old ruler was in many ways a remarkable man. He had never traveled in Europe, yet he adopted many of the ways of civilized nations. He established telegraph lines and connected his capital by telephone with the seacoast many miles away. He built good roads, levied just taxes, and established a mint in which money was coined. Before his time bars of salt, cotton cloth, and other articles which were of value to the people served as money, as they do in parts of Africa today.

Figure 141. This woman has been gathering brushwood for fuel. Why should wood be scarce in parts of Abyssinia?

One achievement which has helped more than anything else to open up the country was the concession given to the French to build the railroad from the boundary of French Somaliland to Adis Abeba, the capital of Abyssinia (see map on page 68). What did you read about this railroad on page 332?

The railroad from Jibuti is the only easy way to enter Abyssinia. If we planned our trip by any other route, we should have to travel by caravan and spend considerable time in making our preparations. We should have to buy camels, mules, tents, provisions for ourselves and the animals, and presents for the chiefs through whose territory we might pass. We should have to hire camel drivers, mule drivers, servants to attend to the luggage and to putting up and taking down the tents, guides for the desert and mountain trails, and a cook to prepare our meals.

On the wharves at Jibuti we begin our acquaintance with Abyssinia, for we see there piles of rubber, bags of coffee, bundles of hides and skins, elephants' tusks, and quantities of beeswax, all products of that inland country.

The train on which we ride inland is carrying many things which the people of Abyssinia need, such as cotton goods, rice, sugar, petroleum, building material, hardware, and many other things. These have come chiefly from European countries, though Asia, Australia, and the United States are all represented in the imports. Which articles do you think may have come from the United States?

Since leaving the coast the train has been steadily climbing the grades, and on account of the height the air is cooler and more comfortable. We are high enough now for the mountains to condense some of the moisture which the winds have brought from the ocean. This causes refreshing showers, which fill the river beds and water the land. Green hills rise above pleasant valleys, wild fig and olive trees grow on the slopes, and rolling, grassy plains are dotted here and there with scattered villages near which cattle are feeding.

Figure 142. These women are gathering grain in the uplands of Abyssinia. Compare the methods of harvesting in this picture and those in the following one. Both photographs were taken in Abyssinia.

There are coffee plantations in this part of Abyssinia, wild trees grow in the west and south, and coffee is an important product. It is said that centuries ago coffee beans were carried from Abyssinia to Arabia and other lands, and that from this small beginning the industry has spread over the world.

As we continue to climb, the air grows cooler. On these higher plateaus we see fewer cattle and more sheep and goats and horses. Adis Abeba, the end of our journey, is about eight thousand feet high. Here the climate is like perpetual spring. The temperature in the cooler months averages about fifty-eight degrees and in the hot season about sixty-one degrees. How does this compare with the temperature where you live?

Figure 143. Harvesting with modern reapers made in the United States.

We could not go far from the railroad without realizing something of the numbers and the variety of the animals which live on the plateau. We see many antelopes, the curious hartebeests, and the striped zebras. Hyenas prey around the camps and towns. Leopards and lions hide in the tall grass, and in the forests we hear the chattering of monkeys. The awkward rhinoceros and the hippopotamus live in the swamps and near the streams. With all the wealth of animal life roaming the plains and skulking in the forests, we do not wonder that hides and skins are an important article of export from Abyssinia. Some of these come from the wild animals and some from the flocks of the natives.

As we approach the capital the little villages grow

THE ABYSSINIAN PLATEAU

more numerous. What odd-looking places they are! From a distance an Abyssinian village looks somewhat like a group of giant toadstools. The little brown houses are round, with cone-shaped roofs of thatch. The inside is as strange as the outside. An inner circular wall parallel with the outer wall separates the house into two parts. In the room between these walls are kept the few tools which are used, perhaps a cow or two, and a mule or pony. The family lives in the inner part. This has an earth floor raised a little higher than that of the outer portion. The earth beds, slightly higher than the floor, serve as seats in the daytime. The fire is built on the ground in the center of the hut, and as there are no chimneys and no windows you can imagine that the air is smoky and the place dirty.

Figure 144. This is a typical village in Abyssinia. Describe the houses.

There seem to be few men in most of the villages. Some of them are away from home hunting and trapping, some are off on the caravan routes driving mules or camels, and some are searching for beeswax in the forest. Many of the men are probably in the king's army or counted among the rebel forces, for fighting is very common in Abyssinia.

The women do most of the work. They attend to the cooking, fetch the water, pound the rice in big wooden vessels with heavy sticks taller than themselves, care for the flocks, work in the gardens, and collect brush for fuel.

The Abyssinians tend to have darkish skin. Many of them look much like the people whom we have seen in the Sahara. Some are of Arab descent. They are straight and tall, and on the whole are rather striking in appearance.

You have never seen nor imagined a capital city like Adis Abeba. It is really a collection of native villages. On a hill in the center is the Gebi, the group of royal buildings where live the king and his family, his officials, and his servants. Some of the buildings in the Gebi are like European houses, while others are such as we might find in India, Arabia, Turkey, or Egypt.

The words "Adis Abeba" mean the "new flower." This town has not long been the capital, the flower of the country. Several places have served as the capital of Abyssinia and have been abandoned one after another because of the lack of wood for fuel. When all the forests around have been cut off and the distance to a fuel supply has become inconveniently great, then a new capital has been chosen. The plain on which Adis Abeba stands had already been robbed of most of its trees when Menelik II, of whom you read on pages 378 and 379, ordered thousands of eucalyptus trees to be planted in and around the capital. The government regulates the cutting of these trees and causes new ones to be planted. So long as this system is enforced, there will be a perpetual supply of firewood, and at present there is little likelihood of any other city's being chosen to take the place of Adis Abeba as the capital.

Abyssinia has great mineral wealth yet unworked. As the people learn more about the customs of civilized nations, mines will be opened, coal may be used as a fuel, new methods of transportation will be introduced, and loads carried by women will become things of the past.

SUGGESTIONS FOR STUDY

I

1. Position and surface of Abyssinia.

2. Progress of the country.

3. The railroad from Jibuti.

4. Village life and occupations.

5. Adis Abeba, the capital.

II

1. Why should the surface of countries like Switzerland and Abyssinia have an effect on the independence of the people?

2. How has the railroad from Jibuti affected Abyssinia?

3. Why should the rainfall on the hills and mountains of Abyssinia be heavier than on the coast?

III

Make a list of the places mentioned in this chapter. Arrange them by countries, cities, rivers, mountains, etc. From the list select those places which you think are so important that you should always be able to locate them and know something about them.

CHAPTER XXIX

THE REPUBLIC OF LIBERIA

THERE is one other independent country in Africa in which the United States is considerably interested. This is the republic of Liberia.

Touching Liberia on the west is the British colony of Sierra Leone. This was founded by English people for slaves liberated in British colonies. Some people in our country thought that it would be a good plan to establish a land in Africa for freedmen of the United States who might like to make their homes in the continent from which they or their ancestors had come. Consequently the little republic was founded and given a name which means land of the free.

Liberia lies near the equator, just where the coast of Africa bends northward (see map on page 193). The climate is very hot and the rainfall heavy. Along the shores are low, steamy swamps covered with mangrove trees whose twisted roots look like great serpents half hidden in the mud and water. Back of the swamps dense tropical forests cover most of the country. Near the coast, where settlements have been made, these forests have been somewhat cleared away, but little has been done as yet to develop the interior. When there are roads and railroads by which the forest products can be taken to the ports, the African mahogany, ebony, and other hard woods, the gums and fibers, and the oil palms and coconut palms will be of great value to Liberia.

Though Africa is the home of the blacks, Liberia is the only division of that great continent which is governed by blacks, the only one in which, according to the law, no whites can become citizens. The people consist of two types, both dark-skinned, but very unlike each other. One class, whom we might call the Americo-Liberians, is made up of the descendants of those blacks who were once slaves in America and who settled in Liberia after they became free. The rest of the population, who make up much the greater part of the inhabitants, are native African blacks belonging to several different tribes. The members of the Kru tribe are the most numerous. What did you read about the Kru men on page 175?

Beyond the mountains, where the rainfall is lighter, the forests less dense, and there are open, grassy areas, are many villages of the Mandingos. These people, like many tribes in Africa, are Mohammedans. Some of these blacks are industrious and spend much of their time collecting the products of the region to sell to the traders. Many of them, however, see no reason why they should work hard in the heat and rain to produce or gather those articles which the foreigner wishes to buy. In this hot land they need little clothing, and their garden patches yield rice, sugar, fruit, and vegetables.

THE REPUBLIC OF LIBERIA

Their cattle, sheep, and goats find plenty of food on the rich grasslands, and the forests around provide building material for their little houses. They can sell ginger root, palm nuts and oil, and hides and skins for the simple articles which they need. These are but few,—perhaps some cooking utensil, some kerosene for their lamp, or some machine-made cloth in prettier patterns and brighter colors than they can make from the cotton grown in their gardens and dye with the juice of some native plant. To be sure, they can neither read nor write, and they have little or no interest outside their own village.

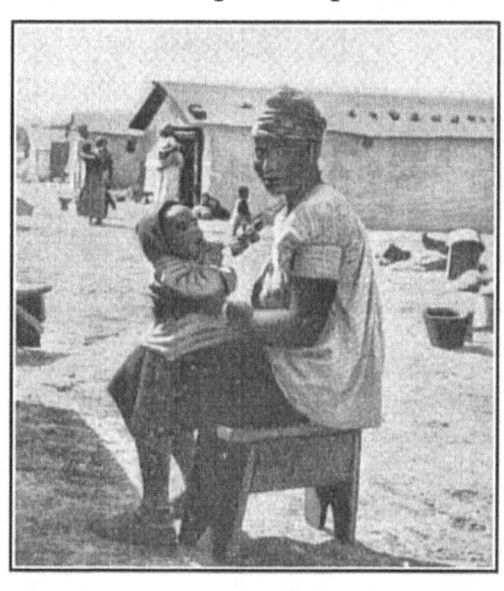

Figure 145. *This woman of Liberia loves her baby as much as mothers in the United States love theirs. How different this baby's life will be from yours. What are some of these differences?*

Along its three hundred and fifty miles of coast line Liberia has no very good harbor. Monrovia, the capital, is the only port of any importance. It rises from the water tier on tier up the green hillside. Many of the houses are brick with tiled or corrugated iron roofs. Some we find two stories high with wide verandas on both floors, reminding us somewhat of the houses in our Southern states. As the Americo-Liberians came to Liberia from that part of our country, it was natural that they should build their houses in the style with which they were familiar.

On the sandy shore near Monrovia is a large village known as Kru Town, where hundreds of Krus live. They are ruled by their own native chief, though of course they obey also the laws of the republic. After their day's work on the wharves and boats and in the warehouses of Monrovia, they go back to their little thatch-roofed huts, eat the supper which the Kru women have prepared over the out-of-door fires, and watch the children roll and play on the sand while the sun sinks into the western waters and darkness steals over the ocean.

Only a few light-skinned people live in Monrovia. These are missionaries, consuls and representatives from different countries, and traders who are interested in selling foreign goods and in buying from the Liberians their native products. In the warehouses down near the water we can see what some of these are. There are casks of palm oil and bags of palm kernels; there are bundles of piassaba fiber, such as you saw being loaded on the ships at Freetown (see page 176). There are kola nuts, which you remember the people of West Africa like to eat (see pages 180 and 181); and there are piles of rubber from the trees and vines in the deep forests. See the bags of ginger root. This is an important export from Liberia. The ginger plant grows on the sunny slopes around many of the villages in the interior. The roots are brought in boats down the streams or carried on the

THE REPUBLIC OF LIBERIA

backs of carriers who trudge through the forest paths to the nearest "factory."

In other warehouses there are quantities of copra, of which you have seen so much in your travels through tropical Africa. There are also bags of coffee and cocoa beans. The trees which bear them grow wild in Liberia. The climate and soil are favorable for their growth, and in the future there will be large coffee and cocoa plantations here.

Liberia is of comparatively little importance today in the world's commerce. It has fewer good seaports, fewer roads and other improvements, is less developed, and is producing less for export to other lands than are most of the other divisions of West Africa.

With our trip in Liberia we finish our travels in Africa. Since we first started on our travels up the Nile River we have learned much about the people and conditions in this part of the world across the great ocean. We have seen what great treasures Nature has stored away in the forests, the grasslands, and in the depths of the earth. We have learned, too, how the people in the large cities and the great manufacturing countries of the temperate zone are depending more and more each year on the materials which come from the forests and farms of tropical and semitropical lands. When the demand for these materials becomes great enough, the changes in these undeveloped countries of Africa will take place faster than ever before.

We have read about many peoples who live in various parts of Africa,—Arabs, Jews, Moors, Boers, and representatives of different European countries. We have visited also many tribes of natives in their villages on the grasslands, in the forests, and along the coast lands of the continent. By reading books of travel, government publications, and other sources of information, and by listening to people who have visited Africa, we should try to become more acquainted with these distant neighbors of ours and understand better the conditions under which they are living and working. We need in our country very large amounts of the products which they can furnish, and they need our products to help them modernize their infrastructure. Strangers cannot help one another as much as friends can. It is only by knowing well the people of any land that we can become their friends and thus enjoy closer relations with them.

SUGGESTIONS FOR STUDY

I

1. Reason for the settlement of Liberia.

2. Position and climate.

3. Conditions and people.

4. Resources and products.

5. Monrovia, the capital.

II

1. How does Liberia differ from all other divisions of Africa?

2. The capital of Liberia was named for James Monroe. When did he hold the office of president of the United States? Why should the capital of this African country be named for him?

3. Why do forests grow on the Gulf of Guinea, grass in the Sudan, and neither in large areas of the Sahara?

III

Make a list of the places mentioned in this chapter. Arrange them by countries, cities, rivers, mountains, etc. From the list select those places which you think are so important that you should always be able to locate them and know something about them.

GENERAL REVIEW OF AFRICA

1. What part of Africa is in west longitude? How much of the continent is in north latitude? What divisions does the equator cross? What divisions are in the temperate zone?

2. Explain the rainfall of northern, central, and southern Africa.

3. Through what divisions of Africa do the Atlas Mountains extend? the Southern Highlands? What divisions are included wholly or partly in the highlands in the east? in the west? What divisions lie in the grasslands? in the deserts? What influence does the natural region in which the divisions lie have on the life and occupations of the people?

4. Name the highest mountain ranges of Africa; the highest peaks; the largest lakes; the four largest rivers.

5. What is the largest city of Africa? the largest river? the highest mountain? the largest lake? the greatest waterfall?

6. Write a list of the chief seaports of Africa. Opposite each one write the name of the division in which it is situated. In a third column write the name of the European nation which controls it.

7. Sketch a map of Africa and show on it the railroads of which you have read and the principal cities on them.

8. What nations control the most of Africa? In what ways have they helped in the development of their colonies? What other nations have colonies in Africa? What countries are independent? Write a list of the possessions of each European nation.

9. What are some of the materials which the United States sends to Africa? What products do we receive from that continent?

10. In which division of Africa have you been most interested? Why?

GENERAL REVIEW OF AFRICA

11. Why are the rivers of Africa of great importance to the countries in which they are located?

12. What parts of Africa are most suitable for light-skinned people to live in?

13. State with what divisions of Africa you associate the following: great lakes, high mountains, mangrove swamps, oases, the veldt, tropical forests, waterfalls; big game, copper, diamonds, gold, irrigation works, ruins; Arabs, Berbers, Bushmen, Kabyles, Blacks, Nomads, Pygmies, Tuaregs, Zulus; animal products, cloves, cocoa, coffee, copal, cork, cotton, dates, dried fruits, embroidery, esparto, grain, gum arabic, ivory, mahogany, olive oil, ostrich feathers, palm nuts and palm oil, peanuts, rubber, sugar, vineyards.

PROBLEMS ON AFRICA

Life in ancient and modern Egypt. How did the position, surface, soil, climate, and other physical features of Egypt help in the early development of the country? In what ways will Egypt be of great future importance?

British possessions in Africa. How will railroads help in the development of the Anglo-Egyptian Sudan? Of what advantage is it to the British to develop their colonies in East Africa? Why do the people of British Somaliland raise cattle and sheep and lead a wandering life, while those of Zanzibar raise fruits, vegetables, and spices? Why is South Africa thinly populated? What are the probabilities of its ever being more densely populated than the United States? What industries may in the future be of more importance in the province of the Cape of Good Hope than diamond mining? Describe the future industries and people of the Orange Free State and Basutoland. How does Natal differ from that part of the Cape Province directly opposite on the Atlantic coast? Why should Johannesburg, rather than Kimberley, Cape Town, or Port Elizabeth, have grown to be the fourth largest city of Africa? Southwest Africa is one of the parts of Africa which will probably develop rapidly in the future. In what ways will it then be different from what it is today? Why is the desert in South Africa not as large as the Sahara in the north? Describe Rhodesia as you think it will be fifty years from now. (Debate) Is it a good investment for England to put large sums of money into harbor improvements, roads, and railroads in West Africa? What makes the Gold Coast and Ashanti valuable? Compare the colony (Liberia) which America established in Africa for freedmen with the one founded by the British (Sierra Leone). Why should Gambia, in the west, be of more value to the British than Somaliland, in the east?

French possessions in Africa. (Debate) Are the French or the British colonies in Africa of more value to the mother country? Describe the people, villages, occupations, productions, transportation, etc. of French Equatorial Africa as you think that they will be half a century from now. Why has Senegal become a more important colony of France than Dahomey or French Guinea? How will it be possible for the Sahara to become of great value to France? As Morocco develops, what exports and imports will increase? Why is Algeria the most important colony of France? Tunis is in about the same latitude, is about as large, and contains about as many people as South Carolina. In what ways is it different from that state? How do you account for these differences? Why is Somaliland of less importance to France than Senegal, on the west coast? Why is Madagascar a prosperous and valuable colony?

The Belgian Congo. (Debate) Which colony will be of the greater value to the world, the Union of South Africa or the Belgian Congo?

Italian possessions in Africa. (Debate) Is it an advantage or a disadvantage to Italy to use men and money to subdue, control, and develop the country of Libya? How does the position of Eritrea affect its importance? Why is Italian Somaliland of less importance than Eritrea?

Portuguese possessions in Africa. In what ways can the colony of Angola help Portugal to become less dependent on foreign nations? (Debate) Which of her two African colonies, Angola or Mozambique, will be of the greatest value to Portugal? Why are the products on the east coast of Africa very different from those of Portuguese Guinea on the west coast? Why do more tourists visit the Madeira Islands than the Azores or the Canaries? How has their position affected the importance of the Cape Verde Islands? Why has the island of St. Thomas become one of the great cocoa-producing regions of the world?

Spanish possessions in Africa. Of what value will the Spanish colonies ever be to the mother country? Is it an advantage or a disadvantage to Spain to hold Spanish Morocco? (Debate) Is it an advantage or a disadvantage to the rest of the world for Spain to hold this land? Rio de Oro is about as large as Colorado. What contrasts in the two places can you find? How have the position and the climate of the Canary Islands affected their importance? Why will Fernando Po become an important place for the production of cocoa and sugar? Why is Rio Muni not as valuable a colony as the Portuguese colony of St. Thomas?

The Abyssinian plateau. What advantages does Abyssinia possess which will tend to increase its importance?

The republic of Liberia. Why is Liberia less developed than other parts of West Africa?

CHAPTER XXX

THE GREAT LAND OF AUSTRALIA

WHAT shall we call Australia—the largest island in the world or the smallest continent? It is surrounded by water, and therefore it is an island. It is about the size of the United States and more than three fourths as large as Europe, so it may well be classed among the continents. In your geography textbook the map of Australia is often made on a smaller scale than those of the other continents. Consequently we do not realize its great size. Imagine Australia occupying a whole page as Europe does, or a double page, like the United States. All its divisions would then appear much larger and its mountain ranges and rivers much longer, and you could better compare them with the mountains and rivers of the other continents.

Australia is a part of the British Commonwealth, and the king is represented there by a governor general. The country, however, enjoys the same freedom that Canada does. The Commonwealth of Australia, formed in 1900, consists of six states: New South Wales, Victoria, Queensland, South Australia, West

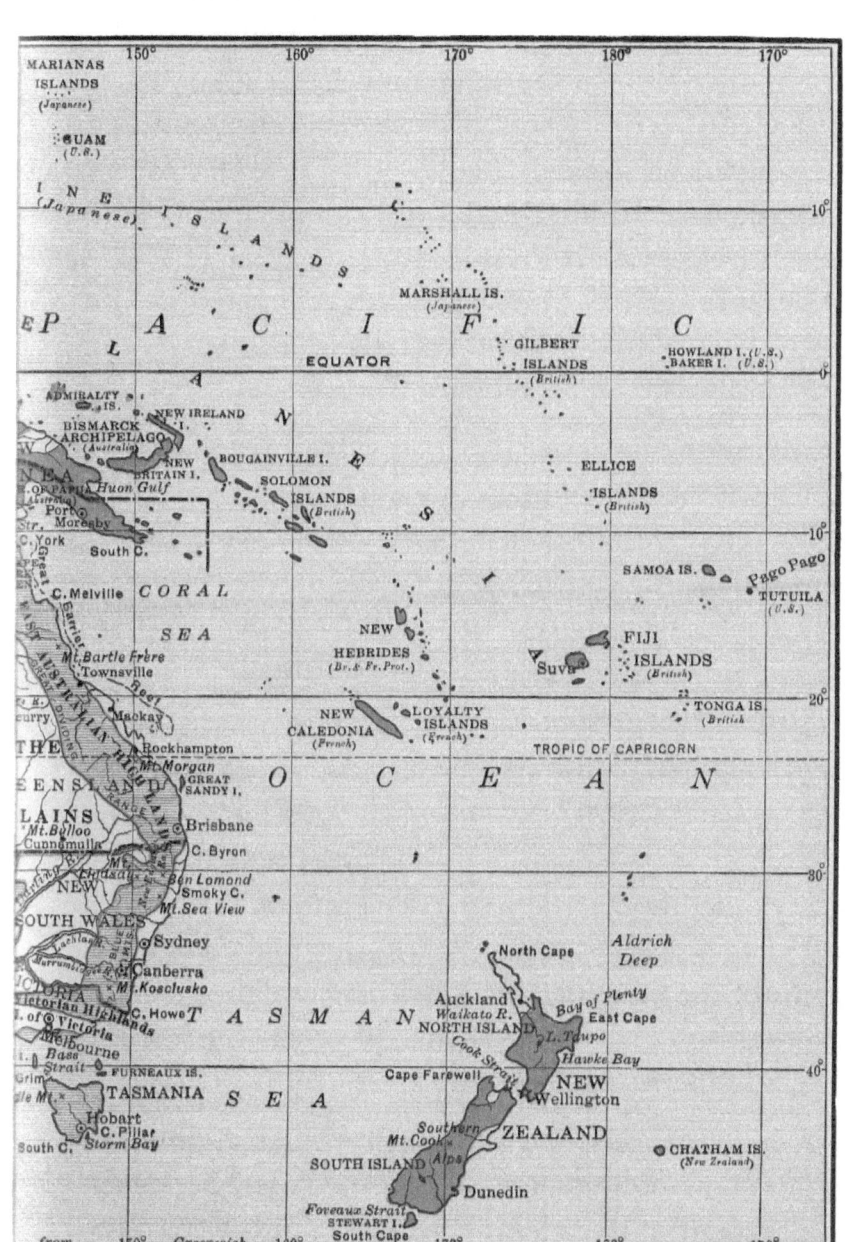

Australia, and Tasmania. Some ten years later South Australia transferred the Northern Territory to the Commonwealth. At the same time an area, known as the Federal Territory, was given to the Commonwealth by New South Wales. This territory is about fifteen times the size of our District of Columbia. Canberra, the future capital, is located in the Federal Territory, as our capital city of Washington is located in the District of Columbia. At present Melbourne serves the Commonwealth as its capital.

Some things about Australia which seem strange to us are the result of its position in the Southern Hemisphere. In our own country the northern part is colder than the southern. In Australia the reverse is true: the northern part is the warmer, and being so near the equator the temperature there during the warmest months is very high.

The hottest part of the year in Australia is in December, January, and February. At this season the sun is high in Australian skies and gives more heat than at any other time of the year. When the sun in June is at its most northerly point and is shining high over lands north of the equator, it is low in Australian skies. Its slanting rays give less heat than at other times of the year, and the Australian winter has begun.

There are plants and animals in Australia unlike any in our country. Some of the trees shed their bark each year instead of their leaves. On some of the trees the leaves hang edgewise to the sun and therefore give less shade than the leaves on our trees do. Exposing less of their surface to the sun they lose less of their moisture by evaporation, which, in this dry land, is a blessing.

One of the peculiar trees in Australia is the grass tree, which sends out its long blades in every direction so that it looks like a ball of grass perched on a short stump. The trunk of another tree is shaped like a bottle. In the north the bamboos, graceful palm trees, and beautiful orchids are much like those of tropical Africa. A common tree in Australia is the eucalyptus, or gum, tree, which sometimes grows more than three hundred feet high. Compare the height of your schoolhouse with one of these tall trees.

The animals of Australia are as interesting as the plants. Of course you have seen pictures of the kangaroo. Its short front legs are much like arms, while its hind legs are very long and strong and enable it to jump great distances. The mother kangaroo carries her babies in a deep skin pocket until they are old enough to use their legs. Some kangaroos are no larger than rabbits, while others are larger than a man. The animals are hunted for their skins, and kangaroo leather is used for bags, belts, shoes, and other articles.

The wombat, which looks somewhat like a small bear, is hunted for its fur. The platypus, another odd animal, has a bill and webbed feet like a duck, but, instead of feathers, it wears a soft, thick fur coat.

In parts of Australia the white ant is as troublesome as it is in parts of Africa. In building houses, laying railroads, and extending telegraph wires these ants have to be reckoned with. They work underground and from the inside, and in a short time make a wooden sleeper, telegraph pole, beam, or joist only a hollow shell which will collapse with the slightest strain.

Look at the map on page 411 and notice that most of the cities are located in the east and southeast. As you know, Nature usually has a large part in determining the position of cities, and it is due to her work that Australian cities are located as they are. The surface of Australia is like a great dish, irregular in shape, with a rim of mountains around the edge (see regional map on pages 400 and 401). This mountain rim is higher

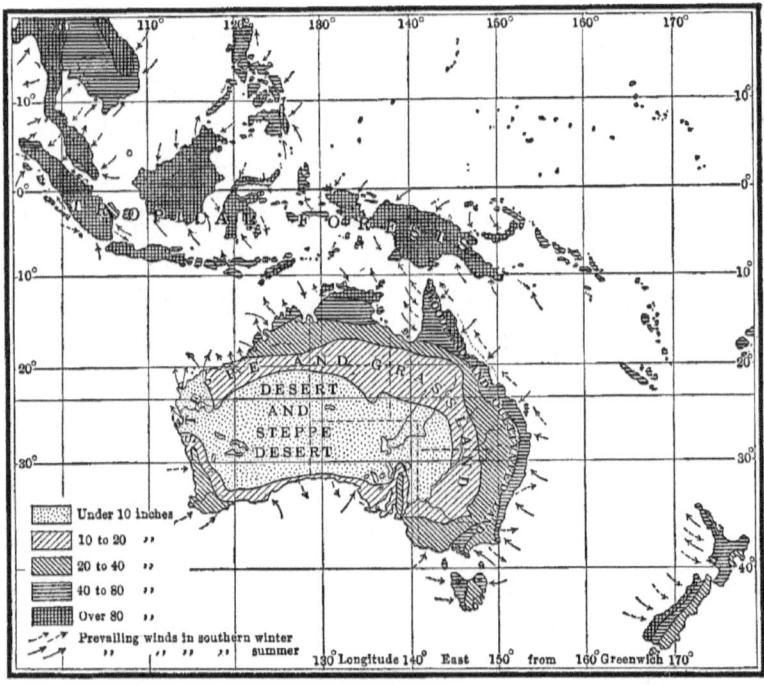

Figure 146. Rainfall map of Australia. Where is the heaviest rainfall? What vegetation do you find in this part of Australia? In what part of the continent is the desert? Why should there be a desert there?

in the east than anywhere else and shuts out from the interior of the continent the moisture brought by the trade winds. When Nature stretched the East Australian Highlands from north to south across the eastern part of the continent and built the Victoria Highland in the southeast, it became certain that large areas west and north of these mountains would be dry (see the rainfall map on page 404).

The northern part of Australia lies in the region where monsoon winds blow. These winds change their direction with the season. In the Australian summer, when the land is more heated than the water, they blow from the ocean to the land, bringing much moisture with them. During the winter season, when the ocean becomes warmer than the land mass, they blow from the land to the water, and therefore at this time little rain falls. Monsoons blow in India also. Have you ever read stories of the dependence of the people on these winds, and of the failure of the crops and the dreadful famines when the monsoons fail to blow?

Look again at the map and find the latitude of northern Australia. What is the latitude of Sydney? of Melbourne? The difference in latitude tells you that it is much cooler and pleasanter in southern Australia, and it is here that we shall find the most important cities and the most people.

West of the East Australian Highlands you find on the regional map an area known as the Great Plains. The soil washed from the mountains is fertile, and much of the land, especially in the south, is watered by great rivers. What are the names of the two largest? The rainfall is light here, but there is an abundance of underground water which can be obtained by drilling wells. As on our own Great Plains, there are many large ranches here and large areas covered with grass, which furnishes food for sheep and cattle.

On the slopes of the highlands are forests of eucalyptus trees. Valuable as these forests are, they were for years a great hindrance to farming. Millions had to be felled and the timber burned to make room for

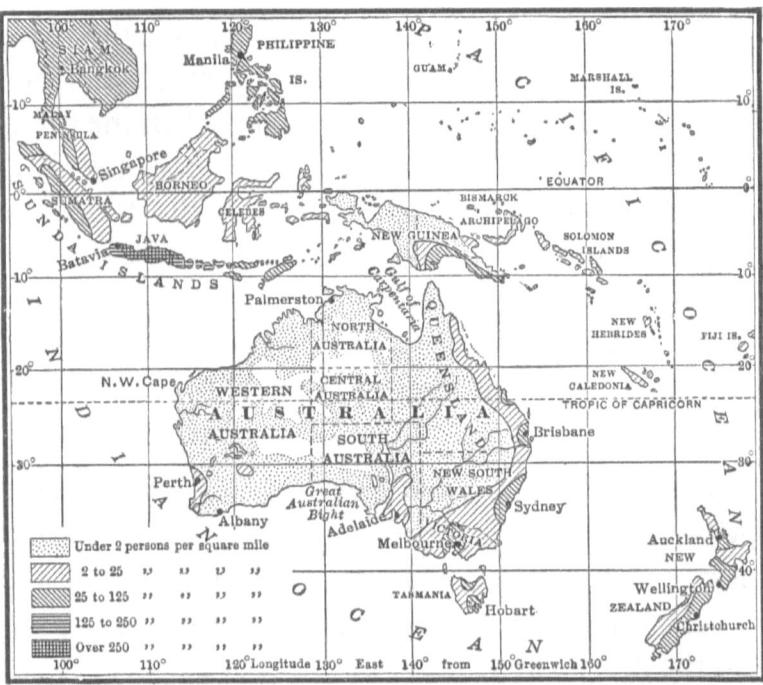

Figure 147. Population map of Australia. In what part of the continent do the most people live? the fewest? How does the map on page 404 help you to explain these conditions?

farms. Such wastefulness always goes on in a new land, but the Australian government is now taking steps to preserve the forest lands and encourage good methods of lumbering.

West of the Great Plains is the Western Plateau. Look again at the map and see how large a part of the continent this plateau occupies. For the most part this is a desert region. Parts of the coastal plain along the western shores receive rain in winter from the westerly winds, and in such regions we find cities and towns and farms and ranches. Where water can be obtained by irrigation, settlers are venturing farther and farther inland, but throughout most of the interior there are no farms, no towns, and no people.

The development of the Western Plateau has been chiefly because of the gold there. You will read later of the mining towns of Kalgoorlie and Coolgardie. Where gold is, there men will go, for many people think that gold is the most valuable thing in the world. Do you think so? Can you think of any desirable thing that gold cannot buy?

SUGGESTIONS FOR STUDY

I

1. Size of Australia.

2. The Commonwealth of Australia.

3. Effect of its position in the Southern Hemisphere.

4. Some plants and animals.

5. Natural regions of Australia.

6. Winds and rainfall.

II

1. If you live north of the tropic of Cancer, you can never see the sun at noon shining directly over your head. Why is this so?

2. How do you account for the fact that your shadow never points directly to the south?

3. What towns or cities in Australia are located almost directly on the tropic of Capricorn? On what date will the people there see the sun shining almost directly over their heads at noon? What season are they enjoying at this time? What season is it in the United States?

4. Cyclopedias will tell you of Australian animals and plants which are not mentioned in the text. What are some of these?

THE GREAT LAND OF AUSTRALIA

5. Why are most of the cities and towns of Australia situated in the south and the southeast?

6. How far is it from Brisbane to Perth? What cities in the United States are about the same distance apart?

7. Four fifths of all the people in Australia live in New South Wales, Victoria, and Queensland. Why should this be so?

III

Make a list of the places mentioned in this chapter. Arrange them by countries, cities, rivers, mountains, etc. From the list select those places which you think are so important that you should always be able to locate them and know something about them.

CHAPTER XXXI

A TRIP THROUGH THE ISLAND CONTINENT

On a trip from the United States to Australia we should probably land at Sydney, the largest city. On which coast is it located? Our steamer glides through a gateway which the ocean has cut in the cliffs, into the wonderful harbor, one of the largest and finest on earth.

Built on the hills sloping up from the sea, Sydney is no less wonderful than its harbor. The fine stone blocks, the splendid public buildings, the attractive stores, and the many busy people, all tell us that we are in a large modern city. From the great warehouses, the crowded wharves, and the many large ships in the harbor we know that we are in one of the world's great commercial ports.

Some of the ships are being loaded with wool, for Australia is the most important sheep-raising country of the world. Others are taking on cargoes of mutton, lamb, tallow, great sides of beef, and thousands of frozen rabbits. In some of the warehouses there are piles of sheepskins, rabbit skins, and cattle hides. In others there

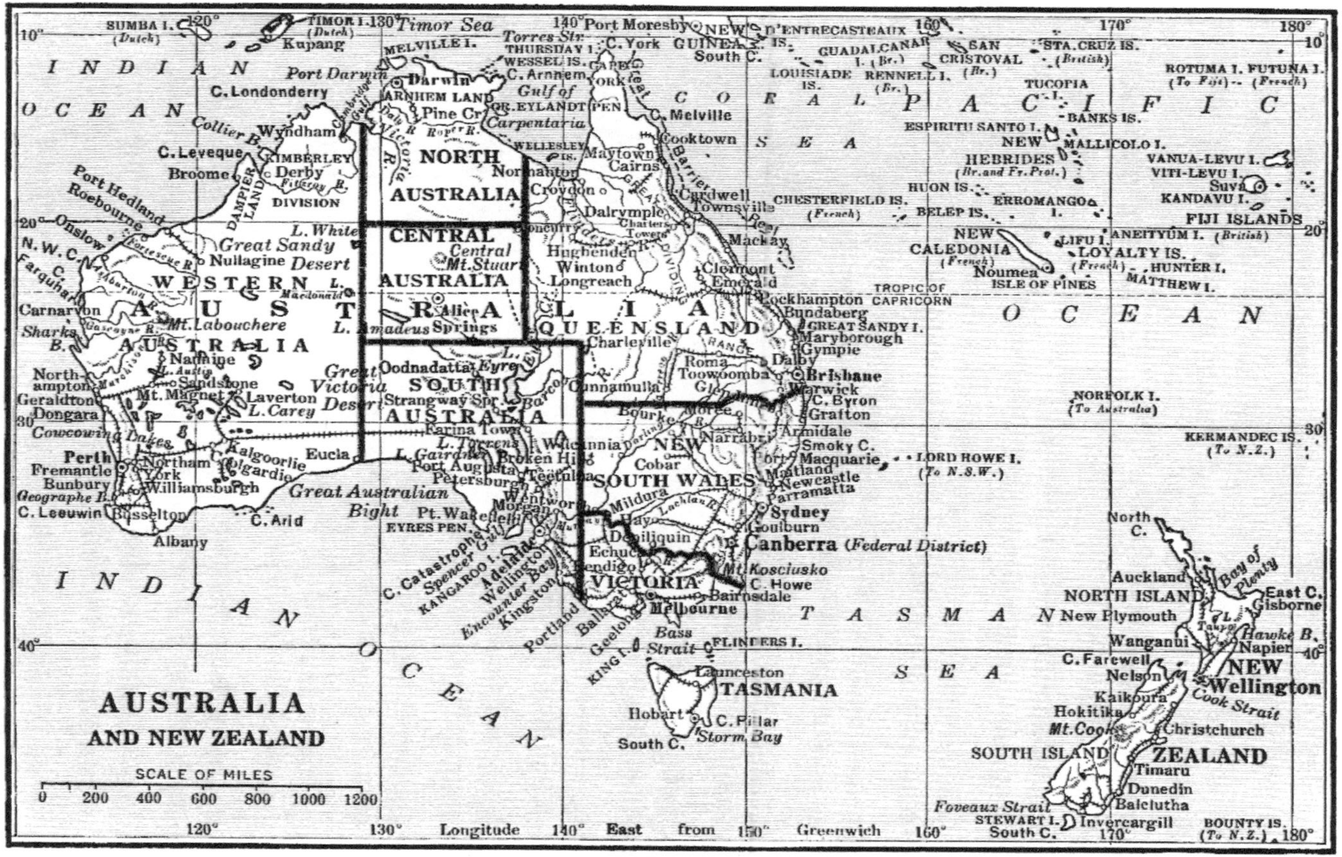

AUSTRALIA
AND NEW ZEALAND
SCALE OF MILES
0 200 400 600 800 1000 1200
Longitude East from Greenwich
INDIAN OCEAN
CORAL SEA
PACIFIC OCEAN
TASMAN SEA
Timor Sea
Torres Str.
Gulf of Carpentaria
Great Australian Bight
Bass Strait
Cook Strait
Foveaux Strait
TROPIC OF CAPRICORN
WESTERN AUSTRALIA
NORTH AUSTRALIA
CENTRAL AUSTRALIA
SOUTH AUSTRALIA
QUEENSLAND
NEW SOUTH WALES
VICTORIA
TASMANIA
NEW ZEALAND
NORTH ISLAND
SOUTH ISLAND
KIMBERLEY DIVISION
DAMPIER LAND
ARNHEM LAND
Great Sandy Desert
Great Victoria Desert
NEW GUINEA
Port Moresby
Darwin
Port Darwin
Wyndham
Derby
Broome
Port Hedland
Roebourne
Onslow
Carnarvon
Geraldton
Dongara
Perth
Fremantle
Bunbury
Busselton
Albany
Kalgoorlie
Coolgardie
Northam
York
Eucla
Oodnadatta
Alice Springs
Port Augusta
Petersburg
Adelaide
Broken Hill
Mildura
Bourke
Cobar
Charleville
Longreach
Winton
Hughenden
Rockhampton
Bundaberg
Maryborough
Gympie
Toowoomba
Brisbane
Townsville
Cairns
Cooktown
Mackay
Armidale
Newcastle
Sydney
Parramatta
Goulburn
Canberra (Federal District)
Mt. Kosciusko
Melbourne
Geelong
Ballarat
Bendigo
Echuca
Deniliquin
Portland
Launceston
Hobart
Auckland
New Plymouth
Wanganui
Napier
Gisborne
Wellington
Nelson
Christchurch
Timaru
Dunedin
Balclutha
Invercargill
Hokitika
Mt. Cook
Kaikoura
Noumea
Suva
FIJI ISLANDS
NEW CALEDONIA
NEW HEBRIDES
LOYALTY IS.
NORFOLK I. (To Australia)
LORD HOWE I. (To N.S.W.)
KERMANDEC IS. (To N.Z.)
BOUNTY IS. (To N.Z.)
STEWART I.
KANGAROO I.
KING I.
FLINDERS I.
MELVILLE I.
SUMBA I. (Dutch)
TIMOR I. (Dutch)
Kupang
CHESTERFIELD IS. (French)
ROTUMA I. (To Fiji)
FUTUNA I. (French)

are many thousand pounds of butter. There are great grain elevators filled with wheat waiting to be loaded on the English steamers in the harbor. We see also copper ingots, bars of gold and silver, and quantities of lead and tin, for Australia, you know, is one of the great mining countries of the earth. Besides the minerals mentioned, it contains also rich deposits of coal and splendid quarries of granite, marble, sandstone, and limestone. These deposits of building material account,

Figure 148. This is a warehouse for storing wool. Foreign buyers are sampling the wool. To what port in the United States may the wool be brought? On what waters will the vessel sail?

partly at least, for the fine public buildings which add so much to the beauty of the cities. Should you like to take a trip through Australia to visit its mines and mining towns? It would take a longer time than we can spare, for there are mining regions in many different parts of the continent. You would see copper mines, as modern as those in Montana and Arizona, and great smelters, where the ore is treated to separate it from the impurities which it contains. You would find lead, zinc, and silver mines which would remind you of those in Missouri, Oklahoma, and Utah. You could visit places where iron is worked from the surface as it is in the open mines of Minnesota, and you could go down in deep mines and see the iron blasted out of the rock, carried to the shaft, and hoisted to the surface in elevators.

In the coal mines of New South Wales you might easily imagine that you were in the mines of Pennsylvania or Illinois, for the work is carried on here on a large scale, and millions of tons are produced each year. What a blessing it is to Australia that Nature included coal among the minerals which she hid in the earth here! Can you imagine what a handicap it would be to the development of Australia if the coal which she needs in her manufactures and commerce had to be brought over the ocean from places thousands of miles away?

It was due to the gold deposits of Australia that settlers were first attracted to this part of the world; and in our trip through the continent we shall find gold mines in every state and in many different kinds of regions, even in the midst of the desert, hundreds of miles from farms and ranches and cities.

It was in 1848 that gold was discovered in California, and the next year the "forty-niners" were making their way over the mountains and deserts of our great West and by long ocean voyages to the gold fields. The gold rush to Australia occurred a few years later, and the people became just as excited over the wonderful nuggets which were found as they did in California. As in our Pacific state, the first gold was taken from the loose sands and gravels. Now in many parts of Australia men are working in the hard quartz rock hundreds of feet below the surface of the earth and mining each year so many millions of dollars' worth of gold that Australia ranks next to Africa and the United States in its production.

The gold of Australia, like that of California, was very important in attracting people to the land, but in both places men have found that other resources may be of equal or even much greater value. Let us see what some of these Australian resources are.

The city of Sydney, at which we landed, is the capital of New South Wales, a state as large as Minnesota, Michigan, Iowa, and Illinois. The eastern slopes of the mountains which extend through the state receive considerable rainfall, but the climate grows drier toward the west. Look at the map on page 411 and you will notice that New South Wales contains more rivers than any other Australian state. In their valleys the soil is very fertile. Water to irrigate the farms can be obtained from the rivers and by sinking wells to the underground supply.

Thousands of cattle and millions of sheep feed in the pastures of New South Wales. These furnish large quantities of wool, meat, hides, skins, and other products. Many of the farmers who raise dairy cattle carry their milk to coöperative creameries, where large amounts of butter and cheese are made.

Figure 149. This is beef hanging in a great packing house awaiting export. In which natural regions of Australia do you think many cattle may be raised? (See regional map and Figure 146)

Nearly twice as many sheep are raised in Australia as in our country. New South Wales has more than any other state, though there are millions in Victoria, Queensland, and other parts of the Commonwealth. On the slopes of the mountains and in the valleys of the Murray and Darling rivers are raised the finest sheep in the world. They are chiefly Merinos, a breed which lived originally on the plateaus of Spain. You would enjoy a visit to a sheep ranch, or station, as it is called in Australia, and the life on the open plains with the herder and his dog. The dog can drive the sheep better than its master can. It looks after the straying animals, turns them back among the others, and guides the whole flock to the feeding grounds which its master has indicated.

Figure 150. See the line of ox teams bringing wool from some distant ranch to a railroad station. Many of the large sheep stations are miles away from a railroad.

When shearing time comes the workmen are busy in the long sheds wielding their power shears, with which they clip off the thick wool. One by one they release the frightened, bewildered animals, shorn of their thick, warm coats. After the shearing is over the wool is loaded on big wagons drawn by several horses or oxen and taken to the nearest railway station. From there it is carried by train down to the warehouses in the seaports.

Did you notice that some of the fields where the sheep were feeding had fences of wire netting? These fences were built not to keep the sheep in but to keep rabbits out. One of the early colonists carried with him to Australia a few rabbits from his English farm. There are no wild animals or long cold winters here to kill off the rabbits, and they have increased so rapidly and have eaten the grass over wide areas so closely that they have become a great pest to the sheep farmers.

Of recent years rabbit furs and skins have grown to be of considerable value, and people in England are using the flesh more and more for food, so that today men are finding it profitable to spend their time in catching rabbits and preparing them for market. Consequently their numbers are beginning to decrease.

From Sydney we can take a train northward to Brisbane, the capital of Queensland. This is a trip of over seven hundred miles. What city is about this distance from your home town? This journey takes us through the cattle-raising area of Australia. There are as many cattle in Queensland as in the other five states of the Commonwealth, and they are raised as far west as water can be supplied. Because of the lack of water in the interior, you can easily understand that irrigation is a very important problem, and farms, ranches, and towns follow its extension. In parts of Queensland the rain which falls on the East Australian Highland is stored in reservoirs and led through canals to farms and ranches as it is in many parts of the western United States. Underground water is obtained by means of artesian wells. Thousands of such wells have been bored, some of them more than a mile deep.

Figure 151. This looks like a scene on one of our great Western farms. It is in Australia, but the combined harvester and thresher shown here was made in the United States.

On the map on page 411 you will find off the coast of Queensland the Great Barrier Reef. This is the most wonderful coral structure in the world. It is marvelous to think of such tiny creatures as the coral polyps building this great sea wall a thousand miles long. In places the top of the reef is still below the surface of the ocean. In other places it rises above the water. Between the coral wall and the coast lies a quiet inland sea which makes a deep, safe channel for vessels plying between Asia and eastern Australia.

Find on the map the tiny island, off the north coast of Queensland, named for the fifth day of the week. Thursday Island is the headquarters of the pearl industry, and we shall be sure to find vessels here from the pearl-fishing grounds. We shall see many boats of the pearl divers also at Broome on the northwest coast.

Pearls are rarely found here, but the shells are valuable for mother-of-pearl, a beautiful coating which lines them. Have you ever seen buttons, knife handles, or box covers made of this lovely iridescent material? Perhaps a jeweler will be kind enough to show you some article made of mother-of-pearl.

Coming back from Brisbane to Sydney and continuing to Melbourne and Adelaide we see fields of waving wheat stretching away on either side of the track. We could see similar sights also around Perth in West Australia. From all the large ports of Australia quantities of wheat are exported. The great plows and harvesters and reapers used in Australian wheat fields are like those which we use on the farms in our central and Western states, and on some of them we might find the words "Made in U.S.A."

As we ride through Australia we see many other products on the well-kept farms besides those which we have mentioned. In places in the Murray River valley you might almost think that you were in a California vineyard. The grapes produced here change in the hot sunshine and dry air into sweet brown raisins, just as they do in southern California. Quantities of smaller grapes also are drying in the fields. These will form little black currants, such as your mother uses in her cakes and puddings.

We are astonished at the amount of fruit produced in Australia. On our trip we have seen orange and lemon groves and orchards of peach, apple, and apricot trees. Besides these there are many olive, cherry, pear, plum, and quince trees, and acres of strawberry vines and raspberry and blackberry bushes. Large quantities of these fruits are made into marmalade, jam, and jelly, and millions of pounds of canned goods are sent to England every year.

Figure 152. See the bags of wheat piled beside the railroad track waiting for a train to take them down to Melbourne. Where is this city?

Victoria, the smallest state of the Commonwealth, is a little larger than Minnesota. Half of the people of the state live in Melbourne, a city about the size of Boston. You would enjoy its "zoo," its botanical gardens, its lovely parks, and its broad streets lined with splendid buildings. There are many beaches along the shore where you would like to play in the hard white sand and bathe in the clear water. You would like, also, to see the large warehouses and wharves, count the big steamers in the harbor, and watch them being loaded with grain, wool, frozen meat, hides and skins, dairy products, and minerals.

Adelaide, in South Australia, is also a beautiful city. Surrounded by blue water and green hills, and with its lovely parks watered by the little river which flows through the city, Adelaide attracts every visitor. It has many imposing blocks of white stone and magnificent public buildings and grounds. Around the city there are rich gardens, orchards, and vineyards.

You will notice on the map that all the cities and towns of South Australia are located near the coast. The northern part of this state belongs to the great Thirst Land, as the desert of central Australia is often called. By taking a trip on the transcontinental railroad from Adelaide to Perth, in the far west, we shall ride through a part of the Australian desert. For some time we run beside large vineyards and splendid orchards. Farther out we pass through a sea of wheat and then through pastures dotted with cattle

Figure 153. *This is one of the main streets in Melbourne. It is as fine a city as any in the United States. With which one of our cities does Melbourne compare in size?*

and with flocks of sheep, each tended by a shepherd and his dog. Still farther west the ranches become more scattered, and soon we are riding over a desert region where there are no farms, no ranches, and no towns.

Out in the desert several hundred miles from other centers are the mining towns of Kalgoorlie and Coolgardie. How wonderful it is that these places, with their electric lights, broad streets, and pleasant homes, should have grown up here in this desolate region. There was not even water near. More than three hundred miles beyond Kalgoorlie the Darling Range squeezes the moisture from the westerly winds which in the winter season blow in from the ocean. Some of this water is collected in huge reservoirs and is led in pipes across the desert to the gold city.

Western Australia will always be an important mining country, not only for gold but for other minerals

Figure 154. This is a scene in the mining region at Kalgoorlie. What can you see in the picture?

as well. Fortunately for its future development, coal is found in abundance.

As we travel north through Western Australia we pass scattered ranches and see cattle and sheep off on the plains. At present this part of Australia is but little developed. Many of the people who have been attracted here by the gold will doubtless settle on the land and become ranchers. With the development of irrigation, farmers will raise wheat and will cultivate vineyards, but stock raising will continue to be the chief industry.

Figure 155. This team is carrying supplies to a lonely sheep station far away from any town. Such regions as this may sometime be covered with prosperous farms. How can this happen?

On the map on page 411 you will find, in the northern part of Western Australia, the town of Kimberley. It is named after the famous mining city in South Africa, but instead of deposits of diamonds it is surrounded by rich gold fields. The few towns along the tropical northern coast of Australia, from the Gulf of

Carpentaria to the western point of the continent, are either mining settlements or the ports leading to them.

While we are in the northern part of Australia we may see something of the natives, descendants of those people whom the early settlers found here. The native Australians have skin of a brownish color. Some of the natives work on the sheep farms, but most of them live far away from any white settlements. The women do the work in the villages and carry the heavy loads on the march. The men hunt and trap and do some fighting with other tribes.

The island of Tasmania is sometimes called the orchard of the Commonwealth of Australia, for it produces many kinds of fruit. Do you suppose that the workers in the strawberry beds and among the raspberry bushes, and in the orchards and jam factories, ever think of the English homes to which the fruit is sent and of the English children who enjoy their bread spread with Australian jam?

Most of the fruit farms are in the fertile valleys of Tasmania. On the uplands and hillsides the shepherds tend large flocks of sheep. Because of its mountains and valleys, its waterfalls, and its lovely scenery, Tasmania has been called the Switzerland of Australia. It has a heavy rainfall, and this keeps its swift streams full. Its abundant water power is very valuable and is being used more each year in developing electricity for lighting and manufacturing. Why is it, do you think, that the use of water power should be increasing so rapidly in all parts of the world?

THE ISLAND CONTINENT

Figure 156. This is a harvesting scene in Tasmania. Notice the height of the grain as compared with that of the horses. Can you tell what the machine does to the wheat?

On account of its climate and its abundant rainfall Tasmania has great forests. Many men find work in felling the trees and in the sawmills, where the splendid hard woods are made into boards, planks, and other forms of lumber. Many other Tasmanians work in the mines. One of the tin mines here is said to be the richest in the world.

On account of its beauty many tourists visit Tasmania, to fish in its streams, bathe in its waters, wander through its woods, and climb its mountains. In later years you may be among its visitors. What should you like best to see here?

The continent of Australia is situated on the other side of the world from the United States and on the opposite side of the equator. In spite of its great distance from us we are interested in its development, for many goods from our mills, factories, and foundries find their way into Australian cities and towns and farm lands. Since we have been in Australia we have seen in the stores cotton goods, underwear, gloves, and many other articles of clothing from our manufacturing centers; we have learned that great quantities of oil, such as benzine, gasoline, kerosene, turpentine, and lubricating oils, have come from our home land; we have found the names of companies in the United States on many articles of iron and steel, machinery, cash registers, tools, sewing machines, typewriters, and on great plows, reapers, and binders for the wheat fields. We have ridden in motor cars made in cities of our Middle West, and in the seaports we have seen large amounts of lumber from our Western forests.

You can easily imagine what the people of Australia send us in return for all these goods. Mixed with the wool of which your coat or sweater is made, there is probably some from Australian sheep. Wool and gold are the most important articles which we receive from Australia, but besides these, ships bring to us other minerals and some copra.

SUGGESTIONS FOR STUDY

I

1. The city of Sydney.

2. Minerals and mines.

3. The cattle and sheep industries.

4. Forests of Australia.

5. The rabbit pest.

6. Rainfall and irrigation.

7. The Great Barrier Reef.

8. The pearl industry.

9. The wheat and fruit industries.

10. A trip on the transcontinental railroad.

11. Cities of Australia.

12. Native Australians.

13. Tasmania.

II

1. How far is Australia from the nearest continent (see map on pages 442 and 443)?

2. Describe the route from your home town or city to Australia. How long would the trip take?

AFRICA, AUSTRALIA, ISLANDS OF PACIFIC

3. Why is more wheat raised in the southern part of Australia than in the northern or the central part?

4. What advantages has Australia as a sheep-producing country?

5. Why is the small state of Victoria the most densely peopled?

6. When it is day in the United States it is night in Australia. When it is summer in the United States it is winter in Australia. Explain these curious facts.

7. Sketch an outline map of Australia. Show the waters around, the names of the states of the Commonwealth, the chief cities, the two chief rivers, and the natural regions.

III

Make a list of the places mentioned in this chapter. Arrange them by countries, cities, rivers, mountains, etc. From the list select those places which you think are so important that you should always be able to locate them and know something about them.

CHAPTER XXXII
IN GEYSER LAND

LIKE Australia, New Zealand is a part of the British Commonwealth. It consists of two main islands and several smaller ones. On the map the group appears to be located at no great distance from Australia, but the trip from Wellington to Sydney occupies four days.

Altogether New Zealand is about as large as Colorado. It is a beautiful place and a very healthful one. North Island contains springs of boiling water and spouting geysers which remind us of those in our own Yellowstone Park. Many people come here to see the wonderful sights and to bathe in some of the hot springs, whose waters, charged with mineral matter, are supposed to be beneficial in the treatment of various diseases.

On South Island are the lovely Southern Alps, with their white, snow-covered tops, their swift mountain streams, their beautiful waterfalls, and their blue glaciers, which rival those of Switzerland. Many visitors come here to camp and rest in the fern-filled valleys and enjoy the wonderful scenery. On the western coast there are many long, deep inlets like the fiords of Norway.

The cliffs rise straight out of the water for hundreds of feet, and over their dark sides pour waterfalls from the snows above. With all these attractions New Zealand is fast becoming one of the world's greatest playgrounds.

Many of the people of New Zealand own large ranches and raise cattle, horses, and sheep. Mountains stretch through the islands, and on the plains and slopes to the east of them are some of the best sheep lands of the world. The grasses are nourishing, water is plentiful, the climate is so mild that the sheep can feed in the pastures all the year round, and there are no wild animals which make it necessary to guard the flocks. Though New Zealand is only about a thirtieth the size of Australia it contains about a third as many sheep.

Figure 157. *This is a scene on a sheep ranch in New Zealand. What advantages has this country for raising sheep?*

Wool is the most important export, and it is shipped away each year in great quantities worth millions of dollars. Some of it comes to the United States. If you would like to know how the number of sheep in these far-away islands and the production of wool compares with the sheep and wool products of the United States, choose someone in the class to write a letter to the Department of Agriculture in Washington asking for this information.

For years certain sections in New Zealand, like large areas in Australia, have been overrun with rabbits which have been a great pest to the sheep and cattle owners. The numbers of rabbits increase so rapidly that if they were not killed off, it would be only a short time before pastures and grainfields would be destroyed. Strict laws have been passed by the government compelling farmers to kill some of the rabbits in order to protect the fields.

With the growing use of rabbit meat and skins in European countries, the rabbit pest is changing into a profitable industry. In some places men are hired to kill the rabbits. Other landowners find it more profitable to allow the rabbits to accumulate, and kill them, rather than to try to raise sheep. In still other cases hunters and trappers give a bonus to landowners for the privilege of killing the rabbits on their property.

In such a mountainous country as New Zealand there is an abundance of water power. This is being used more and more each year in generating electricity for light and power. Considerable manufacturing is carried

AFRICA, AUSTRALIA, ISLANDS OF PACIFIC

on, and some of the wool grown in the pastures is spun and woven into cloth; but the islands will probably always be more important in agriculture, dairying, and stock raising than in manufacturing.

In Dunedin, Christchurch, and other towns, we can visit large meat-freezing establishments. Put on your thickest coat, for the freezing-rooms are very cold. The walls are white with frost, and the thousands of carcasses hanging from the walls and ceiling are frozen stiff. Several hundred million pounds of frozen mutton, lamb, and beef are sent in refrigerator ships to England, the United States, and other countries in different parts of the world.

Figure 158. Isn't this a pleasant scene? It is a cattle ranch in New Zealand. What is said in the text about the cattle industry here?

The dairy products exported from New Zealand are worth many million dollars. Thousands of dairy cattle are raised on the farms, and many of the farmers have milking machines run by electricity and use separators to get the cream from the milk. Some of the butter and cheese factories in the dairy regions are among the largest in the world. One coöperative dairy makes each year nearly ten thousand tons of butter and three thousand tons of cheese, and prepares nearly as much dried milk.

Though the animal industries are the most important in New Zealand, there are also splendid wheat farms, acres of cornlands, millions of fruit trees, and fields where hemp, flax, and many vegetables are produced.

One of the important products of New Zealand is an article of which perhaps you have never heard. This is kauri gum, which is used in large quantities in the making of varnish. Some of this gum is gathered from the forests of kauri pine which are growing on the islands. Much more is obtained in places where forests used to grow. For centuries these ancient trees shed gum from their leaves, limbs, and trunks, and great quantities are buried deep under the soil and leaves. Companies have been formed to obtain the gum from these swamps, and the New Zealand government still holds reservations which are estimated to contain millions of tons.

Makers of paints and varnishes and linoleums in our country are greatly interested in the production

AFRICA, AUSTRALIA, ISLANDS OF PACIFIC

of kauri gum. Are there any manufacturers of these products in your vicinity from whom you can learn more about this valuable product or obtain a sample of it?

Another little-known product of New Zealand is phormium, often called New Zealand flax. The long leaves of this plant yield a valuable fiber which can be used like hemp in making ropes.

When the first foreigners arrived in New Zealand they found many brown-skinned natives already living there. The Maoris, as these natives are called, probably came here from some of the other Pacific islands. Some of them live in the "Hot Lake Region," where they cook their food in the steam or boiling water of the hot springs. Many natives work on the ranches and in

Figure 159. Read the paragraph above and tell who these women are and what they are doing.

the grainfields. Perhaps you would like to visit one of their schools. If you think that you shall find backward methods and dull, uninterested pupils, you will be very much surprised. The Maoris are intelligent and have considerable ability. Some of them do wonderful carving on wood. Some have been educated as lawyers, doctors, and members of other professions, and a few are in the New Zealand government.

Auckland and Wellington are the most important cities of New Zealand. If you wish to see the beautiful government buildings and visit the sessions of congress, you must go to Wellington, for this city is the capital of the islands. Auckland is the largest city. As you walk through the streets of these cities, stop at the fine hotels, shop in the stores, enjoy the theaters, linger in the parks, and watch the traffic on the streets and boulevards, you can hardly realize that you are on the very edge of the civilized world. Everything is as modern and as fine as in the best cities of Europe and America.

We are interested in New Zealand because, next to the British Isles, the United States carries on more commerce than any other country with this group of islands. We receive from New Zealand millions of dollars' worth of hides and skins; frozen meat, tallow, and other animal products; kauri gum, gold, dairy products, hemp, and other articles. We send to the people there a great variety of goods, chief among which are machinery of all kinds and many other iron and steel manufactures; motor cars and trucks; oils, such as benzine, gasoline, kerosene, turpentine, and lubricating oils; textiles, principally of cotton; and tobacco and cigars.

SUGGESTIONS FOR STUDY

I

1. Size and location of New Zealand.

2. Attractions of the islands.

3. Sheep and wool.

4. The rabbit pest.

5. Cattle and cattle products.

6. Kauri gum.

7. The Maoris.

8. Cities of New Zealand.

II

1. How far from Australia is New Zealand (use scale of map on page 411)? Is its position an advantage or a drawback to the development of the island group?

2. In what countries of the world are geysers and hot springs found (see Allen's "North America")?

3. What countries of the world are noted for sheep raising (see Allen's "United States")?

4. What advantages for sheep raising explain the success of the industry in New Zealand?

5. Ship a cargo of wool from New Zealand to the United States. Name the shipping and receiving ports and the waters on which the vessel will sail.

6. What states in our country do you think are most interested in commerce with Australia and New Zealand? With what ports in these states is most of the commerce carried on?

III

Make a list of the places mentioned in this chapter. Be able to locate each place and tell what was said about it.

CHAPTER XXXIII

AMONG THE PACIFIC ISLANDS

The Pacific Ocean covers about a third of the globe. Scattered over its surface are thousands of islands, some of them small bits of land of only an acre or more and some larger than our largest states. Many are the tops of volcanic peaks which rise above the surface of the ocean, while others are formed of the skeletons of coral polyps.

Sometimes with a terrific uproar and outpouring of ashes and lava there is an uplift of the sea bottom, and new islands appear or old ones are enlarged. Sometimes an island which has been long enough above the surface of the ocean to have been covered with vegetation disappears beneath the blue waters. Sometimes a volcanic eruption accompanied by an uplifting of the sea bottom brings above the water some coral formation which, if left entirely to the work of the tiny polyps, might have been centuries in reaching the surface.

There are few places on earth more lovely than these Pacific lands. The white waves break over the low reefs which surround the coral islands, and the waving palm trees on the shelving beach are reflected in the quiet waters inside the reef. On the volcanic islands there are steep mountain masses and high cliffs, dashing streams and lovely waterfalls, and green valleys filled with rich tropical vegetation.

Figure 160. This is a village on one of the Pacific islands. Describe the scenery, the houses, and the people.

The natives are as interesting as their island homes are beautiful, and we shall enjoy visiting some of their villages. Most of the houses have thatched roofs, and in places the huts are raised on piles. On some of the islands they are even built in trees. There is little furniture in the houses—some mats to sleep on, some stones to cook on, and a few dishes of carved wood or coconut shells. Where the villages are near the settlements of foreigners, the natives have gradually adopted some of their customs, dressing and eating and working in a similar fashion.

Missionaries who have made their homes on the Pacific islands have done a valuable work for the people. They have not only taught them about God but have shown them better ways to live and work, have helped them in sickness, and have given them higher ideas of life.

Some of the islands have splendid harbors protected from storms and high waves by coral reefs, and large and deep enough for the world's greatest fleets. Then, too, these stepping-stones across the great ocean are useful for coaling stations, cable stations, and radio stations.

The islands yield valuable products which are needed by the great nations of the world. Many of the natives spend much of their time in gathering coconuts

Figure 161. These people are thatching the roof of their house. Notice the light construction beneath.

and making copra. This has grown to be the most important export from these lands. Some of the people work in cotton fields, on coffee and rubber plantations, and in gold and phosphate mines. We shall find some diving for pearls and others catching huge turtles, the shells of which are used in making combs and other toilet articles.

For long ages these Pacific islands have been the nesting places for enormous numbers of sea birds. The little British island of Nauru, only seven and a half miles long, was one of their favorite haunts. The birds which flocked here fed on the sea food around, nested in the coral rocks, and hatched their feathered families. They deposited here enormous quantities of guano. This, combined with the lime of which coral is composed, has been slowly changed through the long ages into phosphate of lime. This rock when treated with sulphuric acid yields a rich plant food. Men are now quarrying, crushing, and shipping the phosphate rock on Nauru and other islands, and many English farms are yielding rich crops because of this product from these far-distant lands.

The coconut trees which grow on most of the islands are a precious gift to the natives. Where they flourish, there is comfort and happiness; where they do not grow, few people live. On many of the islands the wealth and standing of a person depend on the number of coconut trees he owns. What was said on pages 70-72 about the coconut tree and the copra industry?

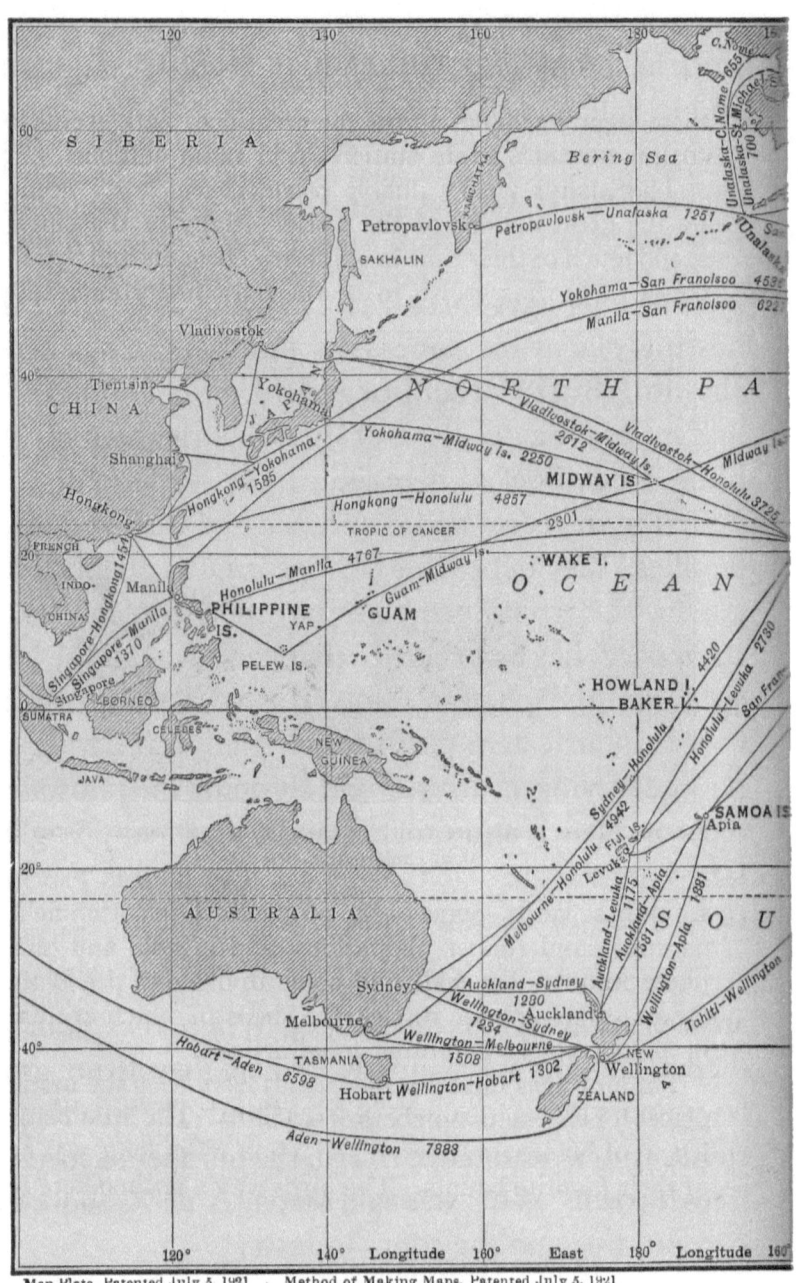

Map Plate, Patented July 5, 1921 . Method of Making Maps, Patented July 5, 1921

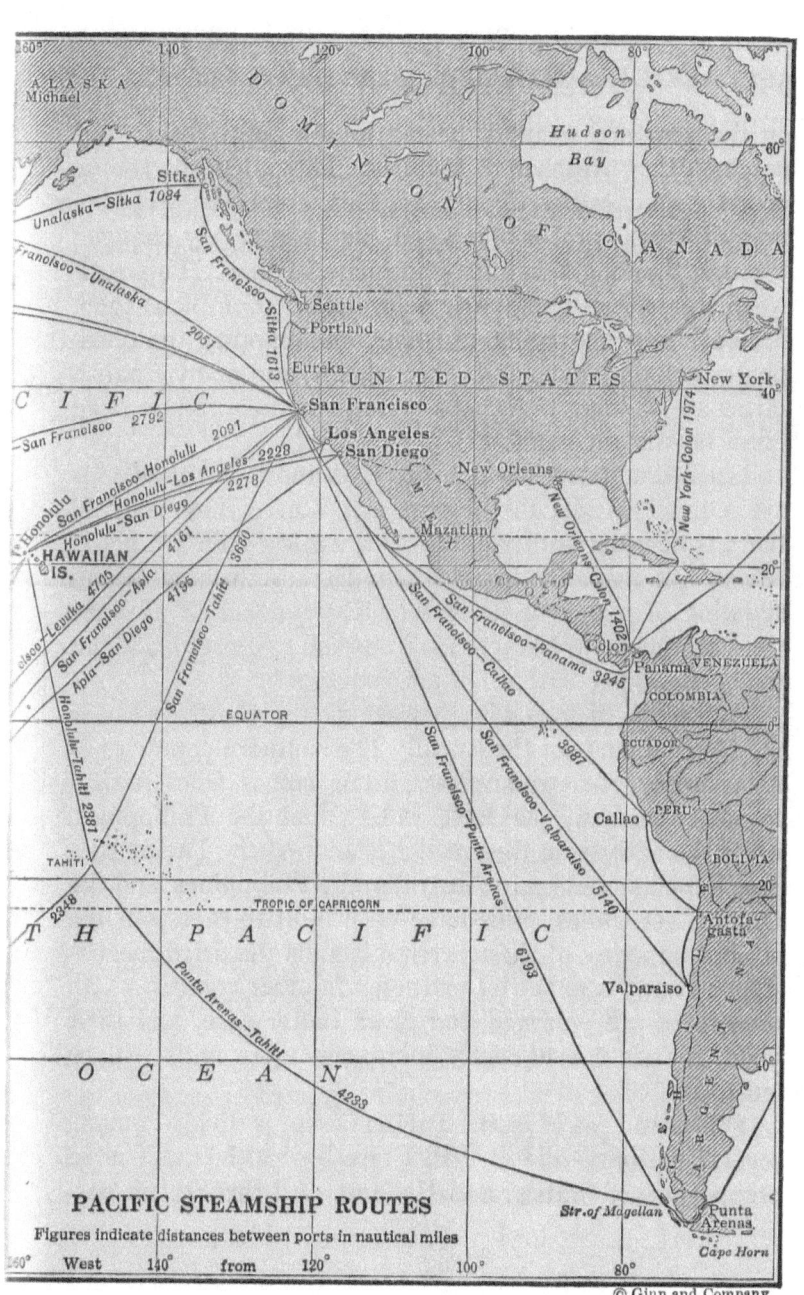

Thousands of tons of copra are produced each year in the tropical parts of the world. The southern countries of Asia supply great quantities. Some comes from Africa, tropical America, the East Indies, and the Philippines, while the natives on the smaller islands of the Pacific prepare large amounts. In Australia, the Philippines, and the Dutch East Indies, mills have been built to press out the oil, but on many of the scattered islands the dried meat is shipped away and the oil extracted in other countries. As the groves are enlarged and given better care, and their yield of fruit consequently increased, more mills will be built.

Figure 162. This is the end of the island of Yap. The natives with their baskets are carrying coal to a vessel which does not show in the picture. Why is Yap important?

This island world of the Pacific Ocean is divided among several nations—the British Commonwealth, the United States, Japan, France, and Holland. All the French possessions and most of those of the British lie south of the equator, while the United States and Japan control most of the land north of that line. Before the World War Germany had valuable possessions here. Among them were Kaiser Wilhelm's Land, a part of New Guinea; the Bismarck Archipelago; the little island of Nauru; some of the Solomon Islands, south of the equator; the Caroline and Marshall islands, north of that line; and all the Marianas, or Ladrone Islands, except Guam, which belongs to the United States.

At the close of the World War Japan received the mandate for the German possessions north of the equator, while those south of it were put under the control of the British through Australia or New Zealand. From the map on pages 400 and 401 find what islands have thus come into the hands of the Japanese. What groups do the British control? See what you can find in a cyclopedia or other reference book about these different island groups.

There is one little islet among these former German possessions in which the United States is more interested than in any other. This is the island of Yap, the most westerly of the Caroline group. The entire island covers a smaller area than some cities do; but small as it is, it is very important, and many discussions between the officials of our government and those of Japan have taken place concerning it. Yap is a crossroads in the Pacific, a crossroads not of routes over the ocean surface but of the cables which lie in its depths. Study the map on pages 442 and 443 and explain how the position of Yap makes it desirable as a center for cable lines.

Though Yap is one of the islands over which Japan

holds a mandate, our rights regarding trade and the control of the cables have been safeguarded by a treaty with that country.

SUGGESTIONS FOR STUDY

I

1. Formation of the Pacific islands.

2. Scenery on the islands.

3. The people and their homes.

4. Occupations.

5. Nauru and its phosphate beds.

6. Coconuts and copra.

7. Ownership of islands.

8. Yap and cable routes.

II

1. Name the oceans in the order of their size (see Appendix, page 505). Which ones have you ever seen?

2. Which do you think is the most important? Which is of the least importance? What are your reasons for so thinking?

3. How can you prove that Nature's work is not permanent but changing?

4. What are the chief industries on the Pacific islands? What products from these islands are used in the United States?

5. What industries mentioned in this chapter are carried on also in Africa?

6. How did the World War affect the Pacific islands? When did this war take place?

III

Make a list of the places mentioned in this chapter. Arrange them by countries, cities, rivers, mountains, etc. From these places select those which you think are so important that you should always be able to locate them and know something about them.

CHAPTER XXXIV

UNITED STATES POSSESSIONS IN THE PACIFIC

The part of our trip in the Pacific Ocean which we shall enjoy most is that which takes us through our own possessions. The Stars and Stripes float over the Philippines, the Hawaiian Islands, a part of the Samoan group, and several smaller islands, some of which are hardly more than dots in the blue water. What do cyclopedias tell you about Wake Island, Baker Island, Howland Island, and Midway? Find these islands on the map on pages 442 and 443.

The Samoan Islands lie on the main route between Australia and New Zealand and the United States. Because of this important position several nations have long been interested in them. Before the World War they were divided between Germany and the United States. Now the British, through New Zealand, have a mandate over the former German possessions.

All the Samoan group are volcanic, but around them the little coral workers have built low reefs. The

UNITED STATES POSSESSIONS IN THE PACIFIC

dark beds of lava extend to the shore, and the sea dashes and roars against the black cliffs.

The largest island of our Samoan possessions is Tutuila. It covers more than seventy square miles. How does this area compare with that of your home town or city? The harbor of Pago Pago is really the crater of an immense volcano of which the side toward the sea has disappeared, making an opening through which ships may enter. On the wharves at Pago Pago we see large quantities of copra which the natives in the different villages have prepared.

While we are here let us visit one of these villages. The people are very hospitable and give us a cordial welcome to their homes, offer us food, and invite us to remain with them. Each village has its native chief who is responsible to the American official for the people in his charge. The men and women are tall and straight with copper-colored skin and dark eyes. They do not like to work very hard, but who can blame them? The little thatch-roofed houses are easily built. Their sleeping mats are made from the fibers of plants, and their dishes from coconut shells and hand-carved wood. Their food is easily produced. The breadfruit tree requires no cultivation, and bananas, yams, and taro, the root of which resembles a sweet potato, need little care after the planting. Fish are plentiful in the waters around. No one is rich, no one is poor, and everyone is happy.

Guam

The island of Guam, the largest of the Marianas, was ceded to the United States by Spain at the close of the Spanish-American War. The rest of the group Spain sold to Germany. Who controls those islands now (see page 445)?

Guam is covered with volcanic hills and mountains and surrounded by low coral reefs. The brown-skinned natives here look much like the Filipinos. They are a happy, care free people, fond of dancing, story-telling, and other good times. They plow their rice fields with the water buffalo, as do their cousins in the Philippines. They dry the meat of the coconut in the warm sunshine and pick the pods from the cacao trees. They catch the fish in the waters around, and in their little gardens they raise some corn, sweet potatoes, and sugar cane.

As yet none of the products of the island are very valuable, and it was for other reasons that we wished to have it under our control. After we obtained the Philippine group it seemed necessary that we have some place not far away where ships of our navy could come, where vessels could be coaled, and where sailors could be stationed in case of trouble. Guam is also an important cable station, and we have built a radio station there by means of which operators can communicate with any part of the world.

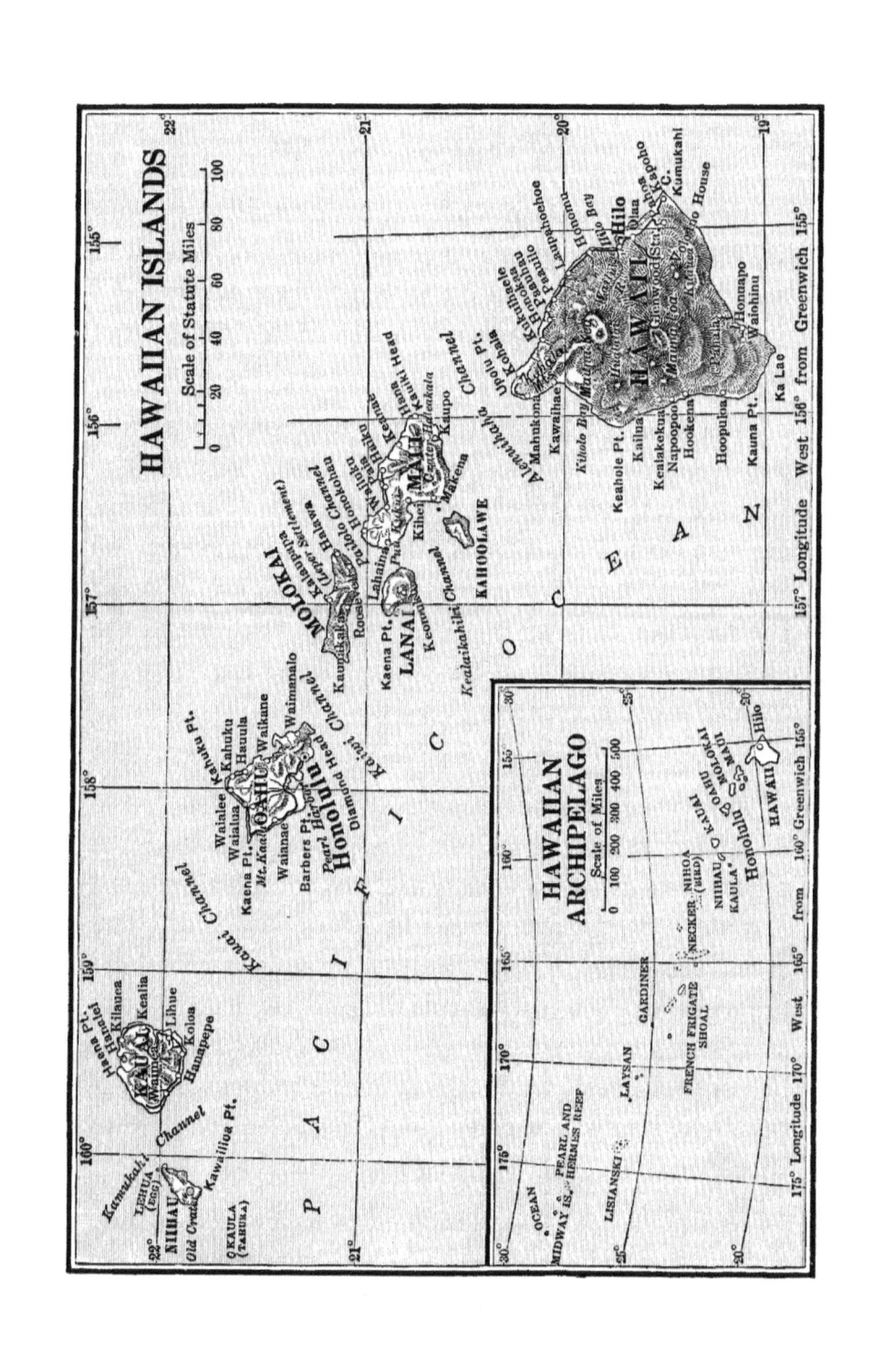

The Hawaiian Islands

The Hawaiian Islands are one of our most important possessions. In the group there are eight inhabited islands, besides several on which no people live. All together they cover an area larger than Connecticut and Rhode Island.

We meet such a variety of people on the islands that we almost wonder in what country we are. The Chinese in the rice fields make us think of China. From the numbers of Japanese, both in the towns and in the country, we might well imagine that we were in Japan. The number of people from Portugal and Spain, the Philippine Islands, and the United States remind us of each of those countries.

The native Hawaiians are brown-skinned, but with so many people from other places having decided to make their homes or go into business on the islands the inhabitants exhibit a wide variety of complexions. The climate is delightful, never too hot or too cold. There are no great land masses within thousands of miles, and the winds bring to the islands the pure air and the even temperature of the ocean. The islands are situated in the belt of the easterly trade winds. These bring most of the rain, which falls in greater quantities on the windward shores than in other localities.

A sail around the islands gives us an idea of their beauty. Rugged mountains clothed in green rise from the blue water. Against high, vertical cliffs, cut here and there by deep gorges, the white-crested waves dash and roar. Now a little river in its green valley comes flowing to the sea. In many places we see the tall, waving cane of a sugar plantation and long rows of pineapples. In the lowlands we catch glimpses of the rice fields.

The Hawaiian Islands are one of the workshops of Nature, and far down below their surface she is tending her great furnaces. From time to time, with many a groan and rumble and display of steam and flame, they throw up, through tall chimneys in the earth, enormous quantities of melted stone and ashes.

The entire group is really the crest of a chain of volcanoes which rise from the bottom of the sea. Mother

Figure 163. This is a side view of the crater of Kilauea. The photograph was taken by the light of the boiling lava.

Nature long since let her fires die out in the furnace of Mauna Kea, the highest peak on the islands, but she is continually busy beneath Mauna Loa and Kilauea. You would have to walk nine miles to travel around the rim of Kilauea's enormous crater. A thousand feet below you in the huge crater is a lake of boiling, bubbling lava. Should you like to go down into this greatest of living craters and walk across the hardened lava floor to the brink of the boiling lake? Its temperature is about seventeen hundred degrees. How many times hotter than the boiling water in your mother's teakettle are the contents of this fiery lake?

There are two kinds of rivers in the Hawaiian Islands, rivers of water and rivers of stone. The rivers of water are wearing away the land. The rivers of stone have helped to build it up. The rivers of water irrigate the land and help to support vegetation. The rivers of stone, when in an intensely heated state, have flowed down from the craters of the volcanoes. They have destroyed crops, cut wide paths through forests, and filled channels and gorges. Finally, with fountains of bluish flames, clouds of steam, and loud hissing, they have plunged into the sea.

The lava rivers have not been entirely harmful. When decayed and crumbled into soil, the volcanic rock is very fertile and has made possible the great farms and plantations which cover such large areas.

Sugar is the most valuable product raised on the Hawaiian Islands. Can you imagine plantations big enough and numerous enough to produce in a single

Figure 164. These men are plowing with an American tractor. How many furrows are being turned at once? The land will be planted with sugar cane.

year over half a million tons of sugar? Someone has called the sugar industry here a "case of farming with brains." The entire industry is in the hands of great corporations, who carry on the work on a large scale and in the most scientific way. In some of the fields we can see the water flowing through the irrigation ditches. This is either brought from the mountains or obtained from artesian wells. Enormous quantities of fertilizer are used in order that the soil may yield its greatest amount. Thousands of Japanese and Chinese work in the fields, cutting the tall cane and loading it on the cars which carry it to the mills. Here the boilers, settling-tanks, vacuum pans, and other machines are as large and modern as any which we might find in a trip through our sugar state of Louisiana.

Figure 165. These workers are loading sugar cane on a railroad that runs through the big plantation. Where will the train carry the cane?

There are laboratories connected with some of the large plantations where experts study every detail of sugar making. They experiment with the amount of water which the growing cane needs and the kind and amount of fertilizer which will give the best results. They know how much juice a pound of cane should yield, how much sugar should be made from it, and the size which the grains of sugar should be. If the results in the mill do not agree with the studies in the laboratory, the experts must find the reason and correct matters. No sights which we have seen in the Hawaiian Islands are more wonderful than these great sugar plantations.

The pineapple plantations on the Hawaiian Islands are the largest in the world, and more of this fruit is produced here than anywhere else. Should you like to stay on the plantations and see the workers pick the

UNITED STATES POSSESSIONS IN THE PACIFIC

pineapples and start them on their way to the canning factory, or should you prefer to visit the factory and watch the machines peel and slice the fruit and pack the cans? The steam kettles where the fruit is cooked are enormous, and the machines which seal and label the cans work so rapidly that one hardly realizes what is being done until the cans roll along in endless rows to the packing room.

On other farms in these islands we can see rice farms in the valleys; coffee trees on the hillsides; tobacco plants completely hiding the ground with their great leaves; stiff necked sisal plants, such as we have seen growing in Mexico; long rows of rubber trees; banana trees, each with its big bunch of fruit; and cotton plants

Figure 166. This is a banana plantation. Notice the bunch of fruit on the tree in the foreground and the great blossom hanging from it.

covered with their fluffy white balls of fiber. None of these crops, however, compare in value with the millions of dollars' worth of sugar and pineapples which are produced each year.

Honolulu, the largest city of the islands, nestles between the mountains and the sea. From the fine streets, buildings, stores, banks, hotels, and the electric cars and lights, we should think that we were in one of the large cities in the United States. Climbing the slopes we see the residential part of the city. The houses are built much like those of California for air, light, and out-of-door life. They have broad piazzas, and lovely gardens brilliant with masses of flowers.

The view from the top of Punch Bowl, a volcano which received its name from the shape of its crater, is magnificent. We look down over the city and out over the great Pacific, whose waves are pounding on the white beach and lava rocks. Coming down from the hill we enjoy a ride through the broad, shaded streets and a trip to the government buildings. Some of these were once the palaces of former native rulers. We visit the Aquarium, one of the best in the world, and see the display of fishes and other forms of sea life. The Museum is even more fascinating. There are wonderful exhibits here of the animals, the plants, and the homes and industries of the people of the Pacific islands. The longer we stay, the better acquainted we feel with this part of the world.

The importance of the Hawaiian group is suggested by the titles which have been given it and the statements which have been made concerning it. It has been called the midway station between the East and the West; an ocean crossroads where routes between Asia and Australia and the American continent converge; a distributing center of the greatest ocean of the world; a stepping-stone to the markets of the East; a coaling station for Uncle Sam's fleet. Which of these titles do you think gives the best idea of the importance of the islands?

The Philippine Islands

We shall not be able to visit all the Philippine Islands, for there are more than three thousand of them. All together their area is about the same as that of Arizona. The largest island, Luzon, is about the size of Ohio, and the next largest, Mindanao, is only a little smaller. The archipelago occupies a large area in the ocean. If it were placed on the United States, with the most northerly point where Duluth, Minnesota, is situated, the most southerly island would touch New Orleans. The distance across the archipelago from east to west is as far as from Detroit to Kansas City.

When we took over the Philippines from Spain we added between eight and ten million people to our population. This means that out of every ten or twelve people one person is a Filipino. The majority of the Filipinos have brownish skin. Most are Christians, some are Mohammedans, and some are heathen. There are many Chinese and Japanese on the islands and also Spaniards and other Europeans and many Americans. Most of the natives are peaceful and friendly, with some remote tribes living in the interior.

Some study of the climate of the Philippines from the map will tell you a good deal not only about the industries but about the character of the people as well, for climate determines these things more than does any other factor of physical geography.

The Philippine Islands are nearer the equator than any part of the United States. Filipino boys and girls wear very light clothing the year round. During our winter and spring the northeast winds bring rain to the eastern slopes of the mountains, and the western parts of the islands have a dry season. The dry season is the idle time in agriculture, thus resembling our winters. Plants do not grow then. But during our summer and autumn, circular storms called "typhoons" bring abundant rain from the Pacific Ocean to all parts of the islands. This is the growing period for crops like rice, sugar, and tobacco, which are harvested in the dry season. In the regions that have no dry season, bananas, Manila hemp, and coconuts are grown, for these need rainfall throughout the year.

When Spain ceded the Philippines to the United States at the close of the Spanish-American War, the Filipinos carried on much of their work in the same crude, primitive way as the people do on many of the other islands. Under Uncle Sam's guiding hand conditions are rapidly changing. The schools have been

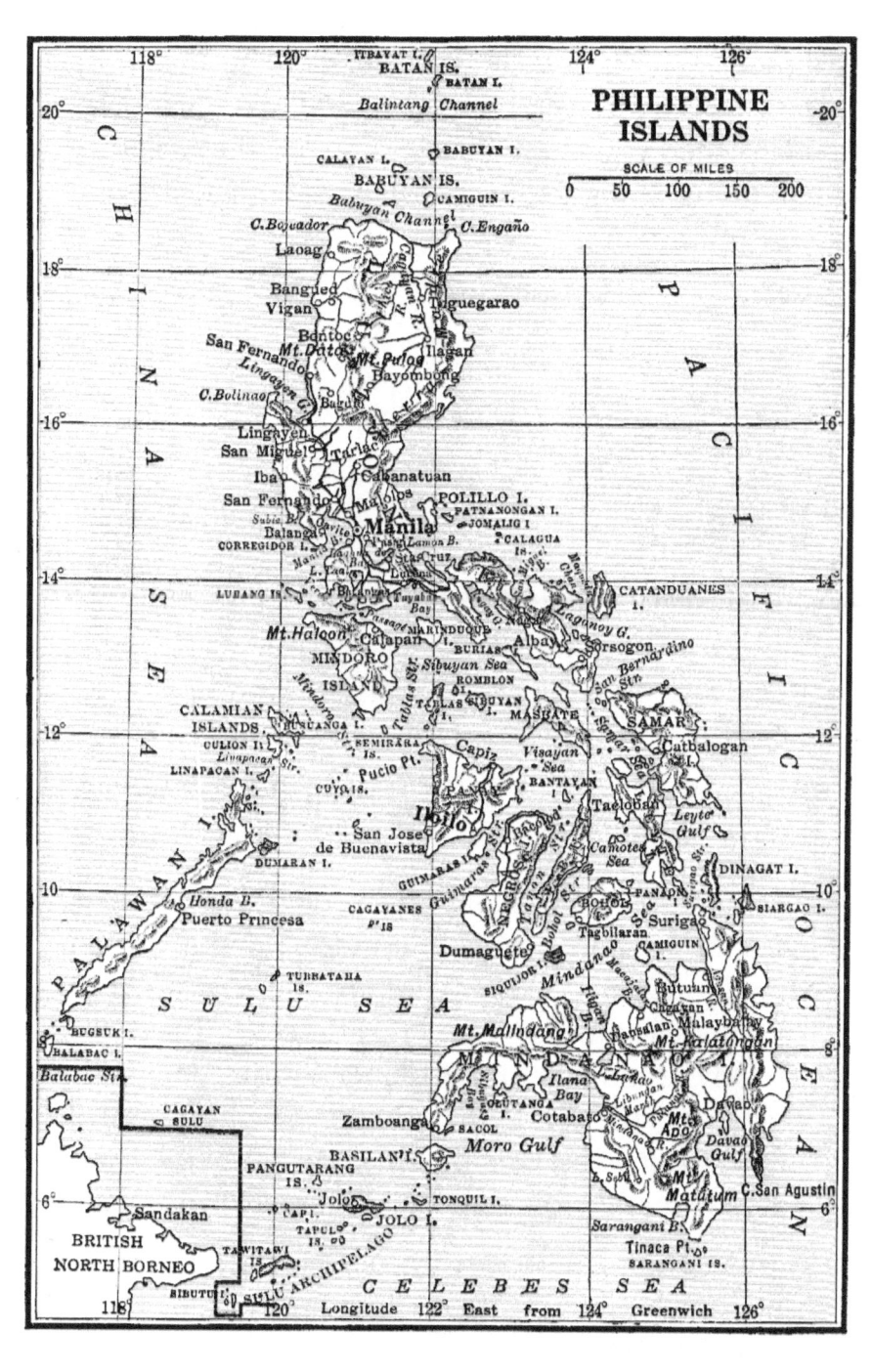

improved, and more and better teachers have been hired to instruct the children and show the people the best way to carry on their farms and raise their crops. Many good roads have been built so that the people can communicate more freely with one another.

Figure 167. These are rafts of coconuts floating down the river to the little seaport. What will be done with them?

Modern factories for pressing out the oil from the coconut have been built, and in the more important sugar-producing areas there are modern mills for crushing the cane and extracting the sugar. The results of all these and other improvements are evident in the character of the people, in the improvement and growth of their industries, and in their growing ability to take upon themselves the responsibilities of government.

The Philippine group lies in the great volcanic belt which stretches along the western shores of the Pacific Ocean. These islands have over a dozen volcanoes, some active. Forests cover many of the mountain ranges, and lumbering is already an important industry. As the climate is tropical you will find here the trees which grow in the hot parts of the world—mahogany, cedar, teak, and others. The palm is common everywhere, and feathery bamboos grow to a height of fifty feet. The forests yield not only lumber but gums, resins, rattan and bamboo, and materials for tanning and dyeing. In the mountains rich deposits of gold are worked. The islands contain many other minerals—silver, copper, sulphur, lead, manganese, coal, asphalt, and several others, some of which are already being mined.

More important to the people than forests or minerals is the rich volcanic soil of the valleys and slopes. In places the mountains look like great flights of stairs. With infinite labor the people have terraced up the slopes with low walls to prevent the soil from being washed away. Everywhere in the valleys and also in all these terraced fields we see rice growing, and we notice the irrigation systems which bring the water to the crops. In the valleys low earth walls surround the fields so that they may be flooded.

Figure 168. The Filipinos in the country regions could hardly get along without the water buffalo. Here is one plowing the rice field.

When it rains the soil becomes a mass of mud. How should you like to plow such a field as you see in the picture on the previous page? Even the Filipino might not be able to do it were it not for his water buffalo, or carabao. This animal does not object to mud and water. It likes to bathe in the streams and canals and wallow in the mud. On the roads we see the buffaloes drawing heavy loads of hemp, copra, tobacco, and other products. Besides doing the farm work and drawing the loads, the buffalo furnishes the Filipino with milk and meat.

In some of the islands humpbacked cattle are used in the fields. These animals look like the sacred cattle in India, of which you have read (see Allen's "Asia").

When the rice is grown the fields are drained and the grain begins to ripen. Later the people will cut it and thresh out the grain from the straw. Rice is their chief food, and each grower saves enough for his family's use, but much larger quantities are shipped to the cities. Although rice is one of the most important products in the Philippines, each year some has to be imported from Indo China (see Allen's "Asia").

The coconut trees in the Philippines are as useful to the people there as they are to the inhabitants of the other Pacific islands and to the people of Africa. Copra is one of the important products, and in many villages we see the people climbing the trees to gather the nuts, cutting them open and preparing the white meat for drying, and carrying the copra to the factories where the oil is pressed out.

UNITED STATES POSSESSIONS IN THE PACIFIC

Figure 169. Describe the preparation of copra.

During our trip through the islands we ride by large fields of tobacco. We shall realize what great quantities are raised if we visit the factories in Manila, where there are hundreds of women and girls rolling cigars and making cigarettes. Many of these are exported, but many also are used on the islands.

You have probably heard of Manila hemp, and you will be interested in this industry not only because of its importance but because it is different from any which is carried on in the United States. We make enormous quantities of rope and twine, but we produce very little of the materials of which it is manufactured. The true hemp grows chiefly in Russia and other European countries, but little cordage is made from its fiber compared with the amounts which are manufactured from the fiber of the sisal plant and from Manila hemp.

AFRICA, AUSTRALIA, ISLANDS OF PACIFIC

Figure 170. This is a big hemp plantation. What must be done to prepare the fiber for export?

Figure 171. This is hemp fiber drying in the sun. What is it used for?

UNITED STATES POSSESSIONS IN THE PACIFIC

When you studied the country of Mexico (see Allen's "North America") you read about the plantations of sisal and the great quantities of its fiber which are exported to the United States. The Philippine fiber is obtained from the abaca, usually called Manila hemp. The plant is a cousin of the banana, which it resembles. The trunk is composed of layers wrapped tightly around an inner stalk. The laborers cut the plant and remove the layers. The white inner layers are scraped and stripped into long, strong fiber. This is cleaned, dried, and twisted like yarn into large hanks. We see the fiber everywhere—on the ground, hung on fences to dry, carried in buffalo carts to the warehouses, and loaded on vessels in Manila harbor.

Figure 172. Why do these Filipino school boys have rice culture as a school project? Why do they wear such large hats? Of what are their hats probably made?

Besides these more important crops which we have mentioned, there are many fields in the Philippines planted with corn and cotton, vegetables and fruits. We should find many of the people in the interior raising cattle and those on the shore engaged in fishing.

We should like to take a trip on one of the many coasting steamers which cruise in and out among the islands and stop at the smaller ports. In such a journey we could see what are the products taken on board, visit the towns of many different islands, become acquainted with the people, and learn at first hand what wonderful progress our Filipino cousins are making.

Before leaving the Philippines we will visit Manila, the most important seaport and the largest city. In its splendid bay all the navies on earth could ride at ease. We see there great ships from many parts of the world. They will take on cargoes of hemp, sugar, tobacco, copra, oil, and other commodities, which they will carry to ports in many countries.

Should you like to make your home in a cargo boat? Several thousand people in Manila live in cargo boats on the Pasig River which flows through the city. The river and the canals which branch from it are crowded with the cargo boats and with launches and larger vessels.

The walled city is the old part of Manila; the narrow streets are lined with Spanish houses with barred windows and hidden courtyards. Very different from this are the newer portions of the city. Here are stores, factories, banks, hotels, and other modern features.

In one quarter of the city all the shopkeepers are Chinese. The stores are very small and so filled with wares that there is little room for customers. There are thousands of Chinese in Manila, and many more are scattered over the islands. Most of them are traders, but a few are farmers.

Our trade with the Philippines is very important, and many millions of dollars' worth of goods are exchanged annually between the United States and these islands. Most important of all the articles which we send to the Philippines are cotton and cotton goods. As industries are developed, roads improved, and railroads extended, the people will need more and more machinery and iron and steel for building roads and bridges, for railroads, and for oil factories, sugar mills, and other establishments. They will need in larger quantities than at present gasoline, oil for lighting and lubricating, farming tools, and foodstuffs of many kinds. As the years go by, the cargoes of hemp, sugar, copra, tobacco, and other products which the Filipinos send to us are sure to increase many times over.

SUGGESTIONS FOR STUDY

I

1. Our Pacific possessions.
2. The Samoan Islands.
3. The island of Guam.

4. Area and population of the Hawaiian Islands.

5. Climate of the Hawaiian Islands.

6. Volcanoes and lava streams.

7. The sugar industry.

8. The cultivation and canning of pineapples.

9. Other products of the Hawaiian Islands.

10. The city of Honolulu.

11. Size and population of the Philippine Islands.

12. Climate and soil of the Philippines.

13. Progress in the Philippines.

14. The cultivation of rice.

15. Copra and tobacco.

16. Manila hemp.

17. The port of Manila.

18. Our trade with the Philippines.

II

1. What is the total area of our Pacific possessions? Arrange these islands in the order of their size (see Appendix, page 503).

2. What islands in the Atlantic belong to the United States (see Appendix, page 503, and Allen's "North America")?

UNITED STATES POSSESSIONS IN THE PACIFIC

3. Which island possession in the Pacific is the nearest to the United States? the farthest away? the farthest north? the farthest south (see map on pages 442 and 443)?

4. What is a mandate? a mandatory?

5. For what two products are the Hawaiian Islands noted?

6. What ports of the United States carry on much trade with the Hawaiian and Philippine islands?

7. On what waters will a ship sail bringing fiber from Manila to New York?

III

Make a list of the places mentioned in this chapter. Arrange them by countries, cities, rivers, mountains, etc. From these places select those which you think are so important that you should always be able to locate them and know something about them.

CHAPTER XXXV

BRITISH POSSESSIONS IN THE PACIFIC

More islands in the Pacific Ocean belong to the British than to any other nation. As you already know, Australia and New Zealand are important parts of the British Commonwealth. Under its control also are the eastern part of New Guinea, the Bismarck Archipelago, the Solomon group, the Gilbert and Ellice islands, the Tongas, the Fijis, and many smaller groups and scattered islets. We shall not have time to visit many of these British possessions, but cyclopedias and books of travel will tell you how the people live, what they do, and whether Nature employed her volcanic agents or her coral workers in building these lands.

The Fiji Islands are one of the most interesting groups in the Pacific. Eighty of the two hundred and fifty islands are inhabited. Years ago few people cared to visit here, for the natives had an unpleasant custom of killing and eating strangers and the prisoners whom they captured from other tribes. Missionaries have done

BRITISH POSSESSIONS IN THE PACIFIC

Figure 173. We shall see all kinds of villages in the Pacific Islands. This is one in Papua. Describe it.

Figure 174. Rubber is produced on many islands in the Pacific. This is a rubber plantation in New Guinea.

a splendid work on the islands, and so most have now settled down to a more peaceful life. Some are employed in gathering coconuts and making copra, some work in the cane fields and the sugar mills, while others care for their flocks and herds.

Now we will sail over the coral seas, past low islands where palm trees wave over white beaches, where flying fishes leap from the blue waters, where sharks swim and porpoises play, to the great island of New Guinea. The western part of the island belongs to the Dutch. The southern part of the eastern portion is known as Papua, and has been for some time a British possession governed by Australia. Since the World War the former German colony in the north has been made an Australian mandate.

Figure 175. What is this native of New Guinea doing to this rubber tree?

Excepting Greenland, New Guinea is the largest island in the world. Its mountains are higher than any in the United States. Its forests are so dense and the undergrowth so tangled with vines and creepers that we should need an ax to chop our way through. Some of its rivers have rich flood plains and deltas and are navigable for thousands of miles.

The nations who control New Guinea have done little more than plant a fringe of settlements along the coast. The interior is inhabited by tribes who live as they did before foreigners touched their shores. They wear little clothing, tattoo their bodies, pierce their noses for ornaments, and have many other curious customs.

The natives bear little resemblance to the brown-skinned, straight-haired people on many of the islands around. They are much more like the black tribes on the Guinea coast of West Africa, and for this reason their island home was called New Guinea.

In the coastal regions the tribes have settled down to peaceful ways, and hundreds of them have become Christians and have adopted many of the foreigners' ways. They work in the coconut groves and on the rubber and sisal plantations. Some are engaged in mining gold, which is an important product of the island. Some find employment in stripping the sheets of bark from the mangrove trees or diving for pearls or pearl shells.

Can you look forward to the time when all the natives of New Guinea will adopt civilized ways, when roads will be built over the island, when locomotives will draw heavy loads of lumber, minerals, and tropical products from many parts of the interior to the seaports, and when well cultivated plantations will take the place of uninhabited forests and jungles? It seems almost impossible to imagine such changes, yet they are no greater than have taken place in other regions. More and more, as the years go on, the civilized nations of temperate zones will need the products which tropical lands like New Guinea can furnish, and the people there will need the products of the mills and factories and foundries in the great cities of the world.

SUGGESTIONS FOR STUDY

I

1. Pacific islands of the British Commonwealth.

2. The Fiji Islands.

3. Size and surface of New Guinea.

4. People and occupations.

5. Future of New Guinea.

II

1. How far is Papua from Australia?

2. Sketch a map of Australia and New Guinea. Show on it the groups mentioned in the text. Show also the equator and the tropic of Capricorn.

3. For what products are the United States and European countries dependent on tropical lands?

III

Make a list of the places mentioned in this chapter. Be able to locate each place and tell what was said about it.

CHAPTER XXXVI

FRENCH POSSESSIONS IN THE PACIFIC

Besides her larger possessions in the Pacific, France owns scores of islands there which are so small that their total area is only a little more than that of Rhode Island. Besides these small scattered islets, the French, in conjunction with the British, control the New Hebrides, a group of islands of great beauty and fertility. Coffee of excellent quality is produced here, the climate is such that three crops of corn can be grown in a year, and large quantities of copra are prepared.

France also controls the Marquesas and Society groups. Have you ever read any of Stevenson's or Melville's stories about these lands? Nature's agents have done a wonderful work here in the ocean. Near the Society Islands the water in places is more than two miles deep. In the center of Tahiti, the largest island of the Society group, there is a volcanic peak which rises nearly a mile and a half above the level of the sea, making a total height from the bed of the ocean of three and a half miles.

FRENCH POSSESSIONS IN THE PACIFIC

Figure 176. This is a village in Tahiti. Describe the place. Where is Tahiti?

You will find Tahiti on the map on pages 442 and 443. It is a beautiful place. With its deep valleys clothed in green, its mountain peaks, its swift little rivers, its blue water fringing the white beach, and its delightful climate it is one of the most charming lands on earth. With the fish in the waters around, the variety of fruit, the taro plant with its tender leaves and nourishing root, and the coconut trees with their thousand uses, it is no wonder that the people do not like to work very hard. Much of the labor of preparing the copra, digging the phosphates, and caring for the sugar-cane plantations is done by Chinese.

Papeete is the largest town on the island of Tahiti, and the French governor in charge of the colony lives here. There is one place in Papeete which you will surely wish to visit. This is a coconut-oil mill, the proprietors of which are men from the United States. Do you suppose that you will ever live and work so far away from your present home?

Of all the French possessions in the Pacific, the island of New Caledonia is the largest and the most important. Find it on the map on page 411. About how far is it from Australia? New Caledonia is nearly the size of New Jersey, but its mountains and valleys, rushing streams, waterfalls, and low coral reefs make it very different from that state. Some of the coral reefs near the island do not as yet reach the surface of the ocean and are therefore dangerous to shipping. The captain takes our vessel very carefully through an opening in

Figure 177. This is a scene along a little river on one of the French islands. Try to imagine the green jungle, the gray rocks, and the blue sky and water.

the reef and over the quiet water beyond to the little seaport.

In former years France used New Caledonia as a prison for some of her criminals. She has now discontinued the practice and is trying to make of the colony a peaceful, prosperous land of honest citizens.

There are fine pasture lands in New Caledonia, and the people raise many cattle and sheep. In the more level parts of the island there are farms which produce crops similar to those produced in other Pacific islands, such as coffee, copra, and rubber. The mineral products, however, are at present more valuable than any others. Chrome ore and manganese, both valuable minerals, are mined in large quantities. Can you find out what they are used for?

When you studied the continent of North America you read about the rich nickel deposits of Canada, from which comes a large part of the nickel supply of the world (see Allen's "North America"). There are few other places in the world where this valuable mineral is found. New Caledonia is one of these, and for this reason the island is of great importance to France. The workmen in the New Caledonian mines produce each year several thousand tons of nickel. What are some of the uses to which it is put?

SUGGESTIONS FOR STUDY

I

1. French possessions in the Pacific.
2. The New Hebrides.
3. The Marquesas and Society islands.
4. New Caledonia and its minerals.

II

1. What other facts than those mentioned in the text do cyclopedias tell you about the French islands in the Pacific?

2. Many of these islands are near the equator. Why are they cooler and pleasanter than the interior of northern Australia?

3. What valuable minerals come from the French possessions?

4. How large an area do the French islands cover? How does this compare with the area of France (Appendix, pages 499 and 503)?

III

Make a list of the places mentioned in this chapter. Be able to locate each place and tell what was said about it.

CHAPTER XXXVII

THE DUTCH EAST INDIES

Our last visit among the Pacific islands will take us to the Dutch East Indies. These include Java, Sumatra, Celebes, most of Borneo, the western part of New Guinea, and some smaller places. Some of these Dutch islands are among the largest in the world. If all of them were placed close together on the United States, they would cover the states of Washington, Oregon, California, Nevada, Idaho, Utah, and Arizona, and a part of New Mexico. From the figures given in the Appendix, page 505, find how Borneo ranks among the islands of the world.

Some of the people in the Dutch East Indies have brownish skins and others black. Most of the foreigners on the islands are Chinese. Few Europeans live here except the Dutch government officials, business people, and the owners of the large plantations. In this hot part of the earth the light-skinned man can do but little hard physical labor and keep in good health. His work is to plan and direct the labor of the natives, who are used to the climate. It is in this way that the riches of tropical regions will be developed.

Figure 178. This is a village in Borneo. Why are there more towns and villages along the coasts of Borneo than in the interior?

Centuries ago, when little was known of these Far Eastern lands, European traders made long journeys over land to central Asia, where they met merchants from the East. Goods were exchanged; and the Europeans carried back to Venice and Genoa in Italy,

THE DUTCH EAST INDIES

then the greatest commercial cities of Europe, many rich products, among them cloves, nutmegs, cinnamon, and pepper. The unknown lands from which these products came were called the Spice Islands. This name, once applied to the entire East Indian archipelago, is now given to a small group there. Find this group on the map on pages 400 and 401.

Today large quantities of spices are produced in the East Indies on big, well-kept plantations. In the blossoming time a clove plantation is an interesting sight, with its long rows of green trees covered with little red flowers. What did you read about clove plantations on pages 85 and 86?

Figure 179. *This girl is making lace. Notice the bobbins with which she works and the pillow on which the lace lies. Do you think that you could work for hours in the position in which she is sitting?*

A nutmeg plantation looks a little like a pear orchard. The blossoms are yellow, however, instead of white like those of a pear tree. The nutmeg, which is the kernel in the pulpy fruit, is taken out and dried in large ovens. Around the kernel is a fibrous covering which is removed and sold as mace. Does your mother ever use mace in her cooking?

If your mother should buy a pound of pepper, it would last her a long time. It seems hardly possible to believe that on the pepper plantations of Sumatra between thirty and forty million pounds are produced each year.

The pepper plant is a tall, climbing bush, and the pepper which we use comes from its little ripe berries. They are picked and dried in the sun, turning black as they dry. To obtain white pepper the shell is soaked off, leaving the little gray-white berry. Before we can use pepper on our tables the berries must be ground into powder.

Java is the most important of the Dutch East Indies. Of the nearly fifty million people on the East Indian archipelago more than three fifths live on this island, making it one of the most densely peopled areas in the whole world. We will land at Batavia, the capital of the Dutch colony. At first sight the neat white houses, the canals, the Dutch people in the street, and the polite Dutch officials in banks, hotels, and other places make us think that we have on the famous seven-league boots and that they have transported us suddenly to Holland. Our second glance, however, shows us the waving palms, banana trees, Chinese merchants, and brown-skinned natives of an Eastern land.

In the business part of Batavia there are many great warehouses. Some are filled with rice, and others with coffee, sugar, cinchona, tobacco, and tea. There are bags of tapioca, copra, and peanuts, and casks of coconut oil and peanut oil. We see also bales of fiber from the kapok tree which will be used later for stuffing mattresses, pillows, and life preservers.

Besides these articles, there are shipped from this busy port quantities of rubber, cocoa beans, gums, spices, nuts and seeds, bundles of rattan, goatskins, buffalo hides and cow hides, and the sweet-scented sandalwood. Many of these things are produced here in Java, while some are sent here from other islands. The variety of articles shipped from the ports of Java gives one an idea of the wealth and great importance of these Dutch possessions.

There are many good roads and railroads in Java, and we shall learn much about the country from the sights which we can see from the car windows. How splendidly the island is cultivated, and what fine plantations and estates there are! They cover not only the valleys and plains but the slopes of the hills as well. These are terraced as you see in the picture to keep the soil from being washed away.

Not only the valleys but the hills are green with rice fields. There are many little shelters where children watch the grain and frighten away the robber birds. In every village we see women pounding the rice to

Figure 180. The natives have built this hillside up in terraces so that the rains will not wash the soil away. The terraces hold the water so that the ground is wet enough for rice growing.

remove the hulls, and beside every little thatch-roofed hut is the granary, where the family rice is stored.

Now we run by large fields of sugar cane, and in the distance we see the mill where the juice is pressed out and the sugar made. Now we pass a tobacco plantation and notice in the fields the sheds where the leaves are dried.

There are some fields where the indigo plant is growing. Men and women are at work cutting the plants, which yield a valuable blue dye. This is extracted by soaking, boiling, and other processes and made into cakes, which are exported and used in European factories.

THE DUTCH EAST INDIES

Does your mother make tapioca pudding? Tapioca, you remember, is made from the manioc, or cassava, plant which we have seen growing in so many native gardens in Africa. What do the people there use manioc for? The plant is cultivated in Java especially for the manufacture of tapioca, and large amounts are exported from the island.

Off on the hillsides there are many acres where the tea plant is growing, and farther on we see the long rows of trees on a coffee plantation. Java exports large quantities of both tea and coffee. The picking, drying, and curing is done in an up-to-date way which improves the quality and therefore increases the value of both products.

On some of the plantations, interplanted with the coffee trees, there are many kapok trees. These grow in many warm parts of the world. We have seen them in several African countries, but nowhere are they so numerous or do they yield so valuable a fiber as in Java. Have you a mattress in your house filled with kapok fiber?

Figure 181. This is a bunch of ripe kapok fruit. Some of the pods have burst open showing the white fiber inside. For what is this fiber used?

In some of your visits to your dentist you may have had cocaine injected into your gum to deaden the pain of pulling a tooth. Cocaine is obtained from the coca plant (see Allen's "South America"). These plants are raised on many plantations in Java, and already thousands and even millions of pounds of leaves have been picked and shipped away from Batavia in a single year.

The sisal plantations which we pass remind us of those which we have seen in Mexico, while the cotton fields look much like those in our Southern states. Now the train stops near a coconut plantation, and we catch glimpses of the natives cutting the meat of the nuts into strips and spreading it out in the sun to dry. Some of the copra will be exported from Batavia and some will be pressed in the oil mills there and the oil shipped away.

Did you ever take that bitter medicine quinine? It is made from the bark of the cinchona tree, which grows in many warm countries. Formerly most of our quinine came from western South America, but so many large plantations of cinchona trees have been planted in the East Indies that most of the quinine sold in the drug stores of the world comes from these trees. The bark is dried, ground into dust, and treated with different substances until it appears in the form of a grayish-white powder. This is made into pills such as you buy from your druggist.

Sumatra, with the little islands along its shores, is three times as large as Java, but it is much less densely peopled. In the coast regions we shall find roads and railroads, and large plantations on which are growing products similar to those which we have seen in Java.

A little distance in from the coast we shall find dense jungles, deep forests, and villages of native tribes who live in the same easy, idle way in which their ancestors lived before they knew of the foreigners and their big plantations where there is always work to be done.

Sumatra has some of the largest rubber plantations on earth. On one of these there are five million trees cared for by twenty thousand workmen. Should you not like to visit such a plantation, watch the Chinese laborers clearing the jungle and planting young seedlings, and the Javanese men and women tapping the trees and collecting the milky juice? The juice is treated with chemicals and then put through machines which press it into long sheets. Some rubber is still obtained from the wild trees and vines. The natives smoke this over their open fires until it hardens in great balls or biscuits. They also collect quantities of gutta-percha, the milky juice of trees and climbers very similar in many respects to the rubber plants of which we have been speaking.

Borneo is as rich in its resources as Java or Sumatra, but only the regions along the coast have been as yet at all developed. The interior is as wild as it was before foreigners landed on its shores.

We should know from the appearance of the palm fringed coast that Borneo is a tropical island. We should realize this more clearly if we should attempt to cut our way through the forests and jungles, where the dense undergrowth and the tangle of ropelike vines bar our progress. The crocodiles in the rivers, the rhinoceroses, the monkeys, the large apes, and the huge snakes which make their homes here live only in tropical regions.

Which part of the island is controlled by the British? Here we find plantations where tobacco is raised, where long rows of coffee trees cover the hillsides, where millions of rubber trees have been planted, and where coconut groves yield large amounts of copra. The mountains are heavily forested, and lumber has already become a valuable export.

In Dutch Borneo there are fewer plantations than in the north. Most of the trade is in native goods which the people can raise in their villages, find in the forests, or obtain from the ocean. Among these are rice, copra, rattans, gums, and fish. The natives bring these in their canoes or on their backs to the ports, where small steamers which coast among the islands collect them and carry them to Singapore or Batavia, where they are loaded on vessels bound for Great Britain, Holland, or the United States.

Find on the map between Borneo and Sumatra the two small islands of Banka and Billiton. They are only about as large as Connecticut and Rhode Island, yet they are important to the manufacturing industry of Europe and America, for they produce large quantities of tin. You will notice on the map that the islands are a continuation of the Malay Peninsula, which produces more tin than any other region. Banka tin is the purest found anywhere in the world.

THE DUTCH EAST INDIES

Tin is a mineral which is not found in large amounts in the United States, yet our manufacturing needs are so great that we import many tons, in some years more than half of all that is mined in the world. Some of this is smelted near the mines where it is produced and is imported in the form of blocks or bars. Some is brought to great smelters in the United States to be refined. Can you think of any reasons why most of our great tin smelters should be located in New York City and on the New Jersey coast?

I do not need to tell you how interested the United States is in the growth and development of the East Indies. Before 1914 most of the commerce of these islands was carried on with European countries, but since the World War their trade with the United States has been much increased. Many things are needed in the islands which our country can very well supply, such as cotton goods and foodstuffs, iron and steel for railroads, bridges, and factories, farming implements and tools, steam engines, and hardware of many kinds. Are there any goods manufactured in your home city which the people of the East Indies need?

There is no part of the world, no matter how far away or how little developed, in which the United States is not interested. We must have markets for the goods which our great mills and factories produce. As the years go by and our population increases we need larger and larger quantities of raw materials for our manufactures, and many articles which, on account of our climate, we cannot produce at home. For these reasons we shall do well to make ourselves as thoroughly acquainted as possible with countries in the torrid zone. Before you boys and girls are grown to manhood and womanhood we shall be making wide use of fibers, fruits, gums, drugs, lumber, and other products of tropical countries of which today you may not even know the names. On what is now jungle and forest land will be raised cotton, rubber, sugar, rice, fruit, oil seeds and nuts, and other crops needed in a world much more crowded than the one in which we live today.

SUGGESTIONS FOR STUDY

I

1. Islands of the Dutch East Indies.
2. Location and climate of the Dutch islands.
3. People of the Dutch East Indies.
4. The Spice Islands.
5. Production of cloves, nutmegs, and peppers.
6. The city of Batavia.
7. Java plantations.
8. Cocaine, copra, and quinine.
9. Development and conditions on Sumatra.
10. The rubber industry.
11. The island of Borneo.
12. Banka and Billiton and their tin mines.
13. Interests of the United States in foreign lands.

II

1. What islands belonging to the Dutch people are not described in the text? What does a cyclopedia tell you about them?

2. On what waters will a vessel sail in going from Batavia to Holland? At what port in Holland will she probably discharge her cargo? Of what articles may this cargo consist? What will she bring back to Batavia?

3. How many islands the size of Borneo would it take to cover the United States (see Appendix, pages 503 and 505)?

4. What British seaport is located on the southern tip of the Malay Peninsula? Why should this city have become one of the most important ports of the British Commonwealth?

5. Why is the United States interested in the development of tropical lands?

6. What are the five largest islands in the world (see Appendix, page 505)?

III

Make a list of the places mentioned in this chapter. Be able to locate each place and tell what was said about it.

AFRICA, AUSTRALIA, ISLANDS OF PACIFIC

REVIEW OF AUSTRALIA AND THE PACIFIC ISLANDS

1. What nations have colonies in the Pacific Ocean? Which one possesses the largest territory there?

2. What is the largest island in the Pacific?

3. How far is it across the Pacific from San Francisco to Manila? to Sydney (see map on pages 442 and 443)? Why are there more routes east and west across the Pacific than north and south?

4. Judging from the map referred to above, what city in United States territory is an important port of call?

5. In what two ways have most Pacific islands been formed?

6. Make a list of the Pacific islands which belong to the United States. Which is our largest possession there? our smallest? Which one do you think is the most important?

7. Which of the seaports of the United States is the nearest to Honolulu? How far away is it?

8. What should you expect to see being unloaded at San Francisco from vessels which have come from Honolulu? from Manila?

9. How does the continent of Australia compare in size with Asia (see Appendix, page 504)?

10. Why are Australia and New Zealand great sheep-producing countries? Why are the cities in these lands larger and finer than those on most of the other islands in the Pacific?

11. What industries are carried on in the Pacific islands? In which one of these are the most people engaged?

12. Why is the Pacific Ocean likely to be of much greater importance in the future than it has been in the past?

PROBLEMS ON AUSTRALIA AND THE PACIFIC ISLANDS

1. How do you account for the difference in the density of population in the United States and in Australia? Will this difference be greater or less in the future than it is at the present time?

2. Is the position of Australia in the Southern Hemisphere an advantage or a disadvantage?

3. How has the climate of Australia helped to determine its industries? What occupation in this continent has been least affected by the climate?

4. Australia is about the size of the United States. In your course of study how long a time is set apart for studying Australia? Is a knowledge of this island continent of sufficient importance to the people of the United States for us to spend more time in learning about conditions there?

AFRICA, AUSTRALIA, ISLANDS OF PACIFIC

5. New Zealand is about as far south of the equator as Japan is north of it. Compare the advantages of the two island groups for developing into importance industrial nations. What topics shall you need to discuss before you can come to a satisfactory conclusion?

6. Judging from the possessions of the different nations in the Pacific, which one do you think possesses the advantage there, commercially and strategically?

7. Of what value to the United States are her small Pacific islands?

8. Compare the advantages of the Philippine and the Hawaiian islands for growth and development.

9. Was it an advantage or a disadvantage to the Philippines to be taken by the United States?

10. What changes have come to the Hawaiian Islands because of United States ownership?

11. Why are tropical lands increasing in importance?

12. How have the Dutch East Indies helped Holland to become one of the great commercial nations of the world?

APPENDIX

TABLES FOR PROBLEMS AND COMPARISONS

TABLE I. AFRICA AND CONTROLLING COUNTRIES

Country	Area in Square Miles	Population
British Isles and British Africa		
British Isles	121,331	47,157,749
London		4,483,249
Glasgow		1,034,069
Anglo-Egyptian Sudan	1,014,400	3,400,000
Basutoland	11,716	500,544
Bechuanaland	275,000	152,983
British East Africa	720,360	9,701,608
British Somaliland	68,000	300,000
Cameroons and Togoland (see page 430		
Gambia	4,130	240,000
Gold Coast and Ashanti	80,000	2,029,750
Kalahari Desert	120,000	
Nigeria	332,000	16,250,000
Nyasaland	39,573	1,201,519
Rhodesia	440,000	1,735,000
Sierra Leone	4,000	75,572
Southwest Africa	322,400	237,237
Swaziland	6,678	133,563
Union of South Africa	473,089	6,928,580
Islands	1,977	601,649
France and French Africa		
France	212,659	39,209,766
Paris		2,906,472
Marseille		586,341

AFRICA, AUSTRALIA, ISLANDS OF PACIFIC

COUNTRY	AREA IN SQUARE MILES	POPULATION
Algeria	222,180	5,800,974
French Equatorial Africa	982,049	9,000,000
Cameroons (British and French)	191,130	2,540,000
French Sahara	1,500,000	800,000
French Somaliland	5,790	65,000
French West Africa	1,800,566	12,283,962
Madagascar	228,000	3,545,575
Morocco	231,500	6,000,000
Togoland (British and French)	33,700	1,032,125
Tunis	50,000	2,093,939
Islands	1,760	270,807
Belgium and Belgian Africa		
Belgium	11,744	7,684,272
Brussels		684,870
Antwerp		333,882
Belgian Congo	909,654	11,000,000
Italy and Italian Africa		
Italy	117,982	38,835,941
Milan		718,304
Naples		780,220
Rome		691,314
Eritrea	45,800	405,681
Libia	406,000	1,000,000
Somaliland	139,430	650,000
Portugal and Portuguese Africa		
Portugal	35,490	6,032,991
Lisbon		489,667
Oporto		203,981
Angola	484,800	4,119,000
Azores Islands	922	242,613
Cape Verde Islands	1,480	149,793
Madeira Islands	314	170,000
Mozambique	428,132	3,015,504
Portuguese Guinea	13,940	289,000
Prince's Island and St. Thomas	360	58,907

APPENDIX

Country	Area in Square Miles	Population
Spain and Spanish Africa		
Spain	194,783	21,347,335
Barcelona		710,335
Madrid		751,352
Valencia		243,783
Annobon Island	7	1,391
Canary Islands	2,808	469,768
Fernando Po	1,185	12,108
Ifni	965	20,000
Rio de Oro	109,200	495
Rio Muni	9,470	89,130
Spanish Morocco	18,147	416,000
Independent countries of Africa		
Abyssinia	350,000	8,000,000
Egypt	350,000 (cultivated and settled area, 12,226)	13,387,000
Liberia	40,000	2,000,000

Largest Cities of Africa

	Population		Population
Cairo	790,939	Port Said (including Ismaïlia)	91,090
Alexandria	444,617	Sfax	85,400
Johannesburg	284,191	Constantine	78,220
Algiers	206,595	Pretoria	73,770
Cape Town	206,558	Lagos	73,766
Tunis	170,381	Tripoli	73,000
Oran	141,156	Tananarivo	63,115
Durban	140,324	Fez	62,693
Marakesh	102,107	Dar es Salam	52,550
Casablanca	101,690	Tangier	50,000
Tafilet	100,000		

Cape-to-Cairo Railroad

Total length	7079 miles
Not yet completed	2700 miles

AFRICA, AUSTRALIA, ISLANDS OF PACIFIC

TABLE II. AUSTRALIA AND NEW ZEALAND

Country	Area in Square Miles	Population
Australia		
Federal Territory	940	2,572
New South Wales	309,432	2,099,763
Northern Territory	523,620	3,870
Queensland	670,500	757,634
South Australia	380,070	495,336
Tasmania	26,215	213,877
Victoria	87,884	1,531,529
Western Australia	975,920	332,213
New Zealand	103,581	1,218,270

Leading Cities

City	Population	City	Population
Sydney	897,640	Christchurch, New Zealand	110,200
Melbourne	784,000	Wellington, New Zealand	107,488
Adelaide	255,318	Newcastle	86,255
Brisbane	209,699	Dunedin, New Zealand	73,470
Auckland, New Zealand	157,757	Hobart	52,163
Perth	154,866		

TABLE III. PACIFIC ISLANDS

Country	Area in Square Miles	Population
British territory in the Pacific		
Australia	2,974,581	5,436,794
Bismarck Archipelago	15,752	188,000
British Borneo	77,106	833,637
British Solomon Islands	11,000	150,750
Fiji Islands	7,083	157,266
New Guinea (mandatary)	89,252	395,000
New Hebrides (British and French protectorate)	5,500	60,000
New Zealand	103,581	1,218,270

APPENDIX

Country	Area in Square Miles	Population
Papua	90,540	251,392
Samoa (mandatary)	1,250	37,051
Solomon Islands (mandatary to Australia)	3,800	17,000
Smaller islands	650	55,063
Dutch territory in the Pacific	735,000	49,161,047
French territory in the Pacific		
New Caledonia and dependencies	8,718	57,208
New Hebrides (French and British protectorate)	5,500	60,000
Society Islands	650	13,255
Smaller islands (not all figures available)	600	17,207
Japanese territory in the Pacific	785	53,500

TABLE IV. SPECIAL STATISTICS OF THE UNITED STATES

	Area	Population
United States	3,026,789	105,710,620
Territories		
Alaska	590,884	55,036
Hawaii	6,449	255,912
Atlantic possessions		
Panama Canal Zone	527	22,858
Porto Rico	3,435	1,299,809
Virgin Islands	132	26,051
Pacific possessions		
American Samoa	77	8,056
Baker Island	.75	
Guam	210	13,275
Hawaiian Islands	6,449	255,912
Howland Island	.75	
Midway Island	1.5	
Philippine Islands	115,026	10,350,640
Wake Island	3.5	

AFRICA, AUSTRALIA, ISLANDS OF PACIFIC

LARGEST CITIES IN THE UNITED STATES

CITY	POPULATION	CITY	POPULATION
New York, N. Y.	5,620,048	Newark, N. J.	414,524
Chicago, Ill.	2,701,705	Cincinnati, Ohio	401,247
Philadelphia, Pa.	1,823,779	New Orleans, La.	387,219
Detroit, Mich.	993,678	Minneapolis, Minn.	380,582
Cleveland, Ohio	796,841	Kansas City, Mo.	324,410
St. Louis, Mo.	772,897	Seattle, Wash.	315,312
Boston, Mass.	748,060	Indianapolis, Ind.	314,194
Baltimore, Md.	733,826	Jersey City, N. J.	298,103
Pittsburgh, Pa.	588,343	Rochester, N. Y.	295,750
Los Angeles, Calif.	576,673	Portland, Ore.	258,288
Buffalo, N. Y.	506,775	Denver, Colo.	256,491
San Francisco, Calif.	506,676	Toledo, Ohio	243,164
Milwaukee, Wis.	457,147	Providence, R. I.	237,595
Washington, D. C.	437,571	Columbus, Ohio	237,031

TABLE V. GENERAL STATISTICS OF THE WORLD

THE EARTH'S LAND SURFACE

CONTINENTS AND ISLANDS	AREA IN SQUARE MILES	POPULATION
Africa	11,500,000	180,000,000
Antarctica	5,000,000	
Asia	17,000,000	900,000,000
Australia	2,975,000	5,437,000
Europe	3,900,000	400,000,000
North America	8,000,000	145,000,000
South America	7,000,000	60,000,000
Islands	4,625,000	9,580,000

APPENDIX

The Earth's Water Surface

Body of Water	Area in Square Miles
Antarctic Ocean	3,600,000
Arctic	5,540,000
Atlantic	31,500,000
Indian	28,350,000
Pacific	64,000,000
Inland waters	750,000

Some of the World's Largest Islands

Name	Area in Square Miles	Name	Area in Square Miles
Greenland	827,300	Madagascar	228,000
New Guinea	330,000	Sumatra	159,800
Borneo	289,800	Great Britain	88,745
Baffin Island	236,000		

Some of the World's Highest Mountains

Name	Height in Feet	Name	Height in Feet
Everest, Asia	29,002	Kilimanjaro, Africa	19,456
Dapsang, Asia	28,250	Misti, South America	19,200
Kanchanjanga, Asia	28,146	Demavend, Asia	18,603
Aconcagua, South America	23,080	Elbruz, Europe	18,465
Illimani, South America	21,188	Tolima, South America	18,432
Chimborazo, South America	20,702	Kenya, Africa	18,373
McKinley, North America	20,300	Orizaba, North America	18,242
Logan, North America	19,539	St. Elias, North America	18,000
Cotopaxi, South America	19,498		

Some of the World's Longest Rivers

Name	Length in Miles	Name	Length in Miles
Missouri-Mississippi, United States	4,221	Amur, Asia	2,900
		Congo, Africa	2,900
Missouri	2,945	Yenisei, Asia	2,800
Mississippi	2,486	Hwang, Asia	2,700
Nile, Africa	4,000	Lena, Asia	2,600
Amazon, South America	3,900	Mekong, Asia	2,600
Ob, Asia	3,200	Niger, Africa	2,600
Yangtze, Asia	3,100	Mackenzie, North America	2,525

Some of the World's Greatest Lakes

Name	Area	Name	Area
Caspian Sea, Asia	170,000	Lake Nyasa, Africa	14,200
Lake Superior, N. A.	31,200	Lake Tanganyika, Africa	12,700
Lake Victoria, Africa	26,828	Lake Baikal, Asia	12,500
Aral Sea, Asia	26,000	Great Bear Lake, N. A.	11,200
Lake Huron, N. A.	23,000	Great Slave Lake, N. A.	10,100
Lake Michigan, N. A.	22,000	Lake Chad, Africa	10,000

Some Important Seas

Name	Area in Square Miles	Name	Area in Square Miles
Mediterranean Sea	1,158,300	Black Sea	165,000
North Sea	192,000	Baltic Sea	160,000
Red Sea	178,000		

Some Famous Canals

Name	Length in Miles	Name	Length in Miles
New York Barge, N.Y.	340	Manchester Ship, England	35½
Gotha, Norway	280	Welland, Canada	26¾
Canal du Midi, France	148	Kronstadt, Russia	16
Suez, Africa	98	Corinthian, Greece	4
Kiel, Germany	61	Soo, United States and Canada	1½
Panama, Central America	50		

GLOSSARY

Key. āle, ăt, câre, ärm, finəl, All; ēve, ĕnd, hẽr, recənt; īce, ĭll, admîrəl; ōld, ŏn, fôr; ūse, ŭp, fûr; fōōd, fŏŏt; ch *as in* chop; g *as in* go; ng *as in* sing; N *as in* ink; th *as in* thin; *th as in* the; ñ *as* ny *in* canyon; oi *as in* oil; ow *as in* cow; ou *as in* noun; N *(the French nasal), nearly like* ng *in* sing.

Abaca (ä bä kä′)

Abyssinia (ăb ĭ sĭn′ ĭ ə)

Acacia tree (ə kā′ shə)

Adelaide (ăd′ ə lād)

Aden (ä′dən)

Adis Abeba (ä′ dĭs ä bā′ bä)

Africa (ăf′ rĭ kə)

Akkra (ăk′ rə)

Alexandria (ăl ĕg zăn′ drĭ ə)

Alfa (ăl′ fə)

Algeria (ăl jē′ rĭ ə)

Algiers (ăl jērz′)

Alhambra (ăl hăm′ brə)

Almonds (ä′ məndz)

Anglo-Egyptian Sudan (ăng′ glō ē jĭp′shən sōō dän′)

Angola (ăng gō′ lə)

AFRICA, AUSTRALIA, ISLANDS OF PACIFIC

Angora (ăng gō´ rə)

Arabs (ăr´ əbz)

Arizona (ăr ĭ zō´ nə)

Asbestos (ăs běs´ təs),

Ashanti (ə shăn´ tē)

Asia (ā´ shə)

Asmara (äs mä´ rä)

Aswan (äs wän´)

Auckland (ôk´ lənd)

Australia (ôs trā´ lĭ ə)

Azores (ə zôrz´) Islands

Bakalahari (bä kä lä hä´ rē)

Balm (bäm) of Gilead (gĭl´ ē əd)

Banka (băng´ kə)

Basutoland (bə sōō´ tō lănd)

Batavia (bə tā´ vĭ ə)

Bathurst (băth´ ûrst)

Bazaars (bə zärz´)

Bechuanaland (Běch ŏŏ ä´ nə lănd)

Bedouins (běd´ ŏŏ ĭnz)

Beira (bě´ ē rä)

Benguela (běn gā´ lə)

Berbers (bẽr´ bẽrz)

GLOSSARY

Billiton (bĭl ĭ tŏn´)

Biskra (bĭs´ krə)

Bismarck (bĭz´märk) Archipelago

Bloemfontein (blŏŏm´ fŏn tān)

Blue Nile (nīl)

Boers (bōōrz)

Boma (bō´ mä)

Borneo (bôr´ nē ō)

Brazil (brə zĭl´)

Brisbane (brĭz´ bən)

British (brĭt´ ĭsh) Commonwealth.

Broome (brŏŏm)

Bulawayo (bōō lə wä´ yō)

Bulus (bōō´ lōōz)

Buttes (būts)

Cacao (kə kā´ ō)

Cæsar (sē´zər)

Cairo (kī´rō)

California (kăl´ ĭ fôr´ nĭə)

Cameroon (kä mə rōōn´)

Canada (kăn´ ə də)

Canary (kə nā´rĭ) Islands

Canberra (kăn´ bĕr ə)

AFRICA, AUSTRALIA, ISLANDS OF PACIFIC

Cape Verde (vĕrd) Islands

Carabao (kä rä bä´ ō)

Caravans (kăr´ ə vănz)

Caroline (kăr´ ō līn)

Carpentaria (kär pĕn tār´ ĭ ə)

Carthage (kär´ thəj)

Carthaginians (kär´ thə jĭn´ ĭ ənz)

Casablanca (kä sä blăng´ kä)

Cassava (kə sä´ və)

Celebes (sĕl´ ə bēz)

Ceuta (sū´tə)

Ceylon (sə lŏn´)

Chad (chäd), Lake

Cheops (kē´ ŏps) King

Chikapa (chĭ kä´pə)

China (chī´nə)

Chocolate (chŏk´ ō lĭt)

Christchurch (krīst´ chûrch)

Chrome (krōm)

Cinchona (sĭn kō´ nə)

Cocaine (kō kān´)

Cochineal (kŏch´ ĭ nēl)

Congo (kŏn´ gō)

GLOSSARY

Constantine (kŏn stän tēn´)

Coolgardie (kōōl gär´dĭ)

Copra (kŏp´ rə)

Cordoba (kôr´dō va)

Couscous (kŏŏs´ kŏŏs)

Dahomey (dä hō´ mā)

Dakar (də kär´)

Dar es Salam (där ĕs sə läm´)

Decatur (dē kā´ tûr)

Dias (dē´ äsh)

Duala (dwä´ lä)

Dunedin (dŭn ē´ dĭn)

Durban (dûr´ bən)

Ecuador (ĕk´ wə dôr)

Egypt (ē´ jĭpt)

El Kantara (kăn´ tə rə)

Ellice (ĕl´ĭs) Island

Eritrea (ā rē trĕ´ ä)

Esparto (es pär´ tō)

Eucalyptus (ū kə lĭp´ təs)

Fernando Po (fẽr năn´ dō pō)

Fez (fĕz)

Fiji (fē´ jē) Islands

Fonduks (fŏn´ dŏŏks)

Fulahs (fōō´ läz)

Funchal (fŏŏɴ shäl´)

Gama, Vasco da (väs´ kō dä gä´ mä)

Gambia (găm´ bĭ ə)

Genoa (jĕn´ ō ə)

Ghadames (gä dä´ mĕs)

Ghat (gät)

Gilbert (gĭl´ bẽrt) Islands

Granada (grə nä´ də)

Guam (gwäm)

Guano (gwä´ nō)

Guardafui (gwär´ dä fwē´), Cape

Guinea (gĭn´ ĭ), Gulf of

Gum copal (kō´ pəl)

Gutta percha (gŭt´ ə pẽr´ chə)

Halfa (häl´ fə)

Hausas (hou´ säz)

Hawaiian (hä wī´ yən) Islands

Hieroglyphics (hī´ ẽr ō glĭf´ ĭks)

Hindus (hĭn´ dōōz)

Honolulu (hō nō lōō´ lōō)

Hottentots (hŏt´ n tŏts)

GLOSSARY

Hovas (hŭv′ əz)

Hull (hŭl)

Ifni (ĕf′ nē)

Java (jä′ və)

Jibuti (jē bōō tē′)

Johannesburg (yō hän′ ĕs bŭrg)

Juba (jōō′ bə) River

Kabyles (kə bīlz′)

Kairwan (kīr wän′)

Kaiser Wilhelm's Land (kī′ zēr vĭl′ hĕlms länt)

Kalahari (kä lä hä′ rē) Desert

Kalgoorlie (kăl gōōr′ lī)

Kangaroo (kăng gə rōō′)

Kano (kä′ nō)

Kapok (kä′ pŏk)

Karnak (kär′ nək)

Kassai (kəs sī′) River

Katanga (kä täng′ gä)

Kauri (kou′ rī) gum

Kenya (kĕn′ yə) Colony

Khartum (ᴋär tōōm′)

Kilauea (kē′ lou ä′ ä)

Kilimanjaro (kĭl ə män jä′ rō), Mt.

513

AFRICA, AUSTRALIA, ISLANDS OF PACIFIC

Kimberley (kĭm´ bẽr lĭ)

Kisumu (kĭ sōō´ mōō)

Kola nuts (kō´ lə)

Kopjes (kŏp´ ĭz)

Krus (krōōz)

Kuka (koo´ kä)

Kumassi (kŏŏ məs´ ĭ)

Ladrone (lə drōn´) Islands

Lagos (lä´ gōs)

Leopoldville (lẽ´ ō pōld vĭl)

Liberia (lī bē´ rī ə)

Libya (lĭb´ ĭ ə)

Limpopo (lĭm pō´pō) River

Livingstone (lĭv´ ĭng stən), David,

Loanda (lō än´ dä)

Lourenço Marques (lō rĕn´sō mär´ kĕs)

Luzon (lōō zŏn´)

Madagascar (măd ə găs´ kər)

Madeira (mə dē´rə) Islands

Mafeking (măf´ ə kĭng)

Mahogany (mə hŏg´ ə nĭ)

Malachite (măl´ ə kīt)

Malay (mə lā´) Peninsula

514

GLOSSARY

Maltese (mäl tēz′)

Mandingos (măn dĭng′gōz)

Manganese (măng gə nēs′)

Mangroves (măn′ grŏvz)

Manila (mə nĭl′ ə)

Manioc (măn′ ĭ ŏk)

Maoris (mä′ ō rĭz)

Marakesh (mä rə kĕsh′)

Mariana (mä rē′ ä nä) Islands

Marquesas (mär kā′səs) Islands

Marseille (mär sa′)

Masai (mä sī′)

Massaua (mäs sou′ ä)

Matadi (mə tä′ dē)

Mauna Kea (mou′ nä kā′ ä)

Mauna Loa (mou′nä lō′ ä)

Mauritania (mô rē tā′ nĭ ə)

Medina (mə dē′ nä)

Mekka (mĕk′ ə)

Melbourne (mĕl′ bûrn)

Menelik (mĕn′ ĕ lĭk) King

Mesas (mā′ säz)

Mindanao (mĭn′ dä nä′ ō)

515

AFRICA, AUSTRALIA, ISLANDS OF PACIFIC

Mogdishu (mōg dĭ´ shōō)

Mohammedans (mō hăm´ ĕd ənz)

Moluccas (mō lŭk´ əz)

Mombasa (mŏm bä´ sä)

Monrovia (mŏn rō´ vĭ ə)

Monsoons (mŏn sōōnz´)

Morocco (mō rok´ ō)

Mozambique (mō zəm bēk´)

Muni (mōō´ nē) River

Murzuk (mōōr zōōk´)

Myrrh (mûr)

Nairobi (nī rō´ bē)

Napoleon Bonaparte (bō´ nə pärt)

Natal (nə täl´)

Nauru (nä´ŏŏ ōō) Island

New Caledonia (kăl ē dō´nĭ ə)

New Guinea (gĭn´ ĭ)

New Hebrides (hĕb´ rĕ dēz)

New Zealand (zē´ lənd)

Niger (nī´ jĕr)

Nigeria (nī´ jē rĭ ə)

Northern Rhodesia (rō dē´ zhĭ ə)

Nyasa (ny ä´ sä), Lake

GLOSSARY

Oran (ō rän´)
Pago Pago (päng´ ō päng´ ō)
Papaw (pə pô´)
Papeete (pä´ pā ā tā)
Papua (pä´ pōō ä)
Papyrus (pə pī´ rəs)
Pemba (pĕm´ bə)
Perth (pĕrth)
Philippines (fĭl´ ĭ pĭnz)
Phormium (fôr´ mĭ əm)
Piassaba (pē ə sä´ bə)
Platypus (plăt´ ä pŭs)
Pretoria (prē tō´ rĭ ə)
Punic Wars (pū´ nĭk)
Pygmies (pĭg´ mēz)
Pyramids (pĭr´ ə mĭdz)
Quinine (kwī´ nīn)
Rabat (rə bät´)
Rameses (răm´ ē sēz)
Rhodesia (rō dē´ zhĭ ə)
Rio de Oro (rē´ ō dā ō´ rō)
Rio Muni (rē´ ō mōō´ nē)
Ripon (rĭp´ ən) Falls

AFRICA, AUSTRALIA, ISLANDS OF PACIFIC

Sahara (Sə hä´rə)

St. Helena (hĕ lē´ nə)

Salisbury (sôlz´ bẽr ĭ)

Samoan (sä mō´ ən) Islands

Santa Isabel (sän´ tä ē sä bĕl´)

Sekondi (sā kōn´ dĭ)

Senegal (sĕn ē gôl´)

Seville (sĕv´ ĭl)

Sfax (sfäks)

Sierra Leone (sĭ ĕr´ə lē ō´nē)

Simoom (sĭ mōōm´)

Singapore (sĭng gə pōr´)

Sisal (sē säl´)

Somali (sō mä´ lē) Coast

Sphinx (sfĭnks)

Sudan (sōō dän´)

Suez (sōō ĕz´)

Sumatra (sŏŏ mä´ trə)

Sus (sōōs)

Swakop (swä´ kŏp) River

Swaziland (swä´ zē lənd)

Tafilet (tä fē lĕt´)

Tahiti (tä´ hē tē)

GLOSSARY

Tamatave (tä mə täv′)

Tananarivo (tə nä nə rē′ vō)

Tanga (täng′ gä)

Tanganyika (tän gän yē′ kä), Lake,

Tangier (tăn jēr′)

Taro (tä′ rō)

Tasmania (tăz mā′ nĭ ə)

Tenerife (tĕn ēr ĭf′)

Tetuan (tĕ twän′)

Thebes (thēbz)

Timbuktu (tĭm bŭk′ tōō)

Timgad (tĭm′ găd)

Togoland (tō′ gō lănd)

Tonga (tōng′ gä) Islands

Transvaal (trăns väl′)

Tripoli (trĭp′ ō lĭ)

Troglodytes (trŏg′ lō dī′ tēz)

Tsetse fly (tsĕt′ sē)

Tuaregs (twä′ rĕgz)

Tuat (tōŏ ät′)

Tugurt (tōŏ gōōrt′)

Tunis (tū′ nĭs)

Tutankhamen (tōōt änk ä′ mĕn)

AFRICA, AUSTRALIA, ISLANDS OF PACIFIC

Tutuila (tōō tōō ē´ lä)

Uganda (ōō gän´ dä)

Ujiji (ōō jē´ jē)

Veldt (fĕlt)

Walfish (wäl´ fĭsh) Bay

Windhoek (vĭnt´ hŏŏk)

Wombat (wŏm´ băt)

Yap (yäp)

Zambesi River (zəm bā´ zē)

Zanzibar (zän zĭ bär´)

Zulus (zōō´ lōōz)

www.ingramcontent.com/pod-product-compliance
Lightning Source LLC
Chambersburg PA
CBHW030236170426
43202CB00007B/29